NABONIDUS AND THE BIBLE

NABONIDUS AND THE BIBLE
Selected Essays

Janet Tyson

Norwich
Pirištu Books
2024

Cover: Author's own design,. Front: Nabonidus' triad of Sîn, Shamash, and Ishtar, plus the serpent; Back: Re on his barque, protected by the *mehen* serpent (Image: Budge, *From Fetish to God*, 166).

British Library Cataloguing in Production Data. A catalogue record for this book is available from the British Library.

ISBN: 978-1-7393154-8-1

CONTENTS

Preface

This selection of essays constitutes the immediate aftermath of my research into Nabonidus in the Hebrew Bible (HB). His tale is dispersed throughout the ancient texts, e.g., the Song of Solomon, the exodus narratives, Daniel, Joshua, and even Genesis. After three books on the subject, there remained so many questions and potential new investigations that I felt compelled to approach one topic at a time. This volume of papers is the first instalment of many, I will wager.

Some of these discussions are lengthy and scholarly, a few are less rigid and more a sharing of a passion, an offering of an alternative perspective. This project has been my main focus of study for five years, and I can honestly say that I have not yet found a single topic I have had to lay aside for want of substantiating evidence. Every personal name and toponym in the material I have analysed, for instance, every number I chose to evaluate, all synchronise with the premise of a 6th Century BCE context for the tale of Abraham, Moses, and Solomon, all three being pseudonyms, or "commission names" as I call them, for Nabonidus, King of Babylon (556-539 BCE).

In order to fully appreciate the magnitude of what this means, and in order to comprehend the historical, literary, and symbolic techniques employed by the Jewish scribes, these essays are best read *after* the first two books. *She Brought the Art of Women*[1] is free to download online; this introduces the tale of Nabonidus and his Egyptian wife, Nitocris, as preserved in the Song of Solomon. The postexilic years, i.e., the 'exodus' years, are assessed in *Arabian Sinai*,[2] which argues that Nabonidus was the inspiration for the Abraham/ Moses stories, each representing a distinct aspect of the exodus … from Babylon, in 538 BCE. Each essay was previously posted online independently, so there may be a little repetition of references to this earlier body of work.

I can honestly say that this research has been the most satisfying and potentially significant of my academic life. It all began with an idea

---

[1] Janet Tyson, *She Brought the Art of Women: A Song of Solomon, Nabonidus, and the Goddess* (Norwich: Pirištu Books, 2023).

[2] Janet Tyson, *Arabian Sinai: Nabonidus and the Exodus* (Norwich: Pirištu Books, 2023).

that my early investigations into the Song of Solomon had not fully uncovered the real Nitocris II, and almost as soon as I had made my mind up to delve deeper into the Song, I had a nightmare that inspired me to venture off the beaten track. I would never have guessed where this new path would lead.

The Song took me three years to unravel but there remained many new questions that just didn't seem to fit, e.g., about Moses! How was the Song of Solomon connected to the tales of Moses?! Within a month of publishing *She Brought*, I began work on these extraneous details concerning the exodus, and within a year I had written *Arabian Sinai*. The process astonished me in its consistency, relative speed, and detail. The exodus narratives seemed to flow seamlessly from the depiction of the King (and his wife) within the Song, and every name, number, and symbolic allusion reiterated a Nabonidus-based paradigm.

I hope you read the entire body of evidence before you make up your mind as to whether I am right or wrong about this suggested rethinking of the exodus years, but understand that I have not knowingly forced anything, or invented anything; I have simply followed the clues written into the texts by those who wished to record multiple levels of their experience with the aging ex-King of Babylon.

These were real, flesh and blood people, not just strange names in the Bible. The repercussions of Nabonidus' involvement with the early Jews has never before seemed so full of potential to biblical exegetes. I hope others will be inspired to investigate this perspective further; perhaps one day the 'true' history will be understood, and some of the hostilities bred from unchallenged preconceptions will come to resolution.

Janet Tyson, November, 2024

1

ANKHNESNEFERIBRE AND NITOCRIS II
A QUESTION OF FILIATION

The following are my working notes thus far on the relationships between Ahmose III, Nitocris II, and Ankhnesneferibre of Egypt's Dynasty 26. The aim is to see if any concrete evidence in the historical record can provide substantiation for a theory that Nitocris was the biological, not merely the cultic adoptive, daughter of the God's Wife Ankhnesneferibre *and/or* that Ahmose was, indeed, married to this God's Wife.

When Ahmose III comes to the throne in 570 BCE, the incumbent God's Wife is Ankhnesneferibre, Pharaoh Apries' sister; she is also Divine Adoratrice, God's Hand, and First Prophet of Amun (i.e., High Priest), a role that had hitherto been exclusively male-dominated.[1] She had held these titles since the death of Nitocris I, the previous God's Wife, in 586 BCE.

The question concerning the filiation between Ankhnesneferibre and Nitocris II stems from the research carried out for *She Brought the Art of Women*, during which it became evident that the "mother" mentioned in the Song of Solomon was a) the female character's *biological* mother and b) had a sacerdotal position in Egypt. From other snippets of information gleaned from various sources it became increasingly clear that the two women in the Song, i.e., the mother and daughter, are none other than Nitocris II (Ahmose III's daughter) and her cultic mentor, Ankhnesneferibre. The first part of this statement is argued in the book but here I wish to focus on Ankhnesneferibre, with the goal of substantiating this mother/daughter relationship alluded to in the Song, and demonstrating how Nitocris in the Song echoes Ankhnesneferibre in both her general depiction and on a deeper, more

---

[1] Gerard P. F., Broekman, "On the Administration of the Thebaid during the Twenty-sixth Dynasty," SAK 41 (2012): 113-35, here 128. For the attribution of God's Hand ("hand of the god"), see Anthony Leahy, "The Adoption of Ankhnesneferibre at Karnak," *The Journal of Egyptian Archaeology* 82 (1996): 145-65, here 149.

personal and philosophical/theological level.

As an independent researcher, I am free to draw conclusions and make statements that may be at odds with convention. It is the way I work, i.e., challenging the status quo is in my nature. With this in mind, the following discussion will probably be rejected out of hand by Egyptologists who have built a reputation promulgating a certain paradigm. Because we now have a broadly accepted perception that the God's Wives were chaste and childless, it seems new questions about them have slowed to a halt. This paper is an exercise in asking "what if …?" What if Ankhnesneferibre was neither celibate nor childless, and what if the Song of Solomon is the missing link that provides just enough information to 'prove' it?

THE SARCOPHAGUS

In 1832, Jacques-Joseph Champollion-Figeac, the famous Egyptologist who first translated the ancient hieroglyphs, wrote to his patrons that he had found a sarcophagus in very good condition.[2] It bore, he said, the cartouches of a queen called Onkhnas, a name he recognized from many of the monuments also bearing the name of Pharaoh Amasis (then Ahmose II)[3]; he assumed Onkhnas to be his wife. The other name he recognized was that of Psametik, which he took to be her family name. This, of course, was Ankhnesneferibre, daughter of Psametik II. Champollion discussed how the sarcophagus contained remains that were once gilded but later burned, concluding that as, traditionally, Cambyses had wreaked revenge on Ahmose for his deception by burning his corpse (i.e., as told by Herodotus, *Hist.* 3.16), his queen must have been burned also. It was later discovered, however, that the casket was re-used by a priest of Montu, Amenhotep-Pimontu, in the early Roman Period, when the gilding of bones was first recorded,[4] so the woman's remains were never actually found.

The identification of "Onkhnas" as the king's wife clinched its

---

[2] See Karine Madrigal, "L'obélisque de Louqsor et le sarcophage d'Ânkhnesneferibrê," ENiM 10 (2017): 51-88.

[3] As of March 2012, this pharaoh is no longer Ahmose II but Ahmose III. See Sébastien Biston-Moulin, "King Sénakht-en-Rê Ahmès of the XVIIth Dynasty," *Égypte Nilotique et Méditerranéenne* 5 (2012): 61-71, here 66.

[4] British Museum, https://www.britishmuseum.org/collection/object/ Y_EA32.

sale to the British Museum, and that is how things remained for generations. The role of the God's Wife was little understood, if at all, in Champollion's day, so it seems an easy mistake to make, *perhaps*.

In 2021, I contacted the person responsible for one of the most recent analyses of the inscriptions on the sarcophagus and asked if there was any suggestion on the casket that Ankhnesneferibre *was* married to Ahmose;[5] I was assured there is no mention of him. It is highly unusual, however, for the funerary inscription of a God's Wife of the later dynasties to include any male name other than that of her royal father (in Ankhnesneferibre's case, Psametik II, whose name is there).[6] It was not the tradition to list the reigning king, as on temple inscriptions, besides which, Ahmose died in 527/6, and Ankhnesneferibre appears on the Karnak Osiris Chapel with Psametik III as monarch just before the Persian invasion of 525 BCE, so *he* would have been the one listed on her sarcophagus, if that were the case.

I dutifully advised the British Museum on the erroneous listing on their website and they responded by deleting the reference to "wife of Amasis," saying the listing had not been changed since the first pamphlet was produced on the item's initial exhibition (nearly two hundred years ago, with the attribution of "Queen Ankhnes-Neferabra"). This saddened me, as it meant Ankhnesneferibre was not as important a figure as I had imagined her to be; not a single person, even one scrutinizing her sarcophagus, had noticed this glaring "error" in her identification in one of the most esteemed institutions. Ankhnesneferibre had been, effectively, distanced from her anticipated afterlife by the usurpation of her sarcophagus (and probable desecration of her mummy) by Amenhotep-Pimontu. My mind, however, kept going back to the finding of King Richard III in Leicester, England, under the "R" (for "Reserved") in a parking lot; a handful of 'believers' never gave up, against all the naysayers, and there he was! What if Ankhnesneferibre's story *is* inextricably linked to that of Nitocris, as true mother and daughter, and to the tale told in the Song of Solomon? As the research for the book continued, the question of the relationship between Ahmose, Ankhnesneferibre, and Nitocris continued to stir up new questions.

---

[5] Mareike Wagner, personal emails, December, 2021.
[6] Ann Macy Roth, "The Absent Spouse: Patterns and Taboos in Egyptian Tomb Decoration," *Journal of the American Research Center in Egypt* 36 (1999): 37-53, here 50.

GOD'S WIFE AS CELIBATE

The current prevailing academic argument is that the God's Wives were celibate, and this has found little refutation, despite the fact that imposed celibacy has "never been positively proved by the citation of any text,"[7] and it certainly was not so restricted in the past. The God's Wives of Dynasties 18 and 19 were often married to the king, e.g., Ahmose-Nefertari, Queen to Ahmose I, was established as the first God's Wife of Amun; Hatshepsut was married with children giving up her role as God's Wife only to become Pharaoh; Thutmose III's wife Merit-Re, mother to Amenhotep II, was a God's Wife. It was an office that began with the concept of hereditary succession but in later generations, as political changes demanded, God's Wives were installed by rulers (usually their father, the king) and the idea of inheritance became synonymous with formal adoption; it was a means of legally ensuring the transfer of property during times of transition, i.e., away from the expected line of inheritance, as demonstrated by the Adoption Stele of Nitocris I.[8]

The idea that these women were bound by duty to be celibate found firm footing in the 1960s, when it was mistakenly declared that a sarcophagus had been found containing a Dynasty 22 "God's Worshipper," Maatkare, and her child. This apparently demonstrated that the woman had "offended the rule of chastity imposed upon her"; the "child" turned out to be the woman's pet baboon. Maatkare, it so happened, had died soon after childbirth but her abdomen had been lovingly packed to indicate that she had born a child. It was no secret, and was not a sin.[9] Amenirdis II (Dynasty 25), who apparently failed to reach the rank of God's Wife and simply disappeared when Nitocris

---

[7] Betsy Bryan, "Property and the God's Wives of Amun," (paper presented at the Women and Property Conference, Centre for Hellenic Studies, Harvard University, 2003): 1-15, here 13.

[8] Emily Teeter, "Celibacy and Adoption Among God's Wives and Singers in the Temple of Amun: A Re-examination of the Evidence," in *Gold of Praise: Studies on Ancient Egypt in Honor of Edward F. Wente*, Emily Teeter and John A. Larson, eds., Studies in Ancient Oriental Civilization 58 (Chicago: Oriental Institute, 1999): 405-14, here 406.

[9] Miriam Ayad, *God's Wife, God's Servant: The God's Wife of Amun (c. 740-525 BC)* (Abingdon: Routledge, 2009), 146 (citing Sir Alan Gardiner, *Egypt of the Pharaohs: An Introduction* [Oxford: Oxford University Press, 1964], 343).

I rose in the ranks, is claimed to have had a husband and child, which she must have had before her installation as Adoratrice.[10]

Scholars have argued that as high-ranking priestesses, the God's Wives were expected to be ritually clean, and that, if symbolically married to Amun, they could not also have an earthy husband.[11] Yet this seems more of a latter-day imposition on a not-so-well-understood, ancient cult; it has the air of a Judeo-Christian sentiment that is not justified in this context. However:

> The association of priestesses with celibacy on account of "purity" seems completely in contrast to what can be gleaned from the Egyptians' own attitude about their cosmos and cult. Sexual imagery—ithyphallic gods, scenes of birth, love poetry—permeated their religious beliefs and daily life. To the Egyptians, sex was not, as in much of the modern world, inherently bad, but rather it was linked to the central theme of Egyptian religion: regeneration.[12]

I, too, am convinced that celibacy was not enforced upon the college of the God's Wives, Adoratrices, songstresses, etc. Sexual activity need not preclude a God's Wife, or any officiate, from her sacerdotal duties (after all, male priests were married, with families), if ritual purity concerns are met. In a relatively recent twist, it has been put forward that the title of God's Wife may allude to the king's "divine descent by a proclaimed marriage of his mother with a god."[13] This, effectively, made the pharaoh a manifestation of the god on earth, in the form of his/her son; Ahmose's name "The Moon is Born" is testament to this notion, i.e., he *was* the lunar deity Iah incarnate. He was also, *de facto*, the earthly representation of Amun. In this context, the God's Wife became a symbolic daughter, rather than a spouse of Amun. This is further attested by the naming of Amun as the God's

---

[10] For details of various claims, see Aiden Dodson, "The Problem of Amenirdis II and the Heirs to the Office of God's Wife of Amun during the Twenty-Sixth Dynasty," *The Journal of Egyptian Archaeology* 88 (2002): 179-186, here 180.

[11] Teeter, "Celibacy," 405.

[12] Teeter, "Celibacy," 410.

[13] C. Koch, *Die den Amun mit ihrer Stimme zufriedenstellen: Gottesgemahlinnen und Musikerinnen im thebanischen Amunstaat von der 22. bis zur 26. Dynastie* (Dettelbach: Röll, 2012) 65; 79-80.

Wife's "father" e.g., on Ankhnesneferibre's stele it is written that upon entering the temple, "She met her father, Amun-Re ...."[14] So, she certainly *could* be married to the pharaoh (the earthly Amun) and bear his children, without insulting the deity. It seems a logical progression, in fact. Also, it is often suggested that the God's Wives were not permitted to marry for fear of raising a pretender to the throne, but this would in no way preclude them marrying the king himself, as any offspring would have been extraordinarily favourable and in line for the throne anyway.

Ahmose III is known as being a retrospective ruler, in that he admired certain aspects of earlier kingdoms; though a bit of a rebel and considered by some as a jokester (*Hist.* 2.174), he forged Dynasty 26 into one of the greatest in Egyptian history. He was keen to make new laws, change the status quo depending on the circumstances, e.g., Herodotus suggests the pharaoh established a law that every man had to prove himself solvent, i.e., earning a living, on pain of death (2.177), and he granted women the right to be their own legal representative in a contract of marriage (soon after Nitocris' death; see Part Two, Epilogue of the book).[15] Ahmose's retrospection seems blended with a degree of progressive enterprise; this might extend to a radical shift in protocol that allowed for the God's Wife to be, once again, the wife of the king, that is, if the practice ever stopped. Although there is simply not enough evidence to prove this, it may just be the case that it was Ankhnesneferibre's father, Psametik II, who instigated a resurgence of the old ways. Was a union of the two ruling entities, i.e., the kings of Tanis and the God's Wives of Thebes part of Psametik's plan?

Anthony Leahy suggests Ankhnesneferibre was possibly a young child when she first went to Thebes and about nine when she was installed as God's Wife.[16] If this is the case, the tall and beautiful

---

[14] Anthony Leahy, "The Adoption of Ankhnesneferibre at Karnak," *The Journal of Egyptian Archaeology* 82 (1996): 145-65, here 148 (line 5).

[15] Annalisa Azzoni, "Women and Property in Persian Egypt and Mesopotamia" (paper presented at the Women and Property Conference, Centre for Hellenic Studies, Harvard University, 2003), 1-28, here 4.

[16] Anthony Leahy suggests that although this would have been risky, given the high level of infant mortality, politically and symbolically it would have been worth the risk, especially if the birth of a daughter coincided with the accession of the king (in "The Adoption of Ankhnesneferibre at Karnak," *The Journal of Egyptian Archaeology* 82 (1996): 145-65, here 160. In the analysis of the

Ankhnesneferibre would be in her early twenties when Ahmose seized the throne, i.e., in her prime. Why would he *not* take her as a wife, unless there was a legally-binding, institutional proclamation denying such an act? This prohibition has never been found, to my knowledge. The Nitocris Adoption Stele preserves a very righteous statement by Psametik I who, in his ninth regnal year, imposed the cultic adoption of his own daughter on the incumbent (Kushite) God's Wife, Shepenwepet II, signifying political and religious unity for Egypt. The statement makes it clear that Psametik I, overtly, had no intention of ousting the extant adoptee (Amenirdis II), which he acknowledged would be wrong, as he wished to be remembered as a righteous "truthful" king.[17] Nevertheless, Amenirdis soon disappeared from the records, possibly covertly ousted anyway. This potentially sets a precedent for pharaohs (surreptitiously) interfering with the priestesses for their own purposes. If scholars are happy to suggest Ahmose married a daughter of Apries to 'legitimize' his reign, surely it is not that big a leap to acknowledge he would have been astute enough to secure not only the most influential and powerful religious and political enterprise, but also the most direct route to the semi-divine bloodline of the dynasty, via the most beautiful and commanding God's Wife.

A conflict of interests is apparent, for on the one hand we insist that the God's Wives were celibate, unmarried, while on the other, we see very strong connections, symbolically, to marriage and motherhood on Ankhnesneferibre's sarcophagus. Would this not be a case of living a lie, i.e., if she secretly adhered to the female-as-sexual-partner-and-mother 'norm' in the privacy of her coffin/tomb? Why create such a powerful, female priestly role that denies the very sexuality, the very act of Creation it is supposed to represent? Often, in papers and books discussing the Sacred Marriage rite, very little, if anything, is mentioned about the original context of that marriage, i.e., to instigate the conception of a special child (Khonsu, Horus, etc.); that is not to say the God's Wife, in her ceremonial role each year had to get

---

Song of Solomon, we see the initial dedication of Ennigaldi-Nanna occur as soon as she is proven 'viable', i.e., at one year old.

[17] Ricardo A. Caminos, "The Nitocris Adoption Stela," *The Journal of Egyptian Archaeology* 50 (1964): 71-101, here 74. Caminos argues against the adoption of Nitocris by Shepenwepet II, claiming Psametik I must have intended for his daughter to be Amenirdis II's successor, as he presents himself as such an honorable man.

pregnant but if and when she did (with the pharaoh as the representative of Amun), surely that would be deemed a sacred re-enactment of divine Creation?

Ankhnesneferibre is associated with deities profoundly representative of sexuality and procreation:

✹ She is partly represented as Hathor on her sarcophagus, i.e., wearing the solar disc and cow's horns (although this is deemed standard iconography for certain God's Wives, suggestive of 'queenship', it should not be forgotten that the composite headdress is also that of Isis, divine consort of Amun and mother of Horus). Hathor, the goddess of fertility and childbirth, music, and dance, is welcomed home (from her killing spree in the desert of Arabia, as the avatar of Sekhmet) with a Festival of Drunkenness (which figures heavily in Part Two, Chapter 7). This festival is known for its celebration of debauchery and sexuality.

✹ Her name appears on a statue of Bastet (UC 36443), the 'domesticated' feline goddess (as opposed to Sekhmet, the ferocious leonine deity) of sex, fertility, and pregnant women. One wonders why a donor, perhaps offering this item in a bid to secure intercession from the God's Wife on her behalf (e.g., to become pregnant?), would choose someone allegedly far removed from all things 'procreational'!

✹ It is also inscribed on a statue of Amun-re-kamutef, the sexually potent version of Amun (i.e., 'mingled' with Min and depicted in ithyphallic form).[18]

✹ Also, there is the *naos* of Pabasa, the chief steward of Nitocris I (Cairo CG 70027), decorated with representations of Taweret, the hippopotamus goddess, and the Seven Hathors; both are pregnancy/childbirth deities!

Why do GWA-celibacy advocates tend to omit these references?

---

[18] Marsha Hill, "Small Divine Statuettes: Outfitting Religion," *Statues in Context: Production, Meaning and (Re)uses*, A. Masson-Berghoff, ed. British Museum Publications on Egypt and Sudan 10 (2019): 35-49, here 39, Fig 2 (BM, EA 60042).

In these latter contexts, perhaps Ankhnesneferibre's role as God's Hand might explain the blatantly sexual/reproductive connotations but then we would be forced to redefine the parameters of the God's Hand office, i.e., we would have to come off the fence and stop referring to it as "perhaps associated with ritual masturbation in cultic ritual" and simply accept that these women were, indeed, highly sexual, not chaste at all. Is it really too much to consider?

Nitocris' "mother" is mentioned in the Song within the context of pregnancy/birth, e.g., "… of her that *conceived* me" (Song 3:4); and of teaching, e.g., "she who used *to teach* me" (8:2). While the latter instance may point to a sacerdotal office, i.e., of God's Wife, with its focus on hierarchy, cultic adoption, mentoring, etc., the former certainly speaks to *physical* motherhood, not symbolic.

DEPICTIONS

There are two statues that prove very interesting in the search for Nitocris' connection to Ankhnesneferibre: 1) Amun-Re seated on his throne, bearing two inscriptions (Chicago D. 30984 / OIM E10584A); 2) Ankhnesneferibre standing, from Karnak (Nubian Museum).

1) The statue of Amun-Re is fascinating because it bears *both* Ankhnesneferibre's and Nitocris' names. One inscription wraps around the base of the statue, whilst the other sits on top of the base, in a small space between the deity's feet and the end of the dais. The former inscription relates to Ankhnesneferibre: "For the Singer in the Interior of the Temple of Amun, Ankhnesneferibre … daughter of … justified."[19] The inscription is corrupted, unfortunately, but judging from other "daughter of" sacerdotal inscriptions, the missing name, in the context of a votive statue of Amun, could be Nitocris I's[20] (it could

---

[19] H. De Meulenaere, "La Famille Du Roi Amasis," *The Journal of Egyptian Archaeology* 54 (1968): 183-87, here 186.

[20] E.g., "The Divine Adoratrice (Ankhnesneferibre) … daughter of the God's Hand (Nitocris)." Laurent Coulon, "The Quarter of the Divine Adoratrices at Karnak (Naga Malgata) during the Twenty-sixth Dynasty: Some Hitherto Unpublished Epigraphic Material," in *Thebes in the First Millennium BC,*

also be that of Psametik II, of course).[21]

De Meulenaere, argues that this Ankhnesneferibre *must* be a different woman to the one we know as the God's Wife, as she does not bear the "songstress" title anywhere else.[22] Another Ankhnesneferibre, in that short space of time, without any adoption ceremony or other mention anywhere, steps into a prominent role (that is second only to the God's Wife)[23] and appears on a statue *with* the current pharaoh's daughter? On the Ankhnesneferibre Stele, however, Ankhnesneferibre's original titles are listed as:

> Great songstress of the residence of Amun, the one who carries the flowers in the chapel, chief of the enclosure of Amun, first prophet of Amun, king's daughter ....[24]

Teeter notes that the name "Ankhnesneferibre" on the side of the base does not appear within a cartouche, as it does in the inscription on the top of the base, so she is also of the opinion this must be a different woman but she supports her claim by stating that Ahmose's wife's name was "Tentheta" (Tentkheta/Tanetkheta).[25] Dodson suggests that

---

Elena Pischikova, Julia Budka and Kenneth Griffin, eds. (Cambridge: Cambridge Scholars, 2014), 565-86, here 577 and 574, respectively.

[21] Leahy suggests that a few scholars have argued that the statue was "dedicated by a northern official ... on behalf of his daughter when she became one of the songstresses of the residence of Amun" (159). He then goes on to discuss the statue in terms of Nitocris I and Ankhnesneferibre, but the inscription pertains to Nitocris, daughter of Ahmose (Amasis).

[22] De Meulenaere, 186.

[23] Jean Li, "The Singers in the Residence of the Temple of Amen at Medinet Habu: Mortuary Practices, Agency, and the Material Constructions of Identity," *Journal of the American Research Centre in Egypt* 47 (2011): 217-30, here 220, note 10.

[24] Leahy, 148.

[25] Emily Teeter, *Ancient Egypt: Treasures from the Collection of the Oriental Institute*, 23 (Oriental Institute Museum Publications: 2003) 84. At the very least, there is evidence for several wives of Ahmose III: Nakhtes-Bastet-reru, who is named as his Great Royal Wife (Inscription from her rock-hewn tomb at Giza. Wolfram Grajetzki, *Ancient Egyptian Queens: A Hieroglyphic Dictionary*, Golden House Publications, London: 2005), (Khetbeneit-erboni II, presumed to be the daughter of Apries; Tadiasir, who has a daughter, Tashereniset (Aidan Dodson, Dyan Hilton, *The Complete Royal Families of Ancient Egypt* [London: Thames & Hudson, 2010], 247); and, perhaps, Ladice,

if a Dynasty 25 or 26 God's Wife is called only by her Adoratrice title, and if her more elevated title does not appear on the same monument, it is probably the case that she was the heiress to the higher role when the inscription was written.[26] The cartouche *is* evident in the second inscription and, as the statue is metal, i.e., made in a mould and not carved in stone, both inscriptions would have been made at the same time. One might propose, therefore, that the first inscription circumscribing the base was in honour of Ankhnesneferibre in recognition of her initial dedication, with a shortened reference to her titles, perhaps highlighting "songstress" because the donor/owner had known Ankhnesneferibre personally, in that capacity (e.g., as a temple songstress herself, which could tally, in part, with Leahy's statement in note 21, above)[27]; the second inscription at the feet of Amun was the intended primary inscription, alluding to a date contemporaneous with Nitocris II's dedication as First Prophet, by which time of course, Ankhnesneferibre *was* Adoratrice/God's Wife and could use the cartouche.

A similar format appears on the Stele of Ankhnesneferibre, in fact, i.e., the first part of the inscription details the initial arrival of the princess at Thebes/Karnak, with her titulary that includes "songstress" and "First Prophet"; her induction as God's Wife, Adoratrice, and God's Hand years later, follows. Both inscriptions are physically contemporaneous but the first inscription reminds us of the past event, to set the context for the main event.

The second inscription on the statue pertains to Nitocris II, on the occasion of *her* dedication as First Prophet of Amun. Here, on the smaller space near Amun's feet, is inscribed (as part of a longer inscription)[28]: "Daughter of the Lord of Two Lands, Amasis-son-of-Neith, living; her mother, the Divine Adoratrice, Ankhnesneferibre,

---

daughter of Battus III of Cyrene (*Hist.* 2:181). Ladice is not mentioned in Egyptian sources.

[26] Aiden Dodson, "The Problem with Amenirdis II," 181-2.

[27] Marsha Hill and Deborah Schorsch discuss a pendent that is potentially an offering made to the cult of the God's Wives, from *within* the cult, i.e., the donor was potentially an 'insider', one in the entourage of the God's Wife (in "A Gilded-silver Pendant of Nephthys Naming Mereskhonsu (with an appended technical examination)," *Revue d'Egyptologie* 66 (2015): 33-49, here 42). This statue of Amun may provide a similar context.

[28] For full English translations of both inscriptions see Teeter, *Ancient Egypt*, 84.

living."[29] While convention holds this filiation pertains to the God's Wife Ankhnesneferibre as Nitocris' cultic "mother" (her religious mentor, an honorific title that possibly has no bearing on potential blood-connections), I argue it points to a biological mother and daughter. A precedent exists, for instance, on the stele of the God's Wife Isis (Manchester Museum 1781), daughter of Ramesses VI (c.1143-1136 BCE): "Her mother, the Great Royal Wife ... Nub-khesbed ..."; "Her father, the king ... Ramesses ...."[30] If cultic relationships are intended on our statue of Amun, why not use the more common "*daughter of* the God's Wife NN" seen in many other inscriptions? I am unaware of any instance where a First Prophet is mentioned in relation to a "mother" (as all, prior to Ankhnesneferibre, were male, taught by their priestly fathers; the male gender is retained for the title held by these two women).

Also, in a purely cultic context, the king would probably not be named as Nitocris' "father"—this would be Amun-Re, e.g., "She met her father, Amun-Re ..." (as discussed above). In the case of Isis, *her* cultic "father" is Osiris. The very fact that both earthly/human parents are mentioned is indicative of biological, not exclusively cultic filiation.[31]

I suggest, therefore that the very simple inscription says what it says: Nitocris II's father is Ahmose and her mother is Ankhnesneferibre.

2) The second statue, of a standing Ankhnesneferibre (from Karnak, and now in the Nubian Museum), depicts the God's Wife with a short, Nubian-style wig and defines her as: "King's Daughter of his Body, Great of Sceptre, God's Wife of Amun, High Priest (First Prophet) of Amun."

The wig is interesting because it reflects her Libyan heritage, through the Psametik/Necho line, as discussed in the book regarding Nitocris being "black" (Part Two, Chapter 1, i.e., applicable whether Nitocris' biological mother was Apries' daughter or sister). Recalling the description of Nitocris' hair being like a flock of goats moving

---

[29] De Meulenaere, 186.

[30] Texts in translation #12: The stela of the God's Wife, Princess Isis (Acc. no. 1781) (2014), https://egyptmanchester.wordpress.com/2014/03/02/texts-in-translation-12-the-stela-of-the-gods-wife-princess-isis-acc-no-1781/.

[31] See the discussion on biological vs. 'adoptive' parents in Teeter, "Celibacy," 407-9.

down a hill/mountain (Song 4:1), which I discussed in terms of being pubic, rather than head hair, it *is* possible that the reference in the Song could be an allusion this traditional wig-form, perhaps worn by Nitocris in emulation of her mother, i.e., the wig hugs the head (the "hill") and is apparently curly (relating to the 'wildness' of pubic hair, demonstrated via the etymology of this scene), bringing to mind a flock of black, coarse-haired goats.

There is one other curiosity regarding depictions of Ankhnesneferibre. In one significant depiction on a wall in the Chapel of Osiris Wennefer Neb-djefau, at Karnak, she is depicted as tall and slim, wearing a see-through shift that reveals something rather odd, i.e., a series of three horizontal lines on her abdomen that Hallman calls "folds of skin."[32] Why would a slim young woman (i.e., in her early twenties) have folds of skin under her navel?

Searching for other instances of such a depiction from ancient Egypt, I came across the image of the goddess Nut as the personification of the sky, in the tomb of Ramesses VI (King's Valley). Nut is the ultimate mother goddess and is depicted in this tomb on two panels comprising a ceiling; she is shown giving birth to Re, the solar deity and has the same horizontal lines on her abdomen, *above* her pubic triangle. These, I posit, are an iconographic allusion to her (recurrent) pregnancy, suggesting either prenatal or postnatal body changes (e.g., stylized stretch marks, or a "mummy-tummy").[33] The

---

[32] Aleksandra Hallmann "Iconography of Prayer and Power: Portrayals of the God's Wife Ankhnesneferibre in Osiris Chapels at Karnak," in *Prayer and Power: Proceedings of the Conference on the God's Wives of Amun in Egypt during the First Millennium*, M. Becker, A. Blöbaum, and A. Löhwasser, eds., Ägypten und Altes Testament 84, Münster 2016: 205-222, here 211; for the image see Figs. 1-2, 206.

[33] Gay Robins argues that ancient Egyptian depictions of women did not suggest the passage of time or changes in body appearance, even regarding pregnancy (unless in a ritualistic context, where the figure is decidedly rounded), and yet depictions of elite males (especially kings) *did* have a motif that suggested body changes, i.e., "explicit rolls of fat under the chest. This represents a mature and successful official who has achieved a sedentary lifestyle with access to plenty of food. It is not applicable to women, because they could not hold office" (in *Women in Ancient Egypt*, [Cambridge: Harvard University Press, 1993], 180. See Fig. 75, p. 173, which uses *three horizontal lines* under the pectorals to suggest a fuller, mature figure. Similarly, a small

figure of Nut reveals similar lines at her throat; although it may be argued that these simply imply a "bending" of the body, there are two arguments against this: 1) The abdominal lines appear on Ankhnesneferibre's chapel depiction while she is in a standing position, and 2) Nut swallows the dying Sun in order to give it new life, so the mouth becomes, in effect, the opening to the uterus (and her entire body functions as such, for the Sun passes through it, nocturnally, before being reborn from her thighs). She is impregnated via her mouth and gives birth via her vagina; the two, as we see in the analysis of the Song (Part Two, Chapter 4), are considered opposing ends of the same "canal" running through the body. A basic search online for ancient Egyptian and Mesopotamian fertility idols will reveal many such depictions of lines on the lower abdomen, above the pubic triangle (often made up of dots, like tattoos, such as with the Egyptian

---

statue of Ahmose himself displays horizontal neck lines (see Marsha Hill, "A Bronze Aegis of King Amasis in the Egyptian Museum: Bronzes, Unconventionality and Unexpected Connections," *Egyptian Museum Collections around the World*, Mamdouh Eldamaty and Mai Trad, eds. [Cairo: American University in Cairo Press, 2002], 545-56, here 551-3). However, Queen Nefertari (wife of Ramesses II), who had at least six children and clearly held the 'office' of Queen, has three very obvious horizontal lines on her neck, even though she is depicted with the body of a young woman. This might suggest she desired to be remembered as the mature, perhaps slightly overweight woman she was when she died (see Project Images: Tomb of Nefertari [1986-1992], The Getty Conservation Institute, https://www.getty .edu/conservation/our_projects/field_projects/nefertari/nefertari_images.html). Perhaps throat lines became a symbol for advanced years (in the case of Nut, she is as old as the universe), not necessarily affluence/indulgence, which would be par for the course for royalty and the elite, i.e., they would not need to be represented with artistic allusions to their status; it was a given. Slaves, workers, or lesser subjects probably did not live long enough to warrant such lines, and were represented objectively and fairly uniformly, not with any sense of portraiture. As Jack Josephson suggests in his discussion concerning a then newly discovered head of Ahmose III, "this period of portraiture was realistic, creative, and dynamic," rather than "bland" and idealistic (in "An Altered Royal Head of the Twenty-Sixth Dynasty," *The Journal of Egyptian Archaeology* 74 (1988): 232-35, here, 35). So, the inclusions of horizontal lines *does* equate to body changes, for men *and* women, but it seems attention has only been paid to throat lines, and to chest lines on men, not the tummy lines on females (of which Ankhnesneferibre may be one of very few examples to date).

priestesses of Hathor).

Hallman suggests that the Chapel of Osiris Wennefer Neb-djefau was constructed during the earlier reign of Ahmose and that it probably predates her other chapels, where Ankhnesneferibre is also depicted (with both Ahmose and Psametik III)[34] but without any hint of the three lines. Is it possible that at the time of the construction of this earlier chapel Ankhnesneferibre was pregnant with, or had just had, Nitocris? I suggest there has to be a logical reason for these lines on the abdomen that disappear from subsequent depictions of Ankhnesneferibre.

Betsy Bryan speaks of the God's Wife office as potentially being "separate from the office holders," and that in this context, the question of celibacy becomes moot.[35] This seems a fundamental perspective that could open the door to a more open and balanced discussion.

TITLES AND EMBLEMS

The statue from Karnak does not list the office of God's Hand, which Ankhnesneferibre received at her dedication as God's Wife (c. 586 BCE, the fourth year of Apries' reign); this in itself is intriguing and may have an explanation in the apparent God's Hand role Nitocris II takes on in the Song, i.e., the role had already been passed down to her when the statue of her mother was made. It also includes something clearly controversial, as I have yet to discover a scholar openly discussing it in reference to Ankhnesneferibre, i.e., Great of Sceptre or, "Great one of the *hetes* sceptre."

There was no term for "Queen" in ancient Egypt, in fact, "most of the queens' titles and epithets related them to the king and [to] the king as the earthly embodiment of the gods, respectively. Only from the Middle Kingdom onward did their titles indicate a ruling function."[36] The title Great of Sceptre can be dated to the end of Dynasty 3, after which it "became the key designation for a royal wife. It fell out of use in the Middle Kingdom, before experiencing a limited

---

[34] Hallmann, 207.
[35] Bryan, 13.
[36] Silke Roth, Johannes Gutenberg-Universität Mainz, *UCLA Encyclopedia of Egyptology* 2009, escholarship.org] https://factsand details.com/world/cat56 /sub404/entry-6142.html.

revival in Saite times …,"[37] i.e., another of the retrospective changes implemented in Dynasty 26. Why is Ankhnesneferibre given this title, if she is not a wife of the king?

It does seem to be an issue that needs clarification, for the roles of God's Wives and "queens" are intricately intertwined, as exemplified by this assessment:

> … many of the rites, costume, paraphernalia, and epitheta of the God's Wives in Egypt were themselves borrowed from a still earlier source—the institution of queenship. Consequently, the adaptation of Egyptian rites and iconography in Nubia rarely allows one to discern whether the woman in question was posing as God's Wife or merely as queen.[38]

In the book, I discuss the role of God's Hand as it seems to relate to Nitocris in her lonely, isolated position in Tayma, with Nabonidus. Within that context, it is argued that the God's Hand was a woman who served as the vessel of the elixir of Life, of Creation (e.g., what is termed today the Elixir Rubeus); she brought the female blood, while the king brought the male 'milk'. She loses her (active) position as God's Hand should she have children, for the blood is thereafter seen as having lost its 'magical' qualities; this might explain why "God's Hand" does not appear as a title on either of the statues or Ankhnesneferibre's sarcophagus, i.e., she had given birth … to Nitocris. It is clear from earlier God's Wives that the title of God's Hand could be retained, e.g., as a sort of 'God's Hand Emeritus', and while both Amenirdis I and Nitocris I used the title regularly, it is possible Ankhnesneferibre did not wish to be remembered as such. This could be a subtle clue to her relationship with Ahmose, perhaps.

As her child is female, Ankhnesneferibre would not be given the title of King's Mother; and as we know Ahmose's Great Royal Wife (GRW) was Nakhtes-Bastet-reru, it is evident Ankhnesneferibre would have been a secondary royal wife. Even though earlier GRWs were the

---

[37] Aiden Dodson, *The Egyptian World,* Toby Wilkinson ed. (Abingdon: Taylor & Francis, 2007), 82.

[38] Jeremy Pope, "The Problem of Meritefnut: A 'God's Wife' during the 25th–26th Dynasties," *Journal of Egyptian History* 6 (2013): 177-216, here 194.

ones normally represented as the king's consort in public depictions,[39] her identification as God's Wife sufficed to afford Ankhnesneferibre the prestige and honour of the pharaoh's consort in all ritualistic contexts. There is a possible further parallel to be drawn from Ayad's description of depictions of the God's Wife Shepenwepet II, who is seen in concert with Pharaoh Taharqa (whose stature she equals), performing a solemn rite of protecting the crypt of Osiris. This God's Wife's identity was, Ayad claims, intentionally obscured for the sole purpose of allowing her to embody the divine wife, Isis, and to act as the female counterpart to the pharaoh.[40] Similarly, due to her title, "God's Wife of Amun," this deity's name had to be removed, in order for the symbolic re-enactment to make sense, i.e., she had to be seen as being Osiris' wife, not Amun's. Although Shepenwepet II sacrifices her GWA identity in order to accommodate the ritual of Osiris' cenotaph, she nevertheless remains the GWA. Ankhnesneferibre's titles might not include King's Wife simply because the GWA title takes precedence, just as her images and cartouches on Ahmose's monuments seem to take precedence over his GRW's (especially if the title relates to the divine birth of the king, as Koch argues [see note 15]).[41] Although the earlier dynasties' God's Wives were acknowledged as both royal wife and deity's consort, it may be that Dynasties 25/26 'changed the rules', i.e., making the reigning God's Wife principally the wife of Amun, and only secondarily the spouse of the king, allowing another, non-sacerdotal woman to take on the role of GRW. As we have no evidence to the contrary, the retrospective yet increasingly innovative Saite rulers (and the college of priestesses) could well have enjoyed the best of both worlds.

Why would Ankhnesneferibre not be *named* as King's Wife, if she

---

[39] Joyce Tyldesley, "The Many Queens of Ancient Egypt," *The Historian* (2020): 11-16, here 12.

[40] Mariam Ayad, "On the Identity and Role of the God's Wife of Amun in Rites of Royal and Divine Dominion," *Journal of the Society for the Study of Egyptian Antiquities* 34 (2007): 1-13, here 7-8.

[41] Anthony Leahy states that on her Adoption Stele, Ankhnesneferibre's "whole name—and not just her father's component of it— was for the first time written in a cartouche, thus completing her transference to regal status"; might this have reflected a marriage to Apries? ("The Adoption of Ankhnesneferibre at Karnak," *The Journal of Egyptian Archaeology* 82 (1996): 145-65, here 159).

were married to the pharaoh? There are many instances of pharaohs' wives not using their "King's Wife" titles, even (or especially) in their funerary inscriptions.[42] Kitchen explains that Ramesses II's mother, Queen Tuya, a God's Wife, is not named as King's Wife in her tomb, yet it is well established that she was Sethi I's wife, and had the title of King's Mother, which was only given to the chief wife who bore the pharaoh his male heir.[43] Ahmose-Nefertari had the titles of "King's Wife" and "King's Mother" but chose to be remembered only as God's Wife; Hatshepsut and her daughter, Neferure, also used the title of God's Wife as their "sole identifying title."[44] It seems Ankhnesneferibre followed suit and chose her eternal names carefully. I suggest she wished to be remembered primarily as God's Wife (God's Adorer) of Amun, leaving behind her God's Hand Emeritus title and her First Prophet title. Obviously Nitocris II had already taken the position of First Prophet (before she left to marry Nabonidus), and I posit in the book that she had also attained the roles of Adoratrice and God's Hand, or was at least 'in training' as such. The only remaining acknowledgement of Ankhnesneferibre's earthly marriage, for the eternal record, is her Great of Sceptre title, simply and quietly stated.

Jane Mulder, in discussing the absence of "King's Wife" titles in royal inscriptions states:

> The fact that the inscription does not contain the title "King's wife" could denote one of two things. Firstly, if she was Pharaoh the title would not be applicable. Secondly, it could indicate that she was a royal princess whose marriage legitimised her (non-royal) husband's title to the throne.[45]

Both of these situations may be applicable to Ankhnesneferibre and Ahmose, for in the first case, there seems to be at least some circumstantial evidence to suggest Ankhnesneferibre was, or saw herself as a pharaoh, or at least a co-regent (see below); in the second case, Ahmose does require a degree of legitimization as he is not of the

---

[42] Teeter, "Celibacy," 410 and see notes 29-31.

[43] K. A. Kitchen, "The Twentieth Dynasty Revisited," *The Journal of Egyptian Archaeology* 68 (1982): 116-25, here 123.

[44] Ayad, *God's Wife, God's Servant*, 6.

[45] Jane Mulder, "Was Khent-Kawes History's First Woman King?" (2014) *Shemu Articles,* https://www.egyptiansociety.co.za/was-khent-kawes-historys-first-woman-king/.

Psametik I lineage, yet he is accepted into the fold of Dynasty 26. Marrying Apries' daughter would have sufficed, perhaps, but why not ally himself with the prestigious and 'superior' sister?

Ankhnesneferibre's regalia, as depicted on her sarcophagus, the power and dominion she represents rests with the iconography of royalty, not merely as a King's Daughter,[46] but as God's Wife *and* a female "ruler." Just like other God's Wives before her,[47] she wears the vulture[48] headdress and uraeus, representing the mother goddesses Nekhbet and Wadjet, adopted by the royal mothers of Dynasties 3 and 4, thereafter a recognized symbol of motherhood; this was the crown the queen wore in the context of the *hieros gamos*.[49] As a point of contrast, the God's Wife Amenirdis I is depicted as a very feminine figure, holding only a "fly whisk,"[50] one of the most frequently depicted elements of New Kingdom queenly regalia. Ankhnesneferibre *is* depicted as feminine (i.e., wearing the queenly crown and the headdress of Hathor) but holding the flail and crook of kingship. The crook is used as the hieroglyph for "ruler" and is generally reserved for the pharaoh; Ankhnesneferibre's prenomen, or throne name, is Hekat-neferu-mut, i.e., "Mut is *regent* of beauty," or "Female *ruler* of perfection is Mut"; the pharaoh's wife traditionally represented Mut (and this was adopted by the God's Wife Amenirdis I, Shepenwepet II, and Nitocris I, but without the allusion to kingship; Ankhnesneferibre's

---

[46] Her title "King's Daughter of his body" is the expanded version of "King's Daughter," signalling a desire to ensure it is known that she is of pure blood, i.e., a true daughter, not adopted, etc.

[47] See Mariam Ayad, *God's Wife, God's Servant: The God's Wife of Amun (c.740-525 BC)* (Abingdon: Routledge, 2009), 53; Dodson and Hilton, 244 (image).

[48] Egyptian legend had it that vultures were only female; the Egyptian word for "mother" (*mwt*) was indicated by a vulture hieroglyph; the word for "womb" (*mwt-rmt*), contains the vulture hieroglyph. See Herman Te Velde, "The Goddess Mut and the Vulture," in *Servant of Mut: Studies in Honor of Richard A. Fazzini*, Sue H. D'Auria, ed., Probleme der Ägyptologie 28 (Leiden: Brill, 2007): 242-5. https://www.jacobusvandijk.nl/docs/Vulture.pdf.

[49] Hallmann, 214.

[50] Dodson and Hilton, 235. See also "Relief, modern cast, Queen Ahmose carrying fly whisk" (ROM 910.53.1), Dynasty 18, Royal Ontario Museum, https://collections.rom.on.ca/objects/187299.

prenomen stands out as "assertive"[51]).

In the chapels at Karnak, Ankhnesneferibre is equal in scale to Ahmose III, illustrating *her* esteemed status; Hallmann suggests that even though "she is rendered in a position hitherto reserved for a ruler, her portrayals are balanced by representations of the ruling king." I am suggesting this is because she *is* (at least) on a par with the king.[52] Ahmose's images in these chapels proceed anticlockwise and appear on the south side, whereas Ankhnesneferibre's proceed clockwise, or towards the left, on the north side; the 'left' side, in terms of temple decoration, took precedence over the 'right' side, possibly suggesting Ankhnesneferibre was, in some respects, superior even to the pharaoh.[53] There is an air of a royal parade, a ritualistic encompassing of the kingdom by the couple—the royal couple, the earthly male-female counterparts to the divine couple, Amun and Mut.

On the walls of the tomb of Pabasa (TT 279), the chief steward of God's Wife Nitocris I (Ankhnesneferibre's predecessor), Pharaoh Psametik I and Nitocris I are also depicted as having equal status; "she is represented as a coregent queen."[54] They appear opposite each other, with analogous representation, e.g., of royal dress, regalia, and titulary, including Horus names. This most ancient title, the Horus name, normally confirmed the legitimacy of the pharaoh as the incarnation of Horus, and thus the true ruler, yet the God's Wives used them. The God's Wife Shepenwepet II (Dynasty 25, also depicted on the same scale as the pharaoh, i.e., Taharqa) was the first of the God's Wives to receive the Horus name; Nitocris I followed suit, and finally, Ankhnesneferibre. "There are only three queens to have claimed a Horus title during the pharaonic era": Neferusobek (Dynasty 12), Hatshepsut (Dynasty 18), and Tausert (Dynasty 19), each of whom

---

[51] Ayad, God's Wife, God's Servant, 29.

[52] Hallmann, 209. Amy Calvert explains that kings are often shown on the same scale as deities, and both royalty and deities "are shown larger than the elite and far larger than the average Egyptian" (in "Egyptian Art," https://www.khanacademy.org/humanities/ap-art-history/ancient-mediterranean-ap/ancient-egypt-ap/a/egyptian-art).

[53] Hallmann, 209 and note 39.

[54] Mamdouh Eldamaty, "The Equality and Presence of Nitocris and Psamtik I in the Tomb of Pabasa (TT 279),"in *Thebes in the First Millennium BC - South Asasif Conference 2 - Program* (25-9 September 2016, Luxor), 17, https://www.academia.edu/29186191.

"ruled Egypt as a king ...."[55]

On her adoption into the priesthood at Thebes (Karnak), Ankhnesneferibre receives *five* special epithets, a number normally attributed to the pharaoh, i.e., "great of kindness, great of praises, lady of grace, sweet of love, mistress of all women." These titles also use language (specific Egyptian words) normally reserved for kings' epithets.[56] On her sarcophagus, she is called: "The Osiris, Ankhnesneferibre, justified, Born [literally engendered] of the great royal wife, foremost of his majesty Tikhawal." This phrasing, so Teeter argues, is unusual, in that the "engendered" filiation is "more often associated with reference to a male antecedent ...."[57]

"Mistress of all Women" suggests true queenship, as we would recognize it:

> ... interpreting the queen's title ... "lady of all women," as a leading position in the context of the harem could be implied by the single known occurrence of the epithet ... "lady of the royal women altogether" of Meritra Hatshepsut (statue of Neferperet, Cairo CG 42121, 18th Dynasty ...).[58]

There is, then, a very clear intention to depict Ankhnesneferibre, posthumously, as quasi-male, a ruler in her own right. This posthumous sexual ambiguity, Egyptologists suggest, is an example of "gender fluidity" that is necessary for women to progress through the necessary rites, rituals, and divine 'associations' required for passage to the afterlife (traditionally ensconced in masculine terminology, etc.). A case in point is that of Nefertari, wife of Ramesses II, whose tomb

---

[55] Eldamaty, 17.

[56] Leahy, 155. Ronald Leprohon (in "Patterns of Royal Name-Giving," *UCLA Encyclopedia of Egyptology*, 1.1 (2010): 1-10, here 3) suggests pharaohs were sometimes named using "anticipatory phraseology," or "wishful thinking," e.g., Amenhotep III, whose Golden Horus name invoked a degree of ruthless aggression seen later in his rule, even though he was only ten years old on his accession. Might the same be said of Psametik II and his ambitions for Ankhnesneferibre? If she were betrothed to her brother, more or less since birth, it would not even be wishful thinking.

[57] Teeter, "Celibacy," 409, note 25.

[58] Silke Roth, "Harem," in *UCLA Encyclopedia of Egyptology*, Elizabeth Frood, Willeke Wendrich eds., (Los Angeles: UCLA, 2012), 3, http://digital2.library.ucla.edu/viewItem.do?ark=21198/zz002bqmpp.

employs representations of both male and female, i.e., queenly and kingly, attributes, without any mention of her much-loved pharaoh-husband.[59] The women in these funerary contexts dispensed with their male counterparts and focused solely on their own regeneration/rebirth.[60] For Ankhnesneferibre, her portrait on the lid of her sarcophagus combines both the feminine/queenly aspect via her vulture headdress *and* the masculine/kingly aspect, via the flail and crook; she has no need for a male counterpart.

Ayad makes an interesting comment that the God's Wife Shepenwepet II "comes across as the one to borrow most extensively from royal iconography. The ritualistic duties of a God's Wife may have peaked during the Kushite period, possibly reflecting an attempt to express Kushite queenship ideology in a manner acceptable to Egyptians." She goes on to say that Shepenwepet went as far as to depict herself taking part in the kingly *sed*-festival (where the king received his priestly office), normally restricted to pharaohs, and concludes that "during this transitional period, the God's Wife and high officials such as Montuemhat (i.e., the First Prophet of Amun) were virtually unaccountable to anyone and probably had complete authority over the Theban region."[61]

The question, therefore, has to be asked: Was Ankhnesneferibre, boldly going into the afterlife dressed as both Queen and King, preserving for posterity her own claim to the throne of Egypt? Could she have been another unrecognized female pharaoh, even if her role was fleeting, or was more of a co-regency?

Christopher Witcombe, in discussing a statue of "Menkaure and His Queen" (2548-2530 BCE, Dynasty 4), argues that dynastic *power* descended through the female line, and states:

> The queen represented in the statue, therefore, was no mere wife. Her position and gestures should be interpreted not as

---

[59] Heather Lee McCarthy, "The Osiris Nefertari: A Case Study of Decorum, Gender, and Regeneration," *Journal of the American Research Center in Egypt* 39 (2002): 173-95.

[60] See also Li, 217-30.

[61] Mariam Ayad, "Gender, Ritual and the Manipulation of Power: The God's Wife of Amun (Dynasty 23-26)," in 'Prayer and Power' Proceedings of the Conference on the God's Wives of Amun in Egypt during the First Millennium BC (2016), 89–106, here 96.

indicating inferiority and submission, but signalling her legitimization of Menkaure as pharaoh. She is shown in the act of presenting him, indicating to the world that he is the man whom she is identifying and establishing as pharaoh. Her pose, in fact, deliberately imitates that of the goddess Hathor in the triad statues and with whom she is clearly intended to be identified. The statue itself is a representation of this act of confirmation, and perhaps even a record of part of an actual confirmation ceremony.[62]

In Part Two, Chapter 5 of my book Nitocris is described as ritually presenting Nabonidus to Amun, identifying him as the one she is 'teaching', her protégée, her "beloved" (*dodi*). She could well have learned from her mother's example that her dominance (something very clearly expressed throughout the Song of Solomon) is her birth right.

Does Ankhnesneferibre inherit this powerful, self-possessed, elitist attitude because she, too, is raised to believe she *is* Pharaoh's equal? Did Psametik I refashion the GWA role as one once again exclusive to royal wives? If Ankhnesneferibre married her brother Apries, she, too, could be seen as the ideal sister-bride (i.e., a precedent for Nitocris in the Song). As there are countless lacunae in the historical record, especially regarding Apries' family, and we know this form of marriage did occur, it is possible that Ahmose seized Ankhnesneferibre as his *own* wife, and as a symbol of the conquest over Apries. If De Meulenaere and Koch are correct in their assessment that the incoming victor of a coup would, necessarily, usurp the position of First Prophet (who would then have been Ankhnesneferibre) for his own offspring,[63] it cannot be too much of a leap to suggest he took the incumbent God's Wife as his own symbol of power (at a visceral level, as a sign of Apries' personal defeat, too).

If Herodotus' account of the initially resented, jokester king is based on any truth (*Hist.* 2.172-4), can it be that Ankhnesneferibre is the power behind the throne? Is it Ahmose's legitimization via his marriage to the powerful, respected God's Wife that supposedly changes his subjects' opinion of him (e.g., would a marriage to an

---

[62] Christopher Witcombe, "Menkaure and His Queen," § 3, http://arthistory resources.net/menkaure /menkaurequeen.html.
[63] De Meulenaere, 79–80.

'ordinary' princess have been enough to sway opinions?)? This may be where the Greek historian gets his notion that Queen Nitocris of Babylon is a formidable ruler and a builder/engineer, without any apparent deference to her husband the king (*Hist.* 1.185).[64] In the Song, too, Nitocris is seen, from the very beginning, as an independent, formidable woman, and during the narrative she honours her mother for teaching her everything she knows.

In *Hist.* 2.100, the Egyptian female pharaoh "Nitocris" is mentioned, forming a link with Nitocris II by virtue of their names. It is interesting that this earlier Nitocris is said to have had a brother who was King, ousted by his own people, and then killed; she is claimed to have taken on his regency for a short while. Apries, of course, is ousted by his own men and later killed; Ankhnesneferibre might well have taken the reins for a while, especially if Ahmose was initially ill-prepared to take on the role of Pharaoh, having had it thrust upon him. The focus of the tale Herodotus relays about this earlier Queen Nitocris is one of a surreptitious revenge that ends with mass murder (via impressive civil-engineering and the redirecting of a river, i.e., projects also attributed to Nitocris of Babylon in *Hist.* 1.185-6) and suicide (a question that arises in the Epilogue of the book and which relates to *Hist.* 1.187 and the supposed tomb of Nitocris). Even the "banquet" alluded to in *Hist.* 2.100, which comes just before the "Egyptian" Nitocris' murder of those responsible for the coup against her brother, reminds us of the festivities just before the invasion of Babylon by the Persians, as preserved in Daniel 5 and *Hist.* 1.191, the latter, *also* in the context of the enemy being submerged by the waters diverted by the Queen.

THE OSIRIS

Ankhnesneferibre appears on her sarcophagus as "The Osiris, Ankhnesneferibre." Roth suggests the female deceased could synchronize with Osiris because the deity was androgynous, i.e., effectively a "woman" (in an ancient myth, Osiris tells his wife "I am a woman like you") because he had no penis (having been 'lost' after

---

[64] Though Herodotus does not suggest our Nitocris is Egyptian, he does link her to the assumed "Queen Nitocris" of Egypt by virtue of her name (*Hist.* 2.100).

his dismemberment).[65] Thus a woman was able to regenerate herself, just as a man could. The iconography of the crook and flail on the sarcophagus lid, though on the one hand suggesting kingship, also suggests a strong Osirian belief system, for these two items are ancient symbols of Osiris. The positioning of the God's Wife's hands is key: Osiris traditionally holds the crook in the left hand, which is positioned below the right hand that holds the flail. The crook extends lower, almost to the thigh, and is held at a different angle to the flail.[66] This is precisely how Ankhnesneferibre is depicted; she is not simply emulating the ideal of Osiris, she identifies as Osiris.

As there are many analyses of the Osirian belief system, mythology, and funerary practices, I wish to focus only on how this may prove significant to an understanding of Nitocris' presentation in the Song of Solomon and, therefore, how it helps us understand the relationship between her and Ankhnesneferibre.

Ayad suggests that Ankhnesneferibre had a very different personal religion to her God's Wife predecessor, Amenirdis I, as exemplified by the choice of funerary texts in both cases (which suggests the office was more political than religious).[67] She explains that the chosen texts of Amenirdis reflect her desire to be remembered as a woman, echoing her feminine depiction, whereas Ankhnesneferibre chose strongly Osirian, and therefore more masculine, texts.[68] Ayad suggests the change in dynastic rule might explain these differences.[69] Thus, once more, we might look to the cultural revolution of Dynasty 26 for the sudden shift in theological

---

[65] Anne Macy Roth, "Father Earth, Mother Sky: Ancient Egyptian Beliefs about Conception and Fertility," in *Reading the Body: Representations and Remains in the Archaeological Record*, Alison Rautman, ed., (Philadelphia: University of Pennsylvania Press, 2000), 187-201, here 198-9.

[66] Griffiths, J. Gwyn. "Osiris and the Moon in Iconography." *The Journal of Egyptian Archaeology* 62 (1976): 153-9, here 154, https://doi.org/10.2307/3856356.

[67] Miriam Ayad, "The Pyramid Texts of Amenirdis I: Selection and Layout," *Journal of the American Research Center in Egypt* 43 (2007): 71-92, here 85.

[68] Mariam Ayad, in "Some Remarks on the Pyramid Texts Inscribed in the Chapel of Amenirdis I at Medinet Habu," in Stephen E. Thompson and Peter der Manuelian (eds.), *Egypt and Beyond: Essays Presented to Leonard H. Lesko* (Providence: Department of Egyptology and Ancient Western Asian Studies, 2008), 1-13, here, 8. https://www.academia.edu/338175.

[69] Ayad, "Pyramid Texts in the Chapel of Amenirdis I," 6.

ideas, which then allows us to more fully ascertain a Dynasty 26 timeframe for the Song of Solomon. If the GWA office was, indeed, more political than religious, then it would not be necessary for any heir to that role to adhere to her predecessor's belief system; it would make perfect sense, however, for a true mother to pass on her beliefs to her flesh and blood daughter. As there is no evidence for Ahmose III's funerary iconography or texts, we cannot know his beliefs but I would wager they were not fully in-synch with Ankhnesneferibre's! He was an outsider, a military man, a clever and astute man, but more a hedonist than an ascetic; his funerary choices would probably have reflected that (albeit imbued with all the expected ritual and pomp of a pharaoh), as this would be his final declaration of who he was and who he intended to be in the afterlife. So, the fact that Nitocris seems to follow the Osirian ideology, i.e., as she is depicted in the Song, suggests she emulates her mother more than her father, which is *also* what we see in the biblical text.

The Osirian mythology, as it relates to the dead, depicts the deity as the chthonic judge, the one who directs proceedings as the deceased's heart is weighed against the feather of Maat. The resulting judgement declares the dead one "Justified" or "True of Voice" (*maat kheru*).

In the Song, as I have attempted to explain, Nitocris takes Nabonidus as a protégée, initiating him into certain rites and rituals; at one point, she creates a poppet of him and 'presents' him to Amun-Re, calling him, in effect, "true of voice" (which has sinister undertones in context). Throughout her attempt to convert the king, Nitocris' teaching is underscored by his listening to and repeating her words, and the power of speech is constantly alluded to throughout; the words of mystical import, the words of ritual, the words of spells—the "utterances"; they are all in the Song. Nitocris is teacher, high priest; Nabonidus is student, novice.

As Tom Hare writes:

> The aim of an Egyptian education is the man who knows how to listen, homo auditor, the man who hears, who obeys, the man attentive, benevolent, and docile, who bows before one who speaks and accepts the counsel which one gives him. The entirety of Egyptian civilization seems to be founded upon and animated by this faculty of listening to one another. The whole

of social life depends on the faculty of understanding one another.[70]

In connection with this emphasis on hearing and obeying the word, and Nitocris' attempt to teach Nabonidus how to do this, is the following extract from *She Brought the Art of Women*:

> Of significance is the fact that the verb "to swallow," as used in the Book of the Dead, came to mean "to know." This is understood to be a specifically Egyptian development within the magical sphere. Inscriptions on Ankhnesneferibre's sarcophagus include "an address to deified 'Perception' (Sia) as 'the Great Swallower'."[71] This may be further evidence for the connection between the Elixir and the God's Hand. King Nabonidus ingests, he "swallows," therefore, he "knows" (in theory).[72]

I claim that Nitocris introduces Nabonidus to the most sacred Elixir rite in a desperate attempt to keep him at bay so she will not become pregnant (again); she wishes to retain her sacred status as this "perpetual fountain." Her plan goes a little awry, however, but the point is, the Song's strong interest in esoteric knowledge, ritual learning, speech and comprehension, culminates in the imbibing of the Elixir, the ambrosia of the gods, the hallucinogenic, mind-bending source of hidden wisdom.

Therefore, it may be that Nitocris' apparent role as God's Hand in Tayma, and her unique position as the source of the Elixir Rubeus, may have a direct correlation with Ankhnesneferibre's tribute to the "the Great Swallower," and the cultic legacy she passed on to her daughter. Although this may not, in and of itself, prove a *biological* filiation, it certainly helps support the theory that it is Nitocris II we are seeing in the Song, and that she is, indeed, emulating her mother, the God's Hand Ankhnesneferibre. It also strengthens the theory of a specific sexual/metaphysical aspect to the God's Hand office.

---

[70] Tom Hare, *Remembering Osiris: Number, Gender, and the Word in Ancient Egyptian Representational System*, (Redwood City: Stanford University Press, 1999), 30.

[71] Robert Kreich Ritner, *The Mechanics of Ancient Egyptian Magical Practice*, ed. Thomas A. Holland, SAOC 54 (Chicago: University of Chicago, 1993), 106-7.

[72] Janet Tyson, *She Brought the Art of Women: A Song of Solomon, Nabonidus, and the Goddess* (Norwich: Pirištu Books, 2023), 123.

Attention is drawn again to Ankhnesneferibre's sarcophagus lid, where she holds the flail and crook. Most discussions concerning these items state they are symbols of earthly power (e.g., the flail as a sign of control, the crook of leadership and restraint, etc.), but there are those who see these as emblems of something far more esoteric and ethereal, which ties in with the more metaphysical aspects of the Song of Solomon.

Nitocris, in the Song's narrative, continues with her priestly rites and rituals, despite Nabonidus' incessant demands for the Elixir. She offers her *dod* to him, i.e., her 'higher love' and tries to convince him to pursue his own *dod*; she shows him the path to enlightenment but he is 'stuck' at the level of the mundane, the profane. The entire Song is constructed around this battle of theologies and wills, with the final outcome being a sombre realisation that the king loses his kingdom because he fails to attain a higher level of consciousness.

This tallies with the metaphysical perception of Osiris in that when a deceased Egyptian's heart is weighed against the feather of Maat, the judgement is not one of assessing one's greatness, or deeds, or riches; it is based solely on what bad, or destructive things one did *not* do in life. It is a test of abstinence, of purity, of enlightenment (*very* broadly speaking). So the Song depicts its main female character (Nitocris) as demonstrating the tenets of an Osirian philosophy; she learned this from her mother who "taught" her.

Many who study ancient esoterica refer to the Osirian crook and flail[73] as a symbolic representation of the opposing forces, the good and evil, the light and dark, etc., that become a 'dance of Mahanaim' for all humans (if you read the book you will understand this allusion) in their quest for eternal salvation.

---

[73] There is an interesting connection between Osiris and the flail, in that the latter is possibly an instrument that was originally used to collect Ladanum, a sweet-scented resin used for special incense (see Percy E. Newberry, "The Shepherd's Crook and the So-Called 'Flail' or 'Scourge' of Osiris," *The Journal of Egyptian Archaeology* 15.1/2 (1929): 84-94). It has been conjectured that the name Osiris originally meant "The Place of the Eye (of Horus)" and that the incense was used in a purification right for the Eye (T. J. Colin Baly, "A Note on the Origin of Osiris," *The Journal of Egyptian Archaeology* 17.3/4 (1931): 221-2, here 222). Baly goes on to suggest that "incense was considered as an exudation of Osiris" (222), and thus equates Osiris with Ladanum itself. Might these snippets of insight have a bearing on understanding the depiction of perfumes and oils in the Song, in the context of Nitocris' priestly rituals?

MUSINGS

All of these little details and related questions form at least a tentative platform from which further investigations into the very *human* arena of Ankhnesneferibre and Nitocris' relationship can be launched. Unorthodox it may be but simply repeating the norm, unquestioned, does nothing to enlighten or move the discussion forward. Something that intrigues me, for instance, is whether all of this might point to Ankhnesneferibre being somewhat resentful of being Ahmose's wife (assuming she was, of course). If she had been forced to marry him, just as Nitocris was forced to marry Nabonidus, and especially if she blamed Ahmose for her daughter's (eternal) death (see the Epilogue to the book), it might explain her desire not to be remembered in her funerary depictions as being King's Wife, i.e., the sole concession being her "Great of Sceptre" title that could just as easily have been privately intended to refer to her (possible) union with her brother, Apries! It might also find a connection with the alleged desecration of the sarcophagi of Ahmose and the rest of his family.

According to Herodotus, recounting a tale he adamantly refutes (*Hist.* 3.16), Ahmose was warned by an oracle that his own tomb would be ransacked and his mummified body desecrated, so he installed a body-double in the tomb to ensure his own passage to the afterlife. This body-double, mistakenly thought to be the pharaoh, apparently received much physical abuse and was then burned. The historian had previously stated that Ahmose was buried alongside Apries and his family (2.169) in a tomb 'guarded' by Osiris. This would have been wholly ironic, don't you think? The tomb has never been found.

The sarcophagi of Ahmose III's wife, Nekhtbastetru, their son Ahmose (Iahmes), and a certain Tashentihet, were all found together in a tomb in Giza in the middle of the nineteenth century.[74] The first two sarcophagi reveal signs of ritualistic and highly targeted defacement in the ancient past; Bolshakov argues that the work had to have been done by someone skilled in carving hieroglyphics (for there is under a millimetre's grace between defacement and eradication), though there would seem to be no motive.[75]

---

[74] Andrey Bolshakov, "Persians and Egyptians: Cooperation in Vandalism?" in *Offerings to the Discerning Eye* (Leiden: Brill, 2010), 45-54.

[75] Bolshakov, 45, note 6. As for the sarcophagus of Tashentihet C, this stood in the court of Cairo Medical School for a while but then disappeared, its

The first explanation that comes to mind, of course, is Herodotus' three-fold tale of the revenge of Cambyses for the wrongful 'palming off' of Apries' daughter, "Nitetis" (who, of course, is Nitocris, as is the claim of my book). John Dillery suggests Herodotus' Egyptian priestly sources expounded the Persian conquest of Egypt in a literary genre that has a strong basis in mythological and prophetic literature dating back to the Middle Kingdom.[76] The combined approaches create a nationalistic narrative with the sequence: King makes bad decisions—the kingdom is lost to outsiders—order is restored. This narrative is founded on the Osiris-Seth legend,[77] with the added 'hope for the future' that traditional prophecy allowed. In times of foreign rule, this was vital.

Looking at Cambyses through this lens, so many things become clearer. We learn that the image of the violent, deranged, revenge-driven Persian king is strongly influenced by an ancient 'coping mechanism' the Egyptian priests promulgated, and Herodotus adopted. As time goes by, more and more atrocities are linked to Cambyses, until he becomes the veritable twin of the arch-nemesis Nebuchadnezzar I, with traits and exploits intermingled between them.[78] Herodotus himself does this with Cambyses and Cleomenes of Sparta (*Hist.* 6.75-84); presumably his audience enjoyed the former depiction, so he rendered Cleomenes similarly.

So, although, once again, there are kernels of veracity in

---

inscriptions unpublished. The name is very similar to Ahmose III's mother, Tashereniset, but I argue in the Epilogue to the book that Tashereniset C could be none other than little Ennigaldi-Nanna, i.e., Ahmose's assumed granddaughter, having been returned to Egypt after the fall of Babylon. (N.B. During the research for *Arabian Sinai* I discovered this is no longer a valid comment, as Ennigaldi remains with her father for much of the 'exodus' and dies on the outskirts of Tayma years later.)

[76] John Dillery, "Cambyses and the Egyptian *Chaosbeschreibung* Tradition," *The Classical Quarterly* 55.2 (2005): 387-406.

[77] Herodotus uses words that link directly to this theme, e.g., "Typhon" (a place name); this was a commonly-used allusion to "external enemies of Egypt," where Typhonic refers to "minions of Seth" (Dillery, 392). Whether Herodotus understood this or not, no one knows, but somehow I doubt it; it was clearly a priestly 'in' reference.

[78] Michal Habaj, "Some Notes on the Tradition of Cambyses/Nebuchadnezzar in Book LI of John of Nikiu's Chronicle," *Egitto E Vicino Oriente* 41 (2018): 151-66, here 159.

Herodotus' stories, it behoves us to be a little more discerning and bear in mind that his may not be the final word on these events. Just as Necho II became the epitome of an 'evil' foreign ruler to the Jews, so Cambyses becomes the personification of Egypt's nemesis and later Xerxes, to the Greeks.

If the damage to the sarcophagi of Ahmose and his family (and, indeed, the cartouches of Ahmose himself, at Abydos) was probably *not* done by Cambyses, nor upon his orders, who could have been responsible? It appears to be a case of "Who? *Me*?" as the Egyptian stone masons hide their chisels behind their backs.

If Ankhnesneferibre was, indeed, married to Ahmose, the fact that her sarcophagus escapes this treatment might be considered suspicious.[79] Did she, perhaps, instigate a ritualistic revenge on the man who killed her brother, forced her into marriage, and then let her daughter suffer a humiliating and everlasting death in a far-off land?

Such an attitude might, on a mundane level, help explain why Nitocris (in the Song) feels she can go to her mother for advice on her marriage/pregnancy situation. Ankhnesneferibre is the "mother" in the Song, i.e., the one who "used to teach" Nitocris; her ability to confer this sort of advice really only makes sense if Ankhnesneferibre is seen as the wife of Pharaoh, i.e., Nitocris' *biological* mother, who would understand about marriage, sex, pregnancy, etc., where a prestigious but celibate priestess would not. Nitocris finds herself in just the same position; she is forced to marry the King of Babylon, considered Egypt's enemy for generations, and she, too, gets pregnant.

That Ahmose is supposedly concerned that a daughter of his would be treated as a concubine in a foreign court (so Herodotus suggests, 3.1), might just be a clue to Ankhnesneferibre's *own* concerns for her daughter, i.e., perhaps it is *she* who insists on Nitocris being given the crown of queenship, the position of primacy and power. Of course this is speculation, but the body of circumstantial evidence does steer us in that direction. Ankhnesneferibre knows from experience as a usurper-king's wife, not as a God's Wife, what Nitocris needs to learn

---

[79] When Psametik II took the throne, the previous Nubian rulers appear to have undergone the same treatment, yet the Nubian God's Wives statues and tombs were left untouched. Lloyd D. Graham (2017-19) "King's Daughter, God's Wife: The Princess as High Priestess in Mesopotamia (Ur, ca. 2300-1100 BCE) and Egypt (Thebes, ca. 1550-525 BCE)," note 715, https://www .academia.edu/34248896.

in her situation in Tayma.

Ahmose III, in his bid to revive the best of 'golden age' Egypt, might well have followed his namesake's lead in making the college of the God's Wives, Adoratrices, and God's Hands far more significant and powerful than before; it would be prudent for him to keep the bloodline as close as possible to his seat of authority. Ahmose Nefertari, for instance, sister and wife of Ahmose I (c.1550-1525 BCE) held the position of Second Prophet of Amun; on being made God's Wife by her husband, she relinquished her Second Prophet position to her stepson. Ankhnesneferibre, who had received the office of First Prophet when initially brought to Thebes (probably as a child) in 595 BCE, relinquishes the role to *her* 'daughter' Nitocris, I suggest, as soon as she is born. This would also be the optimum time for the queen to retire from the God's Hand position, for she had given birth, and as Ankhnesneferibre clearly chose not to be remembered for this role, Nitocris would have assumed the position, possibly, upon beginning menses.

I find it intriguing that scholars who discuss Ankhnesneferibre rarely include her God's Hand title, yet it is one of the many she receives at her inauguration as God's Wife, according to her Adoption Stele (2.12-15); admittedly, it is a subtle title ("hand of the god"), added last, but it is there.[80] If she had been a child (prepubescent), little emphasis would be placed on such a role, perhaps, until she matured, but the fact that it all but disappears from her titulary over the years does point to the possibility of there being someone else in the role and/or to a somewhat tense relationship between her and Ahmose. We tend to think of these ancient Egyptian priestesses, etc., as being defined solely by their sacerdotal duties; we must remember these were just as a much flesh-and-blood folk as you and me, warts and all.

Obviously, much of this discussion is founded on an incomplete historical record and speculation but I have tried to remain faithful to the evidence I have found and the patterns I have seen. My goal was to ask penetrating questions about the potential attribution of a sacerdotal position for her "mother" and the possibility of a biological relationship between the two women based on a possible marriage between Ankhnesneferibre and Ahmose III. I am convinced there is more

---

[80] Even Aiden Dodson does not list her as God's Hand in his suggested chronology ("The Problem of Amenirdis II," 186).

material out there that will help forge this new understanding … I just need to find it!

One day, perhaps, I can go back to the British Museum, put my hand on Ankhnesneferibre's sarcophagus again, and tell them they can relist her as "Wife of Amasis"!

BIBLIOGRAPHY

Ayad, Miriam. "Gender, Ritual and the Manipulation of Power: The God's Wife of Amun (Dynasty 23-26)." Pages 89-106 in *'Prayer and Power' Proceedings of the Conference on the God's Wives of Amun in Egypt during the First Millennium BC*. Ugarit-Verlag, 2016.

____. *God's Wife, God's Servant: The God's Wife of Amun (c. 740-525 BC)*. Abingdon: Routledge, 2009.

____. "On the Identity and Role of the God's Wife of Amun in Rites of Royal and Divine Dominion." *Journal of the Society for the Study of Egyptian Antiquities* 34 (2007): 1-13.

____. "The Pyramid Texts of Amenirdis I: Selection and Layout." *Journal of the American Research Center in Egypt* 43 (2007): 71-92.

____. "Some Remarks on the Pyramid Texts Inscribed in the Chapel of Amenirdis I at Medinet Habu." Pages 1-13 in *Egypt and Beyond: Essays Presented to Leonard H. Lesko*. Edited by Stephen E. Thompson and Peter der Manuelian. Providence: Department of Egyptology and Ancient Western Asian Studies, 2008. https://www .academia.edu /338175.

Azzoni, Annalisa. "Women and Property in Persian Egypt and Mesopotamia." Paper presented at the Women and Property Conference, Centre for Hellenic Studies, Harvard University, 2003. https://classics-at.chs.harvard.edu/wp-content/uploads/2021/05/ca1.2-azzoni.pdf.

Baly, T. J. Colin. "A Note on the Origin of Osiris." *The Journal of Egyptian Archaeology* 17.3/4 (1931): 221-22.

Biston-Moulin, Sébastien. "King Sénakht-en-Rê Ahmès of the XVIIth Dynasty." *Égypte Nilotique et Méditerranéenne* 5 (2012): 61-71.

Bolshakov, Andrey. "Persians and Egyptians: Cooperation in Vandalism?" Pages 45-54 in *Offerings to the Discerning Eye*. Leiden: Brill, 2010.

Broekman, Gerard P. F. "On the Administration of the Thebaid during the Twenty-sixth Dynasty." *Studien zur Altägyptischen Kultur* 41 (2012): 113-35.

Bryan, Betsy. "Property and the God's Wives of Amun." Paper presented at the Women and Property Conference, Centre for Hellenic Studies, Harvard University, 2003. https://classics-at.chs.harvard.edu/wp-content/uploads /2021/05/ca1.2-bryan.pdf.

Calvert, Amy. "Egyptian Art." https://www.khanacademy.org/humanities/ ap-art-history/ancient-mediterranean-ap/ancient-egypt-ap/a/ egyptian-art.

Caminos, Ricardo A. "The Nitocris Adoption Stela." *The Journal of Egyptian Archaeology* 50 (1964): 71-101.

Campbell@Manchester. "The stela of the God's Wife, Princess Isis." Texts in translation #12 (2014). https://egyptmanchester.wordpress.com/2014/03 /02/texts-in-translation-12-the-stela-of-the-gods-wife-princess-isis-acc-no-1781/.

Coulon, Laurent. "The Quarter of the Divine Adoratrices at Karnak (Naga Malgata) during the Twenty-sixth Dynasty: Some Hitherto Unpublished Epigraphic Material." Pages 565-86 in *Thebes in the First Millennium BC*. Edited by Elena Pischikova, Julia Budka and Kenneth Griffin. Cambridge: Cambridge Scholars, 2014.

Dillery, John. "Cambyses and the Egyptian *Chaosbeschreibung* Tradition." *The Classical Quarterly* 55.2 (2005): 387-406.

Dodson, Aiden. *The Egyptian World.* Edited by Toby Wilkinson. Abingdon: Taylor & Francis, 2007.

_____. "The Problem of Amenirdis II and the Heirs to the Office of God's Wife of Amun during the Twenty-Sixth Dynasty." *The Journal of Egyptian Archaeology* 88 (2002): 179-86.

Dodson, Aidan and Dyan Hilton. *The Complete Royal Families of Ancient Egypt.* London: Thames & Hudson, 2010.

Eldamaty, Mamdouh. "The Equality and Presence of Nitocris and Psamtik I in the Tomb of Pabasa (TT 279)." Paper presented at *Thebes in the First Millennium BC - South Asasif Conference 2* (25-29 September 2016, Luxor). https://www.academia.edu/29186191.

Gardiner, Sir Alan. *Egypt of the Pharaohs: An Introduction.* Oxford: Oxford University Press, 1964.

Graham, Lloyd D. "King's Daughter, God's Wife: The Princess as High Priestess in Mesopotamia (Ur, ca. 2300-1100 BCE) and Egypt (Thebes, ca. 1550-525 BCE)." 2017-19. https://www.academia.edu/34248896.

Grajetzki, Wolfram. *Ancient Egyptian Queens: A Hieroglyphic Dictionary.* Golden House Publications, London: 2005.

Griffiths, J. Gwyn. "Osiris and the Moon in Iconography." *The Journal of Egyptian Archaeology* 62 (1976): 153-59. https://doi.org/10.2307 /3856356.

Habaj, Michal. "Some Notes on the Tradition of Cambyses/ Nebuchadnezzar in Book LI of John of Nikiu's Chronicle." *Egitto E Vicino Oriente* 41 (2018): 151-66.

Hallmann, Aleksandra. "Iconography of Prayer and Power: Portrayals of the God's Wife Ankhnesneferibre in Osiris Chapels at Karnak." Pages 205-22 in *Prayer and Power: Proceedings of the Conference on the God's Wives of Amun in Egypt during the First Millennium*. Edited by M. Becker, A. Blöbaum, and A. Löhwasser. Ägypten und Altes Testament 84. Münster, 2016.

Hare, Tom. *Remembering Osiris: Number, Gender, and the Word in Ancient Egyptian Representational System*. Redwood City: Stanford University Press, 1999.

Hill, Marsha. "A Bronze Aegis of King Amasis in the Egyptian Museum: Bronzes, Unconventionality and Unexpected Connections." Pages 545-56 in *Egyptian Museum Collections around the World*. Edited by Mamdouh Eldamaty and Mai Trad. Cairo: American University in Cairo Press, 2002.

____. "Small Divine Statuettes: Outfitting Religion." *Statues in Context: Production, Meaning and (Re)uses*. Edited by A. Masson-Berghoff. British Museum Publications on Egypt and Sudan 10 (2019): 35-49.

Hill, Marsha and Deborah Schorsch. "A Gilded-silver Pendant of Nephthys Naming Mereskhonsu (with an appended technical examination)." *Revue d'Egyptologie* 66 (2015): 33-49.

Josephson, Jack. "An Altered Royal Head of the Twenty-Sixth Dynasty." *The Journal of Egyptian Archaeology* 74 (1988): 232–35.

Kitchen, K. A. "The Twentieth Dynasty Revisited." *The Journal of Egyptian Archaeology* 68 (1982): 116-25.

Koch, C. *Die den Amun mit ihrer Stimme zufriedenstellen: Gottesgemahlinnen und Musikerinnen im thebanischen Amunstaat von der 22. bis zur 26. Dynastie*. Dettelbach: Röll, 2012.

Leahy, Anthony. "The Adoption of Ankhnesneferibre at Karnak." *The Journal of Egyptian Archaeology* 82 (1996): 145-65.

Leprohon, Ronal. "Patterns of Royal Name-Giving." *UCLA Encyclopedia of Egyptology* 1.1 (2010): 1-10.

Li, Jean. "The Singers in the Residence of the Temple of Amen at Medinet Habu: Mortuary Practices, Agency, and the Material Constructions of Identity." *Journal of the American Research Centre in Egypt* 47 (2011): 217-30.

Madrigal, Karine. "L'obélisque de Louqsor et le sarcophage d'Ânkhnesneferibrê." ENiM 10 (2017): 51-88.

McCarthy, Heather Lee. "The Osiris Nefertari: A Case Study of Decorum,

Gender, and Regeneration." *Journal of the American Research Center in Egypt* 39 (2002): 173–95.

Meulenaere, H. De. "La Famille Du Roi Amasis." *The Journal of Egyptian Archaeology* 54 (1968): 183-87.

Mulder, Jane. "Was Khent-Kawes History's First Woman King?" *Shemu Articles* (2014). https://www.egyptiansociety.co.za/was-khent- kawes-historys-first-woman-king/.

Newberry, Percy E. "The Shepherd's Crook and the So-Called 'Flail' or 'Scourge' of Osiris." *The Journal of Egyptian Archaeology* 15.1/2 (1929): 84-94.

Pope, Jeremy. "The Problem of Meritefnut: A 'God's Wife' during the 25th-26th Dynasties." *Journal of Egyptian History* 6 (2013): 177-216.

"Relief, modern cast, Queen Ahmose carrying fly whisk." (ROM 910.53.1). Dynasty 18. Royal Ontario Museum. https://collections.rom.on.ca/objects/187299.

Ritner, Robert Kreich. *The Mechanics of Ancient Egyptian Magical Practice.* Thomas A. Holland, ed. SAOC 54. Chicago: University of Chicago, 1993.

Robins, Gay. *Women in Ancient Egypt.* Cambridge: Harvard University Press, 1993.

Roth, Ann Macy. "The Absent Spouse: Patterns and Taboos in Egyptian Tomb Decoration." *Journal of the American Research Center in Egypt* 36 (1999): 37-53.

____. "Father Earth, Mother Sky: Ancient Egyptian Beliefs about Conception and Fertility." Pages 187-201 in *Reading the Body: Representations and Remains in the Archaeological Record.* Edited by Alison Rautman. Philadelphia: University of Pennsylvania Press, 2000.

Roth, Silke. Johannes Gutenberg-Universität Mainz, *UCLA Encyclopedia of Egyptology* 2009. escholarship.org https://factsanddetails.com/world/cat56/sub404/entry-6142.html.

Teeter, Emily. *Ancient Egypt: Treasures from the Collection of the Oriental Institute*, 23. Oriental Institute Museum Publications: 2003.

____. "Celibacy and Adoption Among God's Wives and Singers in the Temple of Amun: A Re-examination of the Evidence." Pages 405-14 in *Gold of Praise: Studies on Ancient Egypt in Honor of Edward F. Wente.* Edited by Emily Teeter and John A. Larson. Studies in Ancient Oriental Civilization 58. Chicago: Oriental Institute, 1999.

"Tomb of Nefertari (1986-1992)." The Getty Conservation Institute. https://www.getty.edu/conservation/our_projects/field_projects/nefertari/nefertari_images.html.

Tyldesley, Joyce. "The Many Queens of Ancient Egypt." *The Historian* (2020): 11-16.

Velde, Herman Te. "The Goddess Mut and the Vulture." Pages 242–45 in *Servant of Mut: Studies in Honor of Richard A. Fazzini*. Edited by Sue H. D'Auria. Probleme der Ägyptologie 28. Leiden: Brill, 2007. https://www.jacobusvandijk.nl/docs/Vulture.pdf.

Witcombe, Christopher. "Menkaure and His Queen." § 3. http://arthistory resources.net/menkaure/menkaurequeen.html.

2

MITHREDOTH, SHESHBAZZAR, AND THE VESSELS
(IN A NABONIDUS-BASED PARADIGM)

Nabonidus (so I claim) was sent to Jerusalem by Cyrus in 538 BCE, possibly as the first governor, to begin the formal establishment of a new Jewish settlement and temple there;[1] I have argued that Nabonidus was Ezra's "Sheshbazzar."[2] I have also previously argued that the Song of Solomon was written by Jehudijah, Nabonidus' "second-wife" and that in the Song she places "Solomon's" (i.e., a name *she* invented) kingdom in Jerusalem for a specific reason. She sets a curse upon both Nabonidus and Nitocris in the Song, making their names thenceforth unmentionable, so any subsequent allusion to them must be done surreptitiously, via pseudonyms and symbolic etymologies, even for toponyms. Jehudijah sets her poem in a debilitated, meagre Jerusalem (as it would have been in the 6th Century BCE) in order to downplay and ridicule the self-obsessed Nabonidus and to reject the superiority and power of his "kingdom." So, in the Song of Solomon, "Jerusalem" is to be understood as Tayma (i.e., if the poet had mentioned "Tayma" the king's identity would have been too easily construed).

When the time comes to leave Babylonia, Nabonidus takes with him, supposedly, the very vessels he was mockingly drinking from in the final scene of Daniel 5, i.e., the vessels allegedly from the Jerusalem temple, stolen by Nebuchadnezzar II in 587 BCE. According to 2 Kgs 24:13, Nebuchadnezzar supposedly had all the confiscated vessels cut up upon their seizure, and there are several conflicting accounts of how the vessels came to *be* in the temple in the first place and what happened to them, suggesting a certain amount of 'literary license' is at play here, in an attempt to establish historical coherence where there wasn't any.[3]

---

[1] Janet Tyson, *Arabian Sinai: Nabonidus and the Exodus* (Norwich: Pirištu Books, 2024), 43-7.

[2] Tyson, *Arabian Sinai*, 201-2. He is *not* the same as "Zerubbabel."

[3] E.g., Hiram of Tyre and Solomon made them (1 Kgs 7:40-51; 2 Chr 4:11 to 5:1); David already had them (1 Kgs 7:51); Nebuchadnezzar stored them in a temple in Babylon (Dan 1:2); they were destroyed completely (2 Chr 36:18-19).

38

The vessels attributed to Sheshbazzar's exodus were *not*, I suggest, those taken from Jerusalem two generations previously for they most likely *would* have been cut up or melted down and traded or reused.[4]

In *Arabian Sinai*, I conjecture that although Nabonidus leaves Babylonia with Cyrus' consent, he behaves in such a way as to make himself a "fugitive" (hinted at several times in the narratives); he effectively kidnaps his second-wife, Jehudijah, from the temple at Ur, along with his daughter, the *entu*; there is a decisive 'attack' on the temple, and a hurried escape. While I previously suggested that the subsequent pursuit by the priests of Ur was solely because Jehudijah and her daughter were being protected by their temple guardians,[5] now I have worked on this paper, I can see how the stealing of valuable *Babylonian* temple vessels might also have been a factor in the "smash and grab" at Ur! Nabonidus is a man who loves wealth (he is "Solomon" after all); he is not averse to making shady deals and leaving even his best friends out of pocket.[6] He is put in charge of taking these "vessels" to Jerusalem, according to Ezra (1:11), but things aren't that simple.

Look at the name of the man to whom the vessels are given (1:8) to "count out" to Sheshbazzar:

MITHREDOTH

Most translations suggest "given of Mithras" because the assumption is made that this person would be Persian. However, if wordplay is in effect here, as it is with most of the etymologies (of names), I think there is another way of interpreting both this name and the scenario of the transfer of the vessels itself.

I have noticed the frequent employment of a hybrid etymology in the Hebrew Bible (HB), i.e., one that potentially includes two languages: Hebrew (or Aramaic) and Akkadian, which, as elite scribes and professional men, the authors would have grown up with in

---

[4] The "counted" objects and their associated numbers are, without a doubt, gematria-based; I have yet to work on this aspect, so someone might wish to.
[5] Tyson, *Arabian Sinai*, 67-70.
[6] Tyson, *Arabian Sinai*, 71-2.

Babylonia. I argue that most HB names, barring those already known to be historical (such as Tyre, Hiram, etc.), whether personal names or toponyms, are etymological constructs to suit the immediate context.

In this case, if we break "Mithredoth" down into *"mith" "re,"* and *"doth"* there is an intriguing possible etymology that precisely echoes the scene itself.

1. "Mith-"

In Akkadian,[7] the words beginning with *mith* generally pertain to the distribution of something, usually in equal parts, e.g., *mithāriš* ("to distribute, or pay, in equal shares"); *mitharu* ("equal, proportional"). Mithredoth is called a "treasurer," which seems to me to be a case of "we don't know what this word means but as he seems to be counting out goods, 'treasurer' suffices." In fact, all four HB books that refer to a "treasurer" use a different term, i.e., *'atsar* (Neh 13:13; "to lay or store up"); *gedhabhar* (Dan 3:2, 3; "unknown etymology, Strong's says "[Aramaic] corresponding to *gizbar*"), *gizbar* (Ezra 1:8); *cakhan* (Isa 22:15; "to be of use or service," "benefit, profit"). Nehemiah adds that the duty of the "treasurers" was to "distribute to their associates."

We would think of a treasurer being someone who keeps a tally, keeps records, "stores things away" even, which seems to fit the context in Ezra, but the word *gizbar* gives us a clue that needs to be addressed. That it is thought be similar to the term *gedhabhar* from Daniel 3 is interesting because this means both passages *pertaining to Nabonidus* (Ezra 1 and Daniel 3) have a similar perspective on the role of this king's "treasurer." However, the *ged* part of *gedhabhar* stems from the Hebrew verb *gadad*, "to cut, invade, expose (something valuable)"; the noun *gedud* means "a band of raiders"; and the noun *gad* possibly means "fortune." That is quite a shift from a relatively passive record keeper/distributer. The *habhar* part potentially relates to *habhab*, "gift," from *yabab*, "to give," but this can also suggest "to give up, surrender, give over, pay." In Akkadian, *ḫā ' iṭu* is translated (in one sense) as "an official who weighs out."

So, if this understanding of dividing things, perhaps in a context of loot/booty, pay, and an amassed 'fortune', is to be tallied with Ezra's *gizbar,* we should see a similar etymology.

---

[7] Akkadian terms from Sureth Dictionary, "Akkadian," https://www.assyrian languages.org.

The term *gizbar* breaks down into *giz* and *bar*. The Hebrew verb *gez* means "shearing," from *gazaz*, "to shear, cut off"; in Akkadian, *gizzu* means "shearing" or "the yield of shearing." The Hebrew (fem.) noun *gizrah* means "a cutting, separation," while *gezer* (masc.) means "part, portion, piece." So the term *gizbar* does have a corresponding notion of dividing things up, of cutting, or separating a group of things, i.e., the vessels, e.g., into lots.

That just leaves *bar*, which is Aramaic for "son" but it can also mean "to select, choose," and "to act truly," etc. That is, the person doing the divvying up is selecting what to give and to whom, or he is acting according to the agreed division of resources. He's doing his job (cf. Neh 13:13 "they were considered faithful").

For Ezra the vessels are an icon, a symbol of the Jews' emancipation from exile[8] and the reconfiguration of their tribal identity. It wouldn't make any difference if they were in a million pieces, they were still seen as "the vessels." Ezra, in 8:24-30, adopts the role of the "treasurer" and redistributes not just these "holy" relics but also the gold and silver, to twelve[9] "leading priests," emulating the notion of dividing and apportioning the goods 'equally' (in essence, he does exactly the same thing as Mithredoth but with a different rationale; by distributing the pieces, the priests, by association, also become "holy"). Only in Sheshbazzar's case, as Ezra *knows*, things were slightly different; some of the recipients' portions were probably "more equal than others"!

When we shift the paradigm from Jewish lore/dogma to 6th Century BCE pragmatism, and take into consideration that for ease of distribution and transportation (recalling that Nabonidus and his group

---

[8] Just as the vestments of the high priest were a symbol of emancipation, so I have argued, in the Paschal Pardon pericope of John 18:39-40 (Janet Tyson, "The Paschal Pardon: Barabbas, Vitellius, and the Vestments in the Fourth Gospel," www.academia.edu).

[9] The twelve tribes, I have argued, were not an ancient 'reality' but were the result of what happened at Sinai; they were a by-product of the twelve divisions/pillars established by Moses during his metaphysical Qenite/solar-initiation experience (Tyson, *Arabian Sinai*, 256-7). The idea of "twelve" divisions is further explained by "Solomon's" (Nabonidus') twelve district officials (1 Kgs 4:7) who each had to supply the court with produce for one month per year.

travel both in small boats and on camels[10]) anything cumbersome, like "vessels" not required for day to day living *would* be systematically cut into pieces and counted as mobile 'wealth'.

Ballentine provides a relevant comment on the "vessels":

> The removal of cultic objects from their "proper" location constitutes negative treatment and involves both symbolic and direct violence. Forced removal from the temple parallels the forced migration of the people to Babylon and signifies disruption of cultus, while the Kings' account, for example, features cutting the vessels (2 Kgs 24:13). … For violence inflicted upon materials, the range includes the temple vessels (2 Chr 28:24); cutting gold into threads (Exod 39:3); cutting the trimming from laver stands (2 Kgs 16:17); cutting gold off of temple doors and doorposts (2 Kgs 18:16); cutting a spear (Ps 46:9); and cutting chains (Ps 129:4).[11]

Ballentine then argues that Ezra's account of the vessels does not include this "cutting" motif, and that the vessels are semi-miraculously returned without damage or profanation.[12] As we see from the breakdown of the etymology, however, this is, indeed, an aspect of Ezra's account; in fact, it is the very first impression of the vessels, of Sheshbazzar, and of the transference of the vessels from 'exile' to 'freedom'.[13]

2. "-re-"

The middle syllable of "Mithredoth," "re" is, perhaps, a play on (or an abbreviation of) *rea*, "to crush, shatter, break into pieces," reiterating

---

[10] Tyson, *Arabian Sinai*, 51; 65-6.

[11] Debra Scoggins Ballentine, "Exile and Return of the First Temple Vessels: Competing Postexilic Perspectives and Claims of Continuity," *Near Eastern Archaeology* 82 (2019):132-139, here 133-4.

[12] Ballentine, 135.

[13] Balentine plays on this notion to great effect: "Within the cultural memory of exile-and-return, the vessels stand in for cultus as a referent that reaches back in time, thus tying the postexilic community to the pre-exilic. That is, the vessels are part of a 'continuity claim' to the preexilic era" (133). In other words, their return was, *had to be*, symbolic and therefore exempt from the nitty-gritty of the "facts," e.g., that they had, indeed, been "cut up," long ago.

the idea that the objects have been cut up.[14]

On the other hand, "re" might be a play on another form of *rea*, suggesting he is a "companion" or "friend" of the king (thereby affirming this is not a Persian official). There *is* a person who might fit this description, i.e., one of Solomon's most intimate and trusted officials, "Zabud" son of Nathan, who is explicitly defined as the "king's friend" (1 Kgs 4:5).[15] He is a priest, not specifically a "treasurer" but Nehemiah employs a priest as one of his treasurers (Neh 13:13). The name "Zabud" means "to give, bestow," which echoes his role (potentially) as "Mithredoth" in Ezra 1.

3. "-doth"

The Hebrew word *dath* means "law, decree, edict," etc. If, however, Ezra's description of the Edict of Cyrus is exaggerated, e.g., to 'cover up' in inauspicious start to the exodus, perhaps *dath* in this context relates more to a decree from Nabonidus himself. This would be fitting, for at this point, Nabonidus has yet to evolve into his avatar of Moses, who is inextricably linked to the notion of "laws"; perhaps this is an intentional allusion to 'future' events.

The two men, treasurer and ex-king, work together to divvy up the precious metals amongst those who will be on the caravan to Canaan. Ostensibly, this is done in accordance with an ideal that each would receive "equal" payment, but if Nabonidus is in on the allocation, you can bet there's going to be a bit of 'fudging' going on.

Why are the vessels not stored in the temple when Ezra arrives?

---

[14] Also consider the noun *ra'*, "bad, evil," which may be inferred here, from the Jews in Ezra's time who knew the gold/silver was acquired by illicit means. Even without the vowels, the "r" element, i.e., the letter *resh* on its own represents "wickedness, evil." The word *resh* appears in Deut 1:21, in the context of Moses declaring that the Israelites will go and 'take possession' of territories in Canaan. That is, they will seize them, *steal them*. The gold and silver that ends up on the exodus, and that which ends up at Sinai and therefore in the "temple," is just about all stolen, i.e., first from the Babylonians, then from the Egyptians (recall that later, when Nabonidus takes some of the Jews back to Egypt, to retrieve "Joseph's bones," more silver and gold is looted from the locals [Tyson, *Arabian Sinai*, 234-5]).

[15] The title of "King's Friend" is an ancient one and has a parallel in Egyptian royal circles.

Because a) the temple has not been built yet, and b) there aren't any *actual* vessels to store. I have argued that when Nabonidus gets to (the real) Jerusalem, he places a token "vessel" or two as foundation deposits, which is something he was very used to doing in an archaeological/rebuilding capacity as King of Babylon.[16] It may even be the case that it is in Harran, during the stopover (Gen 12:4)[17] that Nabonidus (as "Abraham") trades the pieces of stolen *Babylonian* vessels for the camels and provisions he needs to set out on the exodus-proper. Harran was a central trading hub at the time, and in Gen 12:5, where Abraham "acquires" his goods and "the persons" who will go with him, the word *asah* is used, i.e., "to do, make"; amongst numerous forms, this can suggest making money, making deals, etc.

These illicit, fragmented "vessels" constitute the first level of Nabonidus' trading strategy, i.e., they are his initial assets. We see Abraham building his trading empire from scratch, as he crosses the Levant, making deals and shaking hands with the great and the rich.[18] Later, as "Solomon," of course, trade is central to Nabonidus' success and, eventually, his 'fall' in the eyes of the Jews. He simply gets too rich, and enjoys it too much. On the foundation of this dishonest and seemingly profane act (of cutting up the 'sacred vessels'), over years of appreciation, "the temple" is eventually built, a temple defying almost every stipulation the deity had supposedly made (e.g., that it be simple, unhewn, dark, etc.). This was, however, the temple *at Tayma* (aka "Jerusalem," as in the Song); Jerusalem *itself* still only boasted a modest foundation. With all the gold and silver gathered and used for new vessels, the golden calf, tabernacle accoutrements, etc., those on the trip who did receive a share of the loot probably ended up giving it back anyway (while Nabonidus and his 'officials' kept their share).

---

[16] E.g., Royal Chronicle iii 5b-12a; Nabonidus 13 ii 1-8; 16 ii 20-27, etc. (see Frauke Weiershäuser and J. Novotny, *The Royal Inscriptions of Amēl-Marduk [561-560 BC], Neriglissar [559-556 BC], and Nabonidus [555-539 BC], Kings of Babylon*, The Royal Inscriptions of the Neo-Babylonian Empire, Vol. 2 (University Park: Eisenbrauns, 2020).

[17] People often refer to this as a "five-year" stay but the HB doesn't provide a timescale; I have proposed a potential five-year explanation (*Arabian Sinai*, 70) but only because it cropped up in my analysis. If the HB doesn't provide a specific number, it is not significant to the text in hand, so any gematria, etc., must exclude 'guesses'.

[18] Tyson, *Arabian Sinai*, 74-81.

Ezra uses the term *saphar* (1:8) for "counted"; this means "count, relate, reckon, measure, number," reminding us of Daniel 5 and the "measuring" or "reckoning" of Nabonidus on that fateful night before he lost his kingdom. A different term, *mene*, is used in Daniel,[19] but the inference is the same, for just as Daniel's warning pertains to the decadence and idolatry, etc., of Nabonidus, so Ezra is reminding us that entrusting such a responsibility, such tangible wealth and (allegedly) religiously sensitive 'loot' to such a man was a mistake.

Although Ezra makes the statement that Cyrus' edict had included an order for the returnees to be given provisions—including gold and silver—by those who chose not to leave Babylon (Ezra 1:3-4), I tend to take Ezra's bold declarations with a pinch of salt. I think this is a case of sweeping the unsavoury elements under the carpet, while aggrandising the momentous 'exodus' that was really a relatively small and sporadic affair.

BIBLIOGRAPHY

Ballentine, Debra Scoggins. "Exile and Return of the First Temple Vessels: Competing Postexilic Perspectives and Claims of Continuity." *Near Eastern Archaeology* 82 (2019):132-139.

Sureth Dictionary. "Akkadian." https://www.assyrianlanguages.org.

Tyson, Janet. *Arabian Sinai: Nabonidus and the Exodus*. Norwich: Pirištu Books, 2024.

_____. *Nabonidus and the Queen of Sheba: Roots of a Legend*. Norwich: Pirištu Books, 2024.

_____. "The Paschal Pardon: Barabbas, Vitellius, and the Vestments in the Fourth Gospel." www.academia.edu.

Weiershäuser, Frauke, and J. Novotny. *The Royal Inscriptions of Amēl-Marduk (561-560 BC), Neriglissar (559-556 BC), and Nabonidus (555-539 BC), Kings of Babylon.* The Royal Inscriptions of the Neo-Babylonian Empire, Vol. 2. University Park: Eisenbrauns, 2020.

---

[19] Janet Tyson, *Nabonidus and the Queen of Sheba: Roots of a Legend* (Norwich: Pirištu Books, 2024), 70-2.

3

NABONIDUS, TARSHISH, AND OPHIR

The focus of my studies at present is Nabonidus, the last King of Babylon (556-539 BCE) and his possible association with early Israel, specifically, with the first wave of exiles who left Babylonia under the Edict of Cyrus (538 BCE). After discerning a potential Nabonidus-Nitocris marriage narrative within the Song of Solomon,[1] the extraneous material from my investigation led me to consider that there was a strong correlation between Nabonidus and the character of "Moses" in Exodus. This proved to be the case and much of the discussion in this paper will relate directly to research conducted for my latest book on that topic; rather than repeating information over and over in these papers, I advise at least a fleeting glance at the core material.[2]

The foundation of my continuing research is the premise that at least three major characters in the Hebrew Bible (HB) are based on the historical Nabonidus, i.e., Abraham, Moses, and Solomon. As outlandish as that may seem, there is so much potential corroborating evidence from 6th Century BCE texts, geographical identifications, etymological symbolism, etc., I am convinced this may be the future for biblical exegetes working on verifying the historicity of the HB. With this as a starting point, so much more of the confusing array of seemingly unrelated names, places, and sometimes indecipherable actions, suddenly come into focus and lead to other confirmations, until an entirely cohesive and plausible potential history is laid out (i.e., allowing for the necessary application of informed conjecture to fill the gaps). Nothing is exempt from an exilic/postexilic reinterpretation.

It is necessary to remember that while Nabonidus was King of Babylon in Tayma, Northwestern Arabia, for at least seven years (ten in Arabia but some of that was military expansion, etc., not necessarily residential), what he got up to there remained all but a mystery back in Babylon. Barring a few administrative receipts for delivery of food

---

[1] Janet Tyson, *She Brought the Art of Women: A Song of Solomon, Nabonidus, and the Goddess* (Norwich: Pirištu Books, 2023). Available freely online.

[2] Janet Tyson, *Arabian Sinai: Nabonidus and the Exodus* (Norwich: Pirištu Books, 2024).

46

across the desert, and a yearly note in the Babylonian Chronicle to say the king failed to appear for his expected New Year ritual, it seems no one was really that bothered (at least, according to what has been translated, to date). It seems the establishment was quite content to have Nabonidus at arm's length. He just went about his own business, building his second-capital in Tayma, becoming obsessed with his wife, Nitocris, and doggedly pursuing his dream of having a daughter to dedicate to his beloved lunar deity Sîn, as the first *entu* (high priestess of Sîn) of Ur for centuries. It was a mutually agreeable disassociation.

What I aim to show, here, is the connection between Nabonidus, Solomon, and the biblical references to ports of, and methods of, trade between the mysterious realms beyond, demonstrating that they present a 6th Century BCE political and geographical milieu. The working proposition here, with regard to dating, is that the visit of Moses (Nabonidus) to the Nile took place in 522 BCE; the final crossing of the Israelites into Canaan, *if* the "forty years" is taken as an estimate of how long the group who remained with Nabonidus resided in Tayma, must be ca. 498 BCE, i.e., counted from the departure from Babylonia in 538 BCE.

When it comes to "Tarshish," as with any other apparently unattested or unfamiliar names/toponyms, trying to find its meaning, in context, becomes nigh-on impossible when you are looking at the wrong chronological environment, and/or the wrong filial or geographical relationships. We *have* reached an impasse and need to adjust our assumptions, our preconceptions, if our understanding of these texts is to move forward. It does not mean their significance to whichever religion holds them sacred is lost. It just means we get to understand *why* they were written, *what* they really pertain to in a 'flesh-and-blood' reality and, when we're lucky, even *who* wrote them! Is that not a worthy exchange for outdated presumptions?

I submit the following comments concerning the potential locations of Tarshish and Ophir, and their importance to our understanding of Nabonidus and the biblical "Solomon."

DISCOVERING TARSHISH

There are several longstanding theories as to where, or what, Tarshish was. The following list highlights the most prevalent ideas; I offer my own thoughts on whether or not they are plausible.

1. Tarsus

Josephus claimed Tarshish to be the site of (St.) Paul's birth: "Tharsus to the Tharsians, for so was Cilicia of old called: the sign of which is this, that the noblest city they have, and a metropolis also, is Tarsus: the Tau being by change put for the Theta" (A.J. 1.6.1).

Jonah, in attempting to avoid his mission to Nineveh, headed for Tarshish from Jaffa (Joppa), a Philistine city on the Levantine coast (Jon 1:3). Taking this at face value for the moment, the convention is that he must have travelled westward in order get as far away as possible from where God wanted him to be.[3] However, in Whiston's notes to Josephus' second mention of Tharsus (*A.J.* 9.10.2) he states: "… Josephus understood it, that he went to Tarshish in Cilicia, or to the Mediterranean Sea, upon which Tarsus lay. So that he does not appear to have read the text 1 King. 22:48, … that ships of Tarshish could lie at Ezion Geber, upon the Red Sea."[4] I shall discuss the Ezion-geber connection later, but Cilicia is in Anatolia, today's Turkey, which means Jonah would have been heading northeast, not west.

Covey-Crump goes as far as to suggest:

> In fact, Tarsus (which, by the way, was never a seaport) was a primitive Hittite city dedicated to the deity Tark or Sandan; and we may be absolutely certain that no Old Testament writer would so confuse a tribe of Mongolian Hittites with the white-skinned, blue-eyed Aryans of Greece and the Mediterranean isles as to call Tarshish (meaning Tarsus) a son of Javan.[5]

I am in agreement with this assessment and reject Tarsus of Cilicia as the location of Tarshish.

---

[3] "Tarshish," https://www.jewishvirtuallibrary.org.

[4] William Whiston, trans., *The Works of Flavius Josephus* (London, 1737, 1895), *A.J.* 9.10.2, n. 1.

[5] W. W. Covey-Crump, "The Situation of Tarshish," *The Journal of Theological Studies* 17.67 (1916): 280-90, here 282.

2. Tartessos (Tartessus)

Herodotus (*Hist.* 4.152) mentions the accidental discovery of Tartessos by the Greeks:

> … anxious to reach Egypt [the Samians] made sail in that direction, but were carried out of their course by a gale of wind from the east. The storm not abating, they were driven past the pillars of Hercules, and at last … reached Tartessus. This trading town was in those days a virgin port, unfrequented by the [Greek] merchants. The Samians, in consequence, made by the return voyage a prophet greater than any Greeks before their day ….

He also tells the tale of King Arganthonios of Tartessos who, ca. 550 BCE, invited the Greeks of Phocaea (on the western coast of Anatolia) to come to his land (*Hist.* 1.163-5). Apparently, they declined, meaning that while the site owes much to its *Phoenician* heritage, a thriving *Greek* colony was not manifested at Tartessos.

The kingdom of Tartessos itself fell into decline before 500 BCE and, according to Koch, seems to have been replaced with Celts (whose silver, tin, etc., was being traded with the Tartessians).[6]

They did have time to found Emporion (modern-day Empúries, in Catalonia, Spain) in 575 BCE, but it has been suggested this was not initially for commerce but as a shelter from the powerful east wind that might take them farther out to sea or damage their ships whilst they were in port, trading.[7]

In the Bible "Tarshish" is primarily linked to Solomon who, convention dictates, lived in the 10th Century BCE but the name "Tartessos" is not attested in the Greek or Near Eastern sources until just before the middle of the first millennium BCE. The earliest known references include: Anacreon (6th C BCE); Aristophanes (ca. 445-385); Aristotle (384-322); Ephorus (4th C BCE); Hecataeus (ca. 500); Herodotus (c. 490 - ca. 425); Pherecydes of Athens (5th C BCE);

---

[6] John T. Koch, "Paradigm Shift? Interpreting Tartessian as Celtic," in *Celtic from the West: Alternative Perspectives from Archaeology, Genetics, Language and Literature*, Barry Cunliffe and John T. Koch, eds. (Oxford: Oxbow Books, 2012), 185-302, here 188.

[7] P. Bosch-Gimpera, "The Phokaians in the Far West: An Historical Reconstruction," *The Classical Quarterly* 38.1/2 (1944): 53-9, here 53.

Pytheas (4th C BCE); Stesichorus (6th C BCE); Theopompus (4th C BCE).[8]

In the mid-6th C BCE, Carthage broke free from Phoenician control and began its rise to power, and while the Greeks had been attempting to take over recently abandoned Phoenician maritime markets, Carthage proved the dominant force. The Greeks' veritable monopoly with Tartessos ended with their defeat at the naval battle of Alalia (ca. 540 BCE): "Carthage took over and dominated the Spanish territory and the coastal cities in Africa, thus ending Greece's attempts to go beyond the straits of Gibraltar."[9]

Muhly, citing Carbon 14 tests performed at a silver producing site in Rio Tinto, Spain, states that there was no production, let alone international trading, of silver in this region (at least) before 395 BCE; also, from a selection of 115 Greek silver coins discovered in Egypt (i.e., taken from the Asyut hoard, from Asyut on the Nile, that contained 900 coins), only one contained silver potentially from Spain.[10] Muhly concludes that Phoenician contact with southern Spain was not the norm.[11] This does tend to put the Tartessos theory to the test.

We must either dismiss Tartessos as the inspiration for the alleged 10th Century BCE international trading centre, "Tarshish," used by Solomon, or revise our dating of "Solomon." I do both!

3. "Refinery fleet"

Albright suggests the word *tarshish* was a Phoenician word for "mine" or "smelting plant"; possibly a loanword from the Akkadian meaning

---

[8] Philip M. Freeman, "Ancient References to Tartessos," in *Celtic from the West: Alternative Perspectives from Archaeology, Genetics, Language and Literature*, Barry Cunliffe and John T. Koch, eds. (Oxford: Oxbow Books, 2012), 303-34. Freeman includes the Inscription of Esarhaddon (681-669 BCE) as referring to Tartessos (331).

[9] Carlos Zorea, "Spain in the Bible: From 'Tarshish' to 'Sefarad'," POLIS. *Revista de ideas y formas políticas de la Antigüedad* 28 (2016): 157-188, here 176.

[10] J. D. Muhly, "Copper, Tin, Silver and Iron: The Search for Metallic Ores as an Incentive for Foreign Expansion," in *Mediterranean Peoples in Transition. Thirteenth to Early Tenth Centuries BCE*, S. Gitin, A. Mazar, and E. Stern, eds. (Jerusalem: 1998), 314-29, here 316-17.

[11] Muhly, 324.

"smelting plant, refinery."[12]

López-Ruiz suggests it may be a "morphological construction" (noting that this technique/practice appears "late in biblical Hebrew"), stemming from the "root *rshsh* 'to melt' (in Phoenician and Hebrew formed with a prefix *t-*, *tarshishu*)."[13] Because smelting works were found at Aqaba, Albright considered this the best explanation for "Tarshish" in a Solomonic context.

I think the relevance of this interpretation lies in the fact that many ancient trading ports would have been linked to metallurgical practices as a matter of course, i.e., smithies and workshops prevalent at the docks for making wares, made from imported or local resources, but intended for loading on awaiting ships.[14]

4. India

Those who locate Tarshish in India draw on letter 37 of Jerome (347-420 AD), an interpretation of the word that can also be found later in the tenth-century AD Byzantine lexicon called Souda. First of all, it is possible that both sources were referring to what we call today Ethiopia and not India, an equation that can be seen in other ecclesiastical authors. Furthermore, Jerome's testimony is nothing but confusing; it is clear that the name Tarshish already posed a mystery for him and other ancient authors, who were forced to speculate just as we modern scholars have done and continue doing.[15]

The potential for a connection between Nabonidus and India will be discussed below. Tarshish is not India.

---

[12] W. F. Albright, "New Light on the Early History of Phoenician Colonization," *Bulletin of the American Schools of Oriental Research* 83 (1941):14-22, here 21-2.

[13] Carolina López-Ruiz, "Tarshish and Tartessos Revisited: Textual Problems and Historical Implications," in *Colonial Encounters in Ancient Iberia: Phoenician, Greek, and Indigenous Relations,* Michael Dietler and Carolina Lopez-Ruiz, eds. (Chicago Scholarship Online (2009), 255-80, here 257, DOI: 10.7208/chicago/9780226148489.001.0001.

[14] For a full discussion see Aurélia Masson-Berghoff, et al., "(Re)sources: Origins of metals in Late Period Egypt," *Journal of Archaeological Science: Reports* 21 (2018): 318-33.

[15] López-Ruiz, 258.

5. Africa

In the Hellenistic era Tarshish was thought to be Carthage. The Septuagint translates "Tarshish" both as Carthage and "Africa" generally.

This has its merits, as will be demonstrated below.

6. "Sea"

Hoenig suggests Tarshish is an all-inclusive name for "sea," applicable to regions of sea, sea-faring ships, trade or journeying by sea, etc., and even to a stone called "*tarshish* (there apparently "meaning 'aquamarine', the sea-blue or sea-green variety of the beryl) in the high priest's breastplate" (Exod 28:20).[16]

Again, there is an element of plausibility here, for it is clear Tarshish pertains, on some level, to the sea in almost every biblical use (except for Exod 28:20), whether it be as a boat, a trading port, or a route. I think, however, Hoenig dismisses the context of location too readily and that we must retain the notion of "Tarshish" as a toponym.

ALLEGED EARLY REFERENCES TO "TARSHISH"

1. The Nora Stele

A Phoenician inscription discovered (1773) built into a church wall in Nora, Sardinia, and said to have been produced in the 8th Century BCE,[17] supposedly mentions Tarshish but every argument in favour of this date and interpretation rests on epigraphic assessment and hotly contested translations. The main gist of the text is that a military man fought with someone, drove them out, then found peace in Sardinia.

López-Ruiz suggests that there are

two possible readings of the first preserved letters, depending on where we place word divisions. While some scholars divide

---

[16] Sidney B. Hoenig, "Tarshish," *The Jewish Quarterly Review* 69.3 (1979): 181-2.
[17] For more on the early debates concerning the Nora Stone see Frank Moore Cross, "An Interpretation of the Nora Stone," *Bulletin of the American Schools of Oriental Research*, 208 (1972): 13-19 ; William H. Shea, "The Dedication on the Nora Stone," *Vetus Testamentum* 41.2 (1991): 241-45.

them as *bt-rsh-sh*, vocalized bet-rosh-ʿash, that is, "house or temple of the headland (which … ?)," more read them as *h-trshsh*, that is, "in/from Tarshish" (b∂-tarshish), and assume that this is a mention of the Tarshish of the Bible.

There is a certain the tension between academics, i.e., those who want to prove a link to the biblical Tarshish, and those who just want to decipher the language. Recalling that many ancient societies used one language for common communications and another for formal, legal, or public declarations, etc., we cannot just presume a writing style must fit into a precise timeframe. The Babylonians still used cuneiform long after Aramaic was introduced, yet it would be wrong to suggest all cuneiform writing must be dated to when it was the principal mode of writing (the same can be said for Egyptian hieroglyphs). I fear sometimes there is an overzealousness in determining dates and too often these are not broadly debated but simply accepted, despite sometimes quite convincing evidence to the contrary.

One of the more recent translations of the Nora inscription, by Pilkington, simply reads:

> A house he beat down. And he drove out. In
> Sardinia, he is at peace; his army is at peace. Milkyton,
> son of Shubon, the Commander. For Pummay.[18]

Pilkington suggests that from the archaeological evidence, there seems to have been outbreaks of violence between the Sardinians and the incoming Phoenicians during this time period that might explain the scenario presented in the inscription (a military battle). He also states that the 8th Century invasion was a relatively peaceful process, with the site in question abandoned for nearly two hundred years, until the Phoenicians reoccupied the site in the 6th Century BCE, which caused an even more profound upheaval on a broader scale.[19]

So, it is possible that the stele doesn't mention Tarshish at all. It is also possible that it might bear signs of archaic style, but it might just as easily be dated to the 6th (i.e., when the tumult was worth mentioning), rather than the 9th-8th Century BCE.

---

[18] Nathan Pilkington, "A Note on Nora and the Nora Stone," *Bulletin of the American Schools of Oriental Research* 365 (2012): 45-51, here 47.

[19] Pilkington, 49.

Similarly, the name Pummay is controversial. Cross argues that "Pummay" is Pygmalion, the King of Cyprus (831-785 BCE),[20] while Pilkington, rejecting Cross' "extensive philological reconstruction," argues that the "simplest" form might be best, i.e., the inscription ends with a supplication to the deity, Pummay (as is common to many votive inscriptions). I prefer a simpler interpretation, myself.

In terms of Cross' palaeographic analysis of the Nora material, specifically in this case a smaller item called the "Nora Fragment" (which he dates to the 11th Century BCE), Lipinski makes a valid comment:

> Many of the letter forms persisted for a period of at least 200 years. So it is impossible to tell on the basis of these letter forms alone when the inscription was made …. West Semitic paleography is at a crossroads. It must either admit that it alone has too meager means for dating early inscriptions with a higher degree of precision than within the limits of two or even three centuries, or question the historical, iconographic and factual evidence.[21]

The Sardinian inscription referencing a supposed Phoenician 'battle', seems not to mention "Tarshish" at all. It is of no significance for understanding the biblical toponym, other than to rule it out.

2. The Ostracon

An alleged 7th Century BCE ostracon is thought to be evidence of "Tarshish" within a Jewish context. Its paleo-Hebrew inscription reads: "As Ashyhw [Yoshiah?] the king has ordered you to give into the hand of Zakariahou the silver of Tarshish [*ksp trshsh*] for the house of YHWH, 3 sh[ekels]."[22] The provenance for this object is not known and some consider it a fake but that is where most references to it leave off. As I am working with a 6th Century BCE premise, I went a bit further by researching why and how a Jewish community might insist on silver from this supposedly mysterious, far-off place, to give as an offering to the temple which, if those of us who support a later date for

---

[20] Cross, 17.

[21] Edward Lipinski, "Epigraphy in Crisis: Dating Ancient Semitic Inscriptions, *Biblical Archaeological Review* (July/August, 1990), https://library.biblical archaeology.org/.

[22] López-Ruiz, 6.

the compositions in the HB are correct, had not even been envisioned by the 7th Century BCE.

López-Ruiz goes as far as to say this

> inscription becomes the most valid "external" document attesting the Tarshish of the Bible. Its date and the appearance of the expression "silver of Tarshish" bring the document remarkably close to the use of the word in the Hebrew Bible, if we compare it with the expression "ships of Tarshish" and keep in mind the frequent association of the name with metal trade.[23]

It turns out, there *is* a rationale for this request, but the explanation will have to await the discussion on Esarhaddon's inscription (below).

LOCATING THE PORT OF TARSHISH

The biblical Tarshish, from the very first time it is mentioned, is declared to be of Greek heritage:

> The descendants ["sons of"] of Javan: Elishah, Tarshish, Kittim, and Rodanim. From these the coastland people spread.
>
> Gen 10:4-5

"Javan" is broadly understood to mean Greece. This is not one of those conventions that can be dismissed as outmoded (even by me), for there are textual sources beyond the Bible that attest to this early identification, e.g., the Assyrians called the west coast of Anatolia (Asia Minor) "Jawan" or "Jaman" (Ionia) because it was colonised by Ionians, who had been there for centuries.[24]

In the HB, the name "Javan" comes to identify Greece, rather than just the Ionians, as a *nation*, e.g., in Ezek 27:13, they trade with Tyre; in Joel 4:6 they are considered slave traders; in Zech 9:13 and Dan 8:23; 10:20; 11:2 there is a definite sense of antagonism and the beginnings of a sustained vitriol against the Greeks that will continue into the New Testament.

---

[23] López-Ruiz, 7.

[24] "Javan," Jewish Virtual Library, https://www.jewishvirtuallibrary.org

The actual definition of the term *javan* in Hebrew is "mire, mud," from the noun *yawen*, "mire." How does this relate to Greece in the Hebrew mind? The term seems to have a rather negative, sombre association, as Pss 40:1-2 and 69:1-2 attest, i.e., both refer to the overwhelming despair and fear of finding oneself utterly out of control, where the mire, the watery mud, drags you down and only God can come to the rescue. Intriguingly, however, the term is also related to the noun *yayan*, wine; perhaps the etymological link to Greece comes from mythological associations with Dionysus. I think the drunkenness-revelry-fornication association with Dionysian (bacchanalian) rituals would equal the Babylonian liberality early Jews' abhorred, which is a profound theme in the exodus narratives. Like many other names I have reinterpreted, both from the Song of Solomon and the exodus narratives, "Javan" appears quite simplistic superficially, but penetrate the façade and you find something just a little more sinister. The Hebrew Bible is replete with snide little jabs at individuals *and* nations!

I suggest that if "Javan" in Genesis represents the Greek mother/father country, the "sons of Javan," i.e., the four toponyms of Elishah, Tarshish, Kittim, and Rodanim, represent *not* parts of the Greek isles or other islands in the Mediterranean, which would be unlikely knowledge to the earliest biblical authors,[25] but four locations *on the continent they knew*. The Greeks colonised territories from Anatolia to Libya but to the Jews in a relatively new (postexilic) kingdom of their own, what influenced them *directly* was paramount. Therefore, I suggest that the "sons" represent major coastal regions of the lands that bordered, or affected, the Jews, e.g., the upper and lower

---

[25] André Heller writes about the ignorance of the Greeks concerning Assyria and Babylon, ("Why the Greeks Know so Little about Assyrian and Babylonian History," in *Melammu 7: Mesopotamia in the Ancient World*, Proceedings of the Seventh Symposium of the Melammu Project Held in Obergurgl, Austria, November 4-8, 2013, Robert Rollinger and Erik van Dongen, eds. [Ugarit-Verlag, 2015], 331-48). Similarly, while I acknowledge the possibility of random interactions between the Jews in Babylon and the Ionians they met there during the exile (cf. Heller, 334), or second-hand tales from trading ports (in the manner of Herodotus), I do think it unlikely that those writing the biblical texts, with their attention fixed on their own religious concerns, would have had enough knowledge of the diverse Greek states to know of their geographical origins generations earlier. Greece was, to the early Jews it seems, an unwelcome neighbour and simply came from 'out there'.

Levantine coast, coastlands of the Sinai Peninsula, the Arabian 'corridor' (to the Mediterranean), and Egypt. It is from *these* locations (figuratively "sons," as in offshoots of the parent country) where the first Greek colonists rowed ashore, so to speak, that they inevitably "spread." Anatolia and Libya were too far away to be of immediate concern but, without getting into the headspace of whoever came up with these names, we could suggest they were obliquely included (and this comes up again in the section on Esarhaddon).

I offer the following discussion as a potential (alternative) explanation for Genesis' "sons of Javan," where the etymology of these toponyms reflects the early Jewish perception of *their* "world." This does not preclude the "sons" originating from places such as Cyprus, Crete, etc.; it just means the HB authors have (logically, in my view) invented names for them in the context of their immediate environment. Their intended audiences would thus be able to comprehend the importance of these foreign entities being on the shores of their own homeland, rather than dismiss them as unknowable, vague, and beyond the horizon.

The four "sons of Javan" are:

Elishah: "God supports, God is my salvation," from *el*, God, and the verb *yasha*, to support, or *yasha'*, "to save." A singular deity in a highly Hebraic phrase; how does this compare with Greek polytheism? It seems to be more a reference to the land of Israel, i.e., the Canaanite coastline.

Kittim: "beaters, hammerers" from the verb *katat*, "to beat or hammer." This certainly seems to have metallurgical nuances; perhaps this alludes to the northern coastline of the Sinai Peninsula, with mining/smelting being a predominant staple of the area (copper smelting, turquoise mining, etc.). It also speaks to the Phoenicians, whose quest for raw resources (mainly copper) led them to Cyprus and to Greece (Thrace).[26] It might also allude to the making of boats, which involves similar "hammering" skills; this would correspond with the Phoenician coastline, where the Cypriot Greeks landed.[27]

---

[26] "Phoenician Mining," https://phoenicia.org.

[27] Num 24:24, Balaam's prophecy (a seemingly later insertion), mentions a fleet from Kittim that would come to destroy "Assur and Eber"; Assyria

Dodanim:[28] "slow movers/leaders," from the verb *dada*, to move or lead slowly. To me, this instantly suggests a camel caravan, moving slowly through the desert behind its leader; ships (especially Greek ships) are fast. A potential play on the verb *dwd*, to love, must be considered, for this is a strange prefix for a toponym; *dwd* suggests a sexual form of love. It is a highly significant term in the reading of the Song of Solomon I present in *She Brought*, where *dodi* becomes synonymous with the sexually-orientated initiation of Solomon into his wife's Egyptian religion. This, from *my* research, means that *dod* (*dwd*) is strongly associated with the period of Nabonidus in Tayma; it would then follow that Dodanim pertains to Arabia, a place the biblical Jews knew of all too well.[29] Dodanim may represent the narrow avenue of access commanded by the "King of the Arabs" we learn about from Herodotus' tale of Cambyses crossing the region to Egypt (*Hist.* 3.4-9).

(Assur) at its zenith controlled the entire northern coastline from Anatolia to Egypt, so if Kittim was, indeed Cyprus, as convention holds, this would make sense, as there *would* be access from the sea. But "Eber" is, I contend, the same as "Heber," the territory of Northwestern Arabia, specifically the Tayma/Khaybar region. This seems to fit the reference to "the Qenite" (Num 24:21; and to Amalek in 24:20, whom I have suggested are in the region south of Tayma, in Exodus 17); *Strong's* defines "Eber/Heber" as meaning "the land beyond." How could "ships" from Cyprus get down to this region before the construction of Darius' "canal" (which would give them access via the Nile to the Red Sea and from there to Arabia, in theory)? The question of circumnavigation must be dealt with in that case, and this is fraught with difficulties. It is possible, therefore, that the phrase "ships of Kittim" (e.g., Dan 11:30) represents *an influx of people* (Greeks, but possibly also Phoenicians) not necessarily actual ships (just as Tyre itself is depicted as a "ship" in Ezekiel 27, though of course, it was not).

[28] The NRSV reads "Rodanim" here in Gen 10:4 but at 1 Chr 1:7, the note referring to Gen 10:4 suggests it reads "Dodanim," suggesting either an editorial/notation error, or that Gen 10:4 was changed from Dodanim to Rodanim to mirror 1 Chronicles. The Masoretic Text reads Dodanim.

[29] I. M. Diakonoff notes (in "The Naval Power and Trade of Tyre," *Israel Exploration Journal* 42.3/4 (1992): 168-93, here 189-91) that "Dodanim" is related to *ddn*, or Dedan, Arabia (between al-Wajh and Tayma). He rejects this identification in favour of the alternative "Rodanim" because he claims Dedan itself is mentioned again later in the list of traders (i.e., Ezek 27:23, translated as "Eden" in the NRSV). I am defining Dodanim as a broader allusion to Arabia, which has no bearing on the mention of Dedan in Ezekiel 27.

This tiny stretch of coast belonging to the Arabians is less than 30 km long, if Ienysus is el-Arīsh, and less than 10 if it is Khān Yūnis. Yet it must have served as the outlet for much of the merchandise brought up the Peninsula from ancient Yemen and across the Negev to the Mediterranean. This window on the Mediterranean freed the Arabians from the Phoenicians' virtual monopoly of maritime trade in the region and would have meant that the Arabians could deal directly with Greek and Egyptian merchants and sea-captains.[30]

From each of these coastland regions Greek migrants (or traders who decided to remain) might have expanded deeper inland. It was enough for the biblical scribes, at this point in history, to define these foreigners as having their *roots* in Greece.

So far, then, we have the Levant, i.e., Canaan/Israel (Elishah), the Phoenician coast and/or the Sinai Peninsula (Kittim), and the northern corridor between Arabia and the Mediterranean (Dodanim). The only region left is Tarshish.

Tarshish: Abarim Publications suggests a definition of "breaking, subjection" based on *Jones' Dictionary of Old Testament Proper Names*, which "relates the name to the verb *rashash* meaning "to beat down, shatter"; this may find an echo in another potential association with the word *tarsta*, i.e., "the feared or revered" (BDB Theological Dictionary).[31] Finally, there is a possible link to the noun *shayish*, or white alabaster.

From this short etymological assessment the one place that seems to mirror all potential variations is Egypt. This was *the* place to be feared/revered, for it became the epicentre of the Israelite history, the locus of all their angst and sorrows from distant days ... supposedly ... and certainly a major aspect of their immediate, postexilic experience. I have proposed that the use of "Egypt" is a scribal defence system, as the Jews, newly released from their exile in Babylonia were circumspect about transmitting tales concerning the new Persian ruler(s) lest the same thing happen again. They adopted an ancient,

---

[30] Michael C. A. Macdonald "Arabians, Arabia, and the Greeks: Contact and Perceptions," 1-33, here 8, https://www.academia.edu/4593009.
[31] "Tarshish," https://www.abarim-publications.com.

long-gone "Egypt" as their setting to tell a very immediate and first-hand account of what they experienced on the exodus from Mesopotamia to Canaan (and Arabia) in the 6th Century BCE. The pretence is maintained throughout the HB and has gone relatively unchallenged in scholarship (until very recently). Egypt is the nation, the Hebrew authors claimed, that kept them in captivity for hundreds of years, who beat them into submission as slaves; they were the dreaded ones, "the feared" (i.e., in reality, at least in their collective 'mind', it was the Assyrians first but most profoundly, and within their own lifetime, the Babylonians).

Alabaster, of course, was and still is predominantly quarried in Egypt, in the region of Luxor/Thebes.[32] A type of calcium carbonate formed by sedimentary deposits, the translucency of finely carved alabaster lent itself, perhaps, to the vision of Dan 10:6, where "beryl" in the NRSV is translated from the Hebrew noun *tarshish*. Here, the vision of the resplendent man begins with a body "like beryl (*tarshish*)" and continues on with a list of body parts (and a "belt of gold from Uphaz"; see "Ophir," below) that shine, gleam, etc. If you have ever seen light transmitted through alabaster, you will get a good idea of how this descriptions fits the stone, *tarshish*. In the Song of Solomon's vivid description of the woman's statue/poppet of her lover (Nabonidus, in Song 5:14),[33] *tarshish* is again translated as "beryl," while the term *shesh* is used in 5:15 and is translated as "alabaster" (i.e., "white" stone). In Esther 1:6 *shesh* becomes "marble" (presumably white).

I think it is safe to say the noun *tarshish* represents a prized translucent stone; if alabaster, it probably alludes to Egypt and is an intentional allusion to Nabonidus (Solomon) and his wealth.

Lopez-Ruiz asks a pertinent question: "If the oldest references to Tarshish in the Hebrew Bible referred to Carthage or to Tarsus or to any other well-known contemporary place, why did they not use the familiar names of these places?"[34]

Throughout my research into the influence of Nabonidus on the postexilic Jews, I have maintained that *unless* a name relates to a well-

---

[32] "Egyptian Alabaster Stone," § Egyptian Marble and Granite, https://egyptianmarblegranite.com/natural-stones/egyptian-alabaster/.

[33] I claim in *She Brought* this is Nitocris II, making a poppet of Nabonidus in the symbolic context of a cultic statue.

[34] Lopez-Ruiz, 266.

known city, nation, sea, region, or indeed person, it is probably constructed to suit the immediate context of the narrative (it is possible we have not discovered historical evidence for that particular name, but if it figures large in the narrative, it would seem unlikely no other source would mention it too, whether a location or person of renown). Such names I call commission names, as they often pertain to specific scenarios and can change when the situation changes. This was the intention of a carefully devised etymology, i.e., you can follow the transition of one name (person or place) through the narratives, through other texts even, by understanding the connections made at the etymological level (and you don't have to be a linguist).

In *She Brought*, I broached the idea that Nabonidus' name was anathema to the early Jews, and that the blatant omission of his identification in the HB was a 'group agreement', i.e., his name was cursed by the woman who wrote the Song of Solomon, which was a very early composition; she was on the exodus from Babylonia and had many supporters. This precedent carried forward into all the subsequent accounts of the early post-Babylon years, which is why we cannot read this king's name anywhere in the Bible. The intentional rejection of Nabonidus' name speaks to a great repugnance for the man, yet he is profoundly present throughout several books of the HB, just under pseudonyms. The scribes applied this technique to Nabonidus-linked locations also, creating names to suit the story being told, *not necessarily* for geographical/cartographical reasons. Etymology, as well as gematria (applying numerical values to letters of the alphabet) serves as a sort of shorthand, allowing for multiple levels of meaning to be recorded at the same time, decipherable only by those with the inclination to learn how to decode them. The average early audience would never have considered there might be hidden depths to such names, and the sometimes baffling nomenclature, long distanced from its imaginative creators who had secrets to maintain, became the norm, unquestioned, and misunderstood for millennia.

"Tarshish" is a case in point. It is also unique, to date, for it is both an historical toponym *and* a Hebrew commission name; it is a name that seems to have originated in the Assyrian language and was possibly tweaked for symbolic meaning by the biblical authors.

"Tarshish" is the name for Thonis-Heracleion/Naukratis.

Before I discuss the nature of this site and its significance to Nabonidus, it will help to have a superficial understanding of the apparent machinations of history and linguistic gymnastics that might have created "Tarshish" from "Thonis-Heracleion."

THE NAME "TARSHISH"

There is one inscription from the Assyrian king Esarhaddon (680-669 BC) that some insist refers to Tarshish, while others argue for Tarsus.[35] It is translated as:

> I wrote to all of the kings who are in the midst of the sea, from Iadnana (Cyprus) (and) Ionia to Tarsus, (and) they bowed down at my feet. I received [their] heavy tribute.
>
> Esarhaddon 60 (9-14)[36]

"Tarsus" is, in the transliteration of the text, ***KUR.tar-si-si***.

When this extract from Esarhaddon 60 is used in the debate concerning Tarshish, it is almost always taken out of context, which means the entire reason behind saying these words is lost. Looking at the context we read that Esarhaddon has just extolled the extent of his conquests. He declares first that he has conquered Šubria. This is deemed to be a location in the mountainous region on the northern bank of the River Tigris. Radner makes a significant comment:

> "Šubria" is the Assyrian designation, and this traditional Mesopotamian name simply means "Northland." There are at present no native sources available that would reveal under what name the country was known to its inhabitants ....[37]

---

[35] Such as Jamie Novotny, "Tarsisi" (2020), A Pleiades Name Resource, https://pleiades .stoa.org.

[36] Erle Leichty, *The Royal Inscriptions of Esarhaddon, King of Assyria (680– 669 BC)*, Royal Inscriptions of the Neo-Assyrian Period, Vol. 4, Grant Frame, Jamie Novotny eds. (Winona Lake: Eisenbrauns, 2011), 135.

[37] Karen Radner, "Šubria, a safe haven in the mountains," *Assyrian Empire Builders*, University College London, 2012, http://www.ucl.ac.uk/sargon /essentials/countries/ubria/.

Here we see a) the renaming by the Assyrians of a real location, with its own locally-known name, for their own records and b) the new name is vague and topographical, i.e., "Northland." This is *precisely* what I think happened with "Tarshish."

Šubria is conquered, then Esarhaddon moves on to proclaim victory over Tyre, farther west along the coast. Then, he proudly declares that he has also captured Egypt (671 BCE), thus adding vast swathes of territory to the Assyrian Empire, from east to west. This is a boast, a proclamation of power and (relatively) global authority, made all the more profound by the fact that Esarhaddon had attempted the conquest of Egypt in 673 BCE and had been defeated. The inscription makes a grand gesture of a few carefully chosen words. Had *KUR.tar-si-si* been meant to allude to Tarsus in Cilicia, this proud demonstration of imperial conquest would run no farther than from a few Greek islands and Cyprus to the shores of Turkey (see *Figure 1*, below). On the other hand, if *KUR.tar-si-si* is farther west, on the shores of Egypt, which has just been mentioned as being subjected to Assyrian rule, then the accomplishment is far greater (see *Figure 2*, below). The expanse of territory seized is far broader, i.e., from Šubria in the northern mainland, near the Tigris, via a sweeping victory over everything from Cyprus and at least some of the Greek islands, to the western boundary of Egypt. These are the new demarcations of Assyria, according to Esarhaddon. This is retrospectively reiterated in an alleged "prophecy" said to predict the successful campaign of 671 BCE, which declared: "You shall go forth and conquer the world!" … "And …" the narrator of this prophecy continues … "he went and conquered Egypt."[38] Egypt thus becomes the ultimate symbol of world domination. Tarsus just doesn't cut it.

So this is stage 1, with Esarhaddon applying a relatively generic toponym to a region, based on its topographical situation.

Stage 2 has to do with linguistics. Although I am not a linguist, a fairly simple search into the vicissitudes of the "sh" (usually represented by š) and "s" sounds in Assyrian, Babylonian, and Hebrew, led me to this concise and remarkably apropos summation:

---

[38] State Archives of Assyria, 10.174:10-15, https://oracc.museum.upenn.edu /saao/corpus.

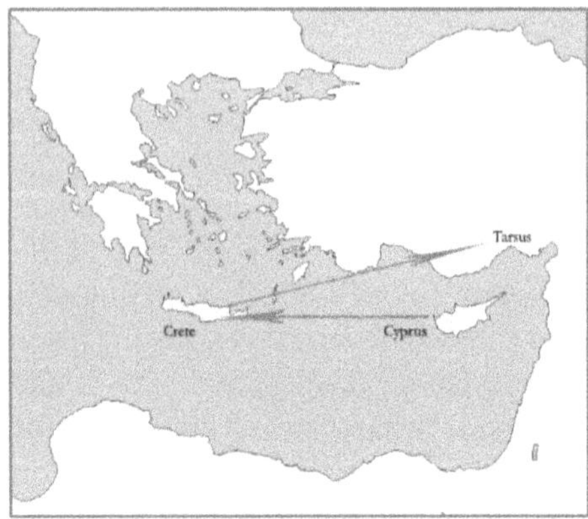

Figure 1. The limited conquest if KUR.tar-si-si is Tarsus (Map, public domain)

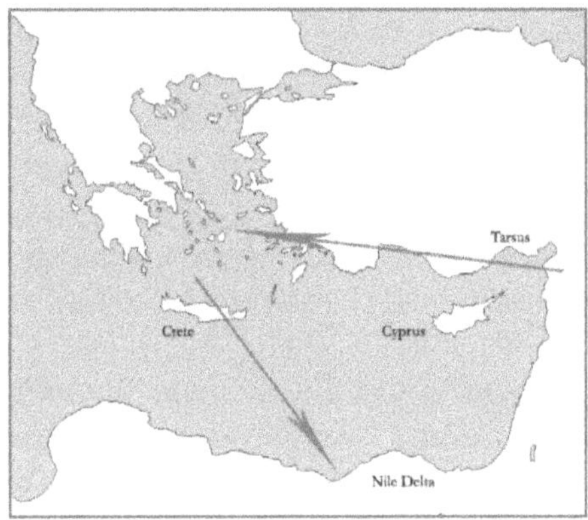

Figure 2. The all-inclusive conquest if KUR.tar-si-si is in Egypt (Map, public domain)

Hebrew *š* stands for two originally distinct sounds: one is a proto-Semitic dental spirant (*ṯ*) … the other is a proto-Semitic sibilant which is the source of many of our present difficulties. That sibilant is represented by *š* in Babylonian (as distinct from the Assyrian dialect of Akkadian) and in Aramaic, as well as in Hebrew; but in Arabic, Amorite, and in Assyria it has the value of *s*.[39]

The name for Tarsus in Esarhaddon's inscription is rendered *KUR.tar-si-si* in the transliteration, not *KUR.tar-ši-ši*, because the source is Assyrian, not Babylonian. Had it been an inscription from Nabonidus, or even from Nebuchadnezzar, for instance, it would probably have been transliterated as *KUR.tar-ši-ši* and we would have had no problem identifying this as "Tarshish(i)."

If the Babylonians inherited the Assyrian toponym "Tarsisi" but pronounced it "Tarshishi," this would, potentially, have been the name the exilic Jews would have heard and replicated in their own Hebrew language. This does not imply identification with Tarsus, however.

---

[39] Ephraim Avigdor Speiser, "The Pronunciation of Hebrew Based Chiefly on the Transliterations in the Hexapla (Continued)," *The Jewish Quarterly Review* 23.3 (1933): 233-65, here 244-5. For further contextual discussion of the two dialects see, A. George, "Babylonian and Assyrian: A History of Akkadian," SOAS Research Online (2007): 31-71, especially 54-64.

According to Schwarzwald, the suffix "-*i*" in Hebrew can denote a "gentilic affiliation, when suffixed to names of locations,"[40] which are themselves "generally derived from non-Hebrew place names or loan words, and are thus linguistically non-integrated."[41] Therefore, as "Egypt-ian" would stem from "Egypt" plus the suffix (in English), so "Tarshishi" *might* have been seen by Hebrew speaking people as referring to 'those of the land of Tarshish'.

In any case, it appears that the Hebrew scribes writing the HB somehow dropped what they saw as a suffix and referred to the geographical place as "Tarshish." This might play into López-Ruiz's "morphological construction" mentioned earlier (i.e., there a blending of Phoenician and Hebrew; here, of Babylonian and Hebrew), i.e., it is simply another expression for "commission name."[42] Thus, I argue that "Tarshish" in the HB is the convoluted result of philological metamorphosis over time.

When searching for a potential rationale behind Esarhaddon's (alleged) naming of Thonis-Heracleion as "Tarsisi", imagining it to be another generic term for the region of the Delta, for instance (as Šubria was for "Northland"), I found this word:

> ***tarṣu*** MA, MB, NA, NB : extent, duration range, scope ; *ana tarṣu* : towards, opposite, against ; *ina tarṣu* : opposite, other way round (?) ; *ištu tarṣu* : from (a place) ; *(ša) tarṣu / ana tarṣu / ina tarṣu* : at the time of ; *ištu tarṣu* : since the time of[43]

As his inscription begins with the eastern Mediterranean regions, then the Levant, and ends with Egypt, one might conjecture that the name reflects the farthest reaches, the lands "opposite" his starting point on the northern coast of Assyria (and the biblical references to "crossing over" to Tarshish implies a degree of distance and geographical opposition, east to west [see below]). So "Tarsisi" would be, perhaps, an allusion to the far reaches of the empire, the "extent" or "scope" of his dominion (whatever it might have been called locally).

---

[40] Ora (Rodrigue) Schwarzwald, "Stress Assignment in Words with -i Suffix in Hebrew," Bar-Ilan University, Israel (111), http://www.skase.sk/Volumes /JTL38 /pdf_doc/06.pdf.

[41] Schwarzwald, 120.

[42] López-Ruiz, 257.

[43] Akkadian Dictionary, https://www.assyrianlanguages.org/akkadian/list.php.

I had also wondered about the following: *tūšaru* (plain, flat land); *ṭišṭišu* (sediment); *tašriḫtu* (splendour); might there be an allusion to the Nile Delta *itself* in "Tarshish"? The lower Delta region *would* be seen as a flat plain, with much sediment, especially after the annual flood; Sais, the seat of Pharaoh, is just upstream from here and would be considered splendiferous. Although the words I list aren't a direct match to "Tarsisi/Tarshish," the idea is that Esarhaddon, on claiming Egypt for Assyria, referred to it as the jewel in the Assyrian crown that it was but also gave it a descriptive toponym to suit its nature.

This may sound far-fetched, and I almost decided not to include these thoughts here, but then I discovered the Decree of Sais stelae that were uncovered by archaeologists working at Thonis-Heracleion and Naukratis. The two identical stelae, one for each location, refer to Thonis as "The-Hone-of-Saïs" and the word *"hone"* is understood to mean, basically, the lower basins formed by the major arms of the Nile, i.e., the river but also the lands it floods.[44] The etymology of the name "Thonis" was, some time ago (1930s), suggested "to be the addition of the article *r3* to the word *ḥnt*"; this was confirmed by the stelae. This means that Thonis is itself named after its topographical situation and/or features.

An informed case of 'copycat' or a case of serendipity? Either way, it would seem *KUR.tar-si-si* in Esarhaddon's inscription, and the original name of Thonis are (potentially) simpatico.[45]

The chances of this conquering king not knowing about Thonis-Heracleion, the greatest sea-port in the Mediterranean at that time, would be slim to nil; in the year Esarhaddon conquered Egypt (671 BCE), however, he probably had never even heard of Naukratis.

---

[44] Anne-Sophie von Bomhard, *The Decree of Saïs: The Stelae of Thonis-Heracleion and Naukratis*, Oxford Centre for Maritime Archaeology: Monograph 7 (Oxford: University of Oxford, 2012), 77-8. Bomhard later expands on this to include the economic sphere of influence of the entire region.

[45] I did also wonder if the name was a play on words, using the two languages a scribe of the 6th Century BCE would have been familiar with, i.e., Akkadian and Hebrew: Babylonian *tarṣu* (correct, proper, descent) + Hebrew *ish* = 'Tarshish' or, "the place of the descent man" (this will make sense if you read *Arabian Sinai*; it refers to Ahmose III).

Naukratis, known locally as Pi-emrô, or *pr-mryt*, the "House of the Port,"[46] appears to have been founded during the reign of Pharaoh Psamtik I (664-610 BCE), who granted lands to the Greek mercenaries who had helped him when he took the throne.[47] Archaeological finds have been dated to c. 630 BCE; its association with Thonis-Heracleion was not immediate.[48]

It was Ahmose III who reorganised Naukratis, allowing the Greek inhabitants the freedom to worship their own deity (Apollo) within their own land (which they did not originally *own*, per se),[49] an act which is evidently alluded to in Exodus, i.e., the pharaoh with the "hardened heart" would not do likewise for the Israelites.

Thonis was, by far, the most practical site for a port, while Naukratis was considered an *empôrion*, i.e., more the brains of the business, the customs office, etc. The Greek inhabitants were residential traders, not citizens but, inevitably, they gradually intermarried with Egyptians and became assimilated into Egyptian society. "Generations of Greeks had coexisted with Carians, Phoenicians, and Egyptians at Naukratis by the time Alexander the Great conquered Egypt in 332 BCE."[50] Thus, it is fair to say that Naukratis was one of the most successful, long-term settlements (if not an official colony) of the mother/father country, Greece, i.e., a true "son of Javan" to the early Jewish mind.[51]

---

[46] Bomhard, 5.

[47] Astrid Möller, *Naukratis: Trade in Archaic Greece* (Oxford: Oxford University Press, 2000), 118.

[48] Bomhard, 98.

[49] Möller, *Naukratis,* 196.

[50] Chrysopoulos, https://greekreporter.com.

[51] Although some scholars emphasise the "Egyptian" element of Naukratis, Möller states that it was "a purely Greek *empôrion*, the assumption of an Egyptian quarter being based on misinterpretation" (*Naukratis,* 118-19). Stephan Pfeiffer suggests "Naukratis appears to have achieved the political status of a *polis* during the last period of Egyptian independence" ("Egypt and Greece before Alexander," UCLA Encyclopedia of Egyptology (2013): 1-12, here 5, http://escholarship .org/uc/item/833528zm. For more on this topic see Astrid Möller, "Naukratis as Port-of-Trade Revisited," *Topoi. Orient-Occident* 12.13.1 (2005): 183-192.

THE SHIPS OF TARSHISH

The "ships of Tarshish" are mentioned in Isa 23:1: "Wail, O ships of Tarshish, for your fortress is destroyed." Here, Isaiah is speaking of the fall of Tyre, emphasising the profound reliance of Tyre on the trade ships, and vice versa. The "fortress" is the safe trading harbour, which is mentioned again in 23:10: "this is a harbour no more." More interestingly, 23:3-6 explains that Tyre has been reliant on their trade with Egypt, i.e., the "harvest of the Nile," and vv. 5-6 read:

> When the report comes to Egypt,
> they will be in anguish over the
> report about Tyre.
> Cross over to Tarshish—
> wail, O inhabitants of the coast!

The inference is that those suffering from the loss of the trading port at Tyre, i.e., those who trade predominantly with Egypt, should "cross over," i.e., *to* Tarshish. It is clear from 23:1 that Tarshish is not Cyprus, as the ships of Tarshish leaving there learn of the fall of Tyre on route.

Gilbert suggests that Cyprus might not have had "suitable products for elite consumption in Egypt" and that ships trading in the eastern Mediterranean might have been in the region solely to exploit the northerly winds (south of Cyprus) to help them get back to Egypt.[52] He also states that there is a regular anti-clockwise route taken by such trading vessels:

> The new maritime trade routes in the Eastern Mediterranean formed a large trade circle, with the majority of ships sailing anticlockwise with the prevailing winds around the Mediterranean Sea from Egypt, to the Syrian coast, to Cyprus and the Southern coast of Turkey, to the Greek islands, to Crete, to the Libyan coast and back to Egypt. The archaeological material uncovered at sites around the Eastern Mediterranean has imports that support this circular trade route.[53]

---

[52] Gregory P. Gilbert *Ancient Egyptian Sea Power and the Origin of Maritime Forces*, (Canberra: Sea Power Centre, Australia, 2008), 94.
[53] Gilbert, 94.

The ships of Tarshish leaving Cyprus, then, are the same ones that are defined in the following verses of Isaiah as bringing news of the fall of Tyre to the Egyptians; they are probably already on the way home, having learned of the situation from small ships fleeing Tyrian waters. In Isa 23:12, the Sidonians are warned that they will not find "rest" in Cyprus' ports, which means this island cannot be the same place as the Tarshish, so vehemently hailed as the place the traders *should* go (to escape the mayhem).

There is only one other option, geographically, for the ships of Tarshish (and/or the Tyrian traders) to "cross over" *to*, be it from Cyprus or Tyre, i.e., Thonis-Heracleion.

From Isa 23:10 we learn that the ships of Tarshish *do* have a designated origin: "Cross over *to your own land*, O ships of Tarshish." Here, once again, there is mention of Egypt and (in the Hebrew but not in the English translation) even the Nile, i.e., "Overflow through your land like the Nile, daughter of Tarshish," emphasising the strong, figuratively filial relationship between Egypt and Tyre (the 'daughter' follows the mother-land's example).

Also, Ezek 38:13 provides an all-encompassing image of northward trade from South Arabia, through Northwestern Arabia, and on into Egypt: "Sheba and Dedan and the merchants of Tarshish"; had Tarshish been some island out in the Mediterranean, this juxtaposition wouldn't make sense.

Therefore, for Isaiah at least, the "ships of Tarshish" seem to be international trading vessels whose port of origin is Tarshish, i.e., the port through which all vessels seeking to trade with Egypt had to pass at some time or other; it was seen as the greatest, the safest, the most secure, etc. This was Thonis at its zenith. Once the gateway port to Egypt from the Mediterranean, it was damaged by an earthquake and tsunami sometime in the 5th Century BCE and gradually sank beneath the waves over the next few hundred years, but in Nabonidus' day, it served Naukratis, which held, by royal decree, the monopoly on trade into and out of Egypt via the Nile.[54]

---

[54] Möller, *Naukratis,* 204.

TRADING SHIPS

Möller argues that it is

> unlikely that ships were built here: how could they have been constructed in an Egypt without wood, where every piece of timber required for building had to be imported? Surely it would have been much easier to transport the completed ships to Egypt. On the other hand, one may suppose the existence of ship-repairing facilities. [55]

I disagree, especially in light of the discovery of the famed harbour of Thonis-Heracleion in 2000. What the archaeologists discovered was a trove of almost perfectly preserved sunken Egyptian ships that could be analysed in detail. The famous Ship 17 turned out to be an almost exact match to the ship Herodotus called a *baris* (*Hist.* 2.96), which the historian claimed was made from "acantha (thorn)," or Cyrenaic acacia. "Acacia was also the wood of choice used for the construction of other ships from Thonis-Heracleion. The wood of acacia, and especially of *Acacia nilotica* (*Snt*), was employed in Egyptian boatbuilding from ancient times."[56]

While larger, truly seafaring ships *were* made from imported cedar (from Lebanon, for instance), boats used on the Nile, and even on the Red Sea, were predominantly locally sourced and constructed.[57] The *baris*-ship/boat was a "Nilotic freighter"; it had a

> shallow draft and a flat keel [that] was perfectly suited for the navigational conditions of the Delta that included shallow waters and numerous sandbanks. Alternatively, these ships could have been used for the lightening of cargo on to or off of large sea-going freighters that may have anchored in the deeper waters of the port of Thonis-Heracleion.[58]

---

[55] Möller, *Naukratis,* 198-9.

[56] Alexander Belov, "Archaeological Evidence for the Egyptian *baris* (Herodotus *Historiae* 2.96)," in *Thonis Heracleion in Context*, Damian Robinson and Franck Goddio, eds. (Oxford Centre for Maritime Archaeology, 2015), 195-210, here 196.

[57] Belov, 206-7. See especially n. 110 (206), which describes a riverboat being used as a ferry between the Egyptian coast and the Sinai Peninsula.

[58] Belov, 207.

These boats were of "considerable tonnage"; Ship 17 (at 28 by 8 meters) could hold 112-151 metric tonnes, but by Hellenistic times ships on the Nile were carrying 450 tonnes.[59]

The Egyptians had, for centuries, devised and constructed ships according to the environment. They had various names for the types of ships/boats, such as *h'ww*-boats that were "loaded with all the treasures of Egypt" and were used both on the river Nile and at sea; there were *s3ṯ*-boats that were used for the transportation of massive construction materials for royal building projects (such as stone for obelisks, etc.; often towed by smaller craft); and *wsḥ.t*-boats (made from Nubian acacia) that could traverse the marshlands with ease carrying very heavy loads.[60] There were "divisions of riverine vessels of the Kepen type, traditional keel-less 'flexible boats'" that multi-tasked.[61] One of the largest seafaring cargo ships appears in the ancient sources "using a classifier" that looks just like our massive container ships today![62] So for all the talk of and fascination with Phoenician maritime prowess, we tend to forget that the Egyptians ruled the waves too!

One of the most significant types of ship for this discussion, perhaps, was the seafaring "Byblos boat" … which was so named, it is conjectured, because of the regular 'run' from Egypt to Byblos, one of Egypt's main trading partners.[63] These ships, like the "ships of Tarshish" in the Bible, are used for other runs, too (i.e., in 1 Kgs 22:48, Jehoshaphat plans to use Tarshish-ships to sail to Ophir), i.e., an Egyptian inscription tells of a Byblos boat being used for a journey down the Red Sea to Punt.[64]

Ezek 27.25, referring to the fall of Tyre (ca. 586-573 BCE) says: "The ships of Tarshish travelled for you in your trade," which is akin to acknowledging the Byblos-boat run from Egypt to the Levant.

---

[59] Belov, 206, n. 104.

[60] Serena Esposito, "Riverboats and Seagoing Ships: Lexicographical Analysis of Nautical Terms from the Sources of the Old Kingdom," in *Stories of Globalisation: The Red Sea and the Persian Gulf from Late Prehistory to Early Modernity*, Andrea Manzo, Chiara Zazzaro, and Diana Joyce De Falco eds. (Leiden: Brill, 2018), 32-41.

[61] "Egyptian Navy," https://naval-encyclopedia.com/cold-war/egyptian-navy.php#.

[62] Esposito, 50.

[63] Esposito, 48.

[64] Esposito, 77.

Thus, the "ships of Tarshish," in Nabonidus' 6th Century BCE world, could be vessels constructed on the basis of the cargo vessels used prolifically for the transportation of goods within the marshland environment of the Nile Delta, but also, with modifications perhaps, on the Red Sea. The regular 'run' to Tarshish, i.e., to Thonis-Heracleion/Naukratis, would provide the inspiration for the biblical commission name "ships of Tarshish."

NABONIDUS' FLEET

If "Solomon" is Nabonidus, as I claim, and is living in Tayma, the location of Ezion-geber, where we are told "Solomon" kept his fleet (and Jehoshaphat kept his), is significant. Research for *Arabian Sinai* uncovered what I think is the most obvious and strategic location for "Solomon's" fleet at Ezion-geber.

The following is an excerpt from this book:[65]

-Start of excerpt-

The conventional location of Ezion-geber is said to be at the north-eastern tip of the Gulf of Aqaba. I have never felt comfortable with this, and since researching the influence of Nabonidus on the HB, I am utterly convinced this is wrong. Because Ezion-geber is such a prominent site in the story of Nabonidus-Solomon, and because it is also on the Red Sea, its location needs to be confirmed, for this is where Nabonidus-Moses is headed.

A Note on Aqaba

The site of Aqaba, archaeologically, shows no evidence of having been a major sea port (i.e., tradition holds it is "Solomon's" grand port) at any time before the Byzantine era from (ca. 300-500 CE) and the later Islamic Period (from 610 CE); the earliest attested name for the site is "Aila" (Byzantine) while the Islamic name is "Ayla," and for most of its history, "the settlement has ... taken its name from the root attested in

---

[65] Tyson, *Arabian Sinai*, 130-6.

the Bible, Elath (Eloth) ...."[66] So, here we have, again, the circular reasoning that because someone attributed the site to a place mentioned in the Bible, it is all but universally accepted for millennia, without any material or even further textual evidence to support the claim. A multitude of other places and events are then linked to this site to prove the biblical precedent (and a solely Canaanite heritage). It is very difficult to break free from this but we must, if the understanding of the exodus (and Solomon) narratives is to take a step forward.

Hiram's crews, we know, are used to moving their ships cross-country, disassembled, like flat-packs,[67] so it is feasible that vessels could be transferred from the Nile to the Red Sea by land, even before the canal was functional. Thus, Hiram might maintain a presence there permanently, which would mean he would probably have precedence, if not a monopoly, in both gulfs. The two biblical fleets can sail together for trade purposes (1 Kgs 10:22) with their respective trading harbours far enough away from each other (i.e., like Abraham and Lot) and Hiram can easily send his sailors over to Solomon's ships when needed, from Memphis to Arsinoe, or another port on the western shore of the Sea. It seems most unlikely they would keep two major fleets in the same little harbour and have no presence on the rest of the Red Sea shoreline. That lacks business acumen.

Besides, from a biblical author's perspective, having Solomon's fleet tucked away in this otherwise insignificant place, would not demonstrate his position as the greatest king; he would have to have the prime spot. If, from the historical perspective, the fleet of Solomon was, indeed, right at the tip of a gulf that doesn't even appear on early maps, the location would have been recorded as being in a secluded bay, etc. As it

---

[66] Donald Whitcomb, "Aqaba," in *Oriental Institute 1994-1995 Annual Report,* William M. Sumner, ed. (Chicago: Oriental Institute, 1995), 14-17, here 15.

[67] Barry J. Beitzel, "Was There a Joint Nautical Venture on the Mediterranean Sea by Tyrian Phoenicians and Early Israelites?" *Bulletin of the American Schools of Oriental Research* 360 (2010): 37-66, here 47, n. 26; "The city of Opis is where the Assyrian king Sennacherib famously had Syrian-built ships dragged overland on rollers from the Tigris River to the Euphrates River in 694 BCE" (Frauke Weiershäuser and J. Novotny. *The Royal Inscriptions of Amēl-Marduk (561-560 BC), Neriglissar (559-556 BC), and Nabonidus (555-539 BC), Kings of Babylon,* The Royal Inscriptions of the Neo-Babylonian Empire, Vol. 2. [University Park: Eisenbrauns, 2020], 11 n. 100).

stands, 1 Kgs 9:26 claims Solomon's ships are based "on the shore of the Red Sea," which suggests the Sea *proper*, not the very tip of a narrow gulf.

Some have suggested that Nabonidus' sojourn into Arabia might have been for the purpose of "exerting his authority over the trade-routes in the west and of gaining control of the eastern shore of the Red Sea" because "the old alliance with the Medes had broken down" and he could not make a deal for access; the Persian Gulf had been silting up over a long period, "leaving the king without seaports."[68] If trade is the overwhelming incentive for Nabonidus to build a port on the shores of the Red Sea, why not place it in a convenient halfway point, more specifically on the eastern shore, where ships can be unloaded and goods packed off in caravans waiting on the far side of the harbour, ready to set out on the inland trade routes? Why take cargo right to Aqaba, where the immediate trade route is accessed predominantly by the King's Highway, toward the northern regions?[69] This is more convenient for Tyre. During Nabonidus' reign, the goods *he* traded for would be heading for either Tayma or Babylonia. The quickest route would be to Tayma and from there, across the desert to Babylon (via Adummatu).[70] There would be no need to double back or go far north and then down the Euphrates.

Therefore, I suggest it is Hiram, with his Egyptian investors/trade-partners, who dominates ports in both the Gulf of Suez *and* the Gulf of Aqaba, while Solomon (Nabonidus) has his ships somewhere along the shore of the open Red Sea, to service his interests in Arabia. It would make sense for this port to be relatively close to his Tayma kingdom.

---

[68] J. M. Wilkie, "Nabonidus and the Later Jewish Exiles," *JTS* 2.1 (1951): 36-44, here 39.

[69] "The road seems to have eased traffic and trade in a north-south direction between the territories of Edom, Moab and Ammon, and probably beyond, but the true path of this route is still unconfirmed" (Fawzi Abudanah, Saad Twaissi, et al., "The Legend of the King's Highway: The Archaeological Evidence," *ZOA*, Band 8 [2015]: 156-187, here 157, n. 1; 158).

[70] See Hanspeter Schaudig, "Edom in the Nabonidus Chronicle: A Land Conquered or a Vassal Defended? A Reappraisal of the Annexation of North Arabia by the Late Babylonian Empire," in *About Edom and Idumea in the Persian Period: Recent Research and Approaches from Archaeology, Hebrew Bible Studies, and Ancient Near East Studies,* B. Hensel, E. Ben Zvi, and D. V. Edelman, eds. (Sheffield: Equinox 2022), 251-64, here "Figure 10.1: The main caravan routes in North Arabia in the time of Nabonidus," 252.

***

The evidence for the location of Solomon's port within the biblical texts has remained almost untouched because it was so cleverly hidden—but it *is* there! With a little investigation, the precise location of "Ezion-geber, near Eloth" can be discovered. It is nowhere near Aqaba.

The etymology of "Ezion-geber" is profoundly instructive. The verb *asam* relates to a skeletal structure i.e., a "backbone" that supports the larger structure. The noun *osem* means "might or skeleton," while the noun *osma* means "strength"; the adjective *asum* means "mighty or numerous." The root verb *asam* denotes "strength in numbers," "to be mighty" (Gen 26:16, Dan 8:8), or "to be numerous" (Exod 1:7, Isa 31:1). The BDB suggests, on the other hand, "a land abounding with the trees" (*es* means "tree," *esa* "trees").

The verb *gabar* also means "to be strong or mighty" (Job 21:7, 1 Chr 5:2), or "to prevail" (Exod 17:11, Gen 7:18). Note that the Exodus example is the scene at Rephidim, with Moses having his hands held up during the battle between Joshua and Amalek. Ezion-geber is, perhaps, a commission name that simply reflects a military site, i.e., a naval base); it is a place of numerous mighty ships (and sailors).

This could be a potential reason for suggesting that Solomon forms an alliance with Hiram, who has similar notions of expanding trade to farther realms perhaps, or in order to strengthen their mutual security, i.e., safety in numbers, as *asam* denotes.

If Nabonidus *is* the inspiration for "Solomon," as I claim, the most logical place to build a port for a "fleet" of large ships is at or near the harbour we know today as al-Wajh. About 600 km down the coastline from the tip of the Gulf of Aqaba, al-Wajh lies at a very strategic point on the Red Sea's eastern shore, i.e., where a well-trodden caravan route leads to the criss-crossing trade trails from the interior, i.e., from Tayma, to Babylon, to the north, and to the south.

In 2013-19 a survey, and then an expedition, was undertaken to examine the potential for ancient caravan access between al-Wajh and al-Ula.[71] The most relevant findings for

---

[71] Zbigniew T. Fiema, et al., "The al-ʿUlā–al-Wajh Survey Project: 2013 Reconnaissance Season," ATLAL: 28.2 (2020): 109-31, https://hal.science/hal-03064753/document. For the 2019 summary see Laïla Nehmé, "Land

this discussion were:

✹ The same routes Doughty took in the 19th Century (*Fig. 10*) turned out to be the more viable ones the expedition tested (though they made no reference to him), i.e., one that took them through the volcanic fields and one that went around

✹ The most plausible trade route was the one that took the longest time but was much safer and more easily accessible for people and load-bearing beasts

✹ This route, via the Wadi al-Jizl and Wadi al-Hamd, proved more hospitable, with more frequent access to ground water, forage for camels, and greater easiness underfoot

Num 33:35 says: "They set out from Abronah and camped at Ezion-geber."[72] "Abronah" means "passage, pass" from the verb *abar*, "to pass over, through" (the term "Hebrew" originally implied "nomads" or "travellers").

Similarly, Deut 2:8 reads: "We turned away from the Arabah road ("away from the road of the plain/desert"), which *comes up from* Elath (Eloth) and Ezion-geber, and travelled along the road of the Wilderness of Moab." Doughty mentions an Arabian tribe who frequented a passage from Aqaba to al-Wajh that hugged the shores of the Red Sea; on his map (*Fig. 10*) it is marked by a black line and runs through a region called "Aarab Agaba." "Agaba" in Arabic is the same as Numbers' "Abronah," i.e., "passage/pass"[73]; "Aarab" refers to the nomadic Arabs or Bedouins.[74] Aarab Agaba is thus equivalent to the HB's "Abronah" or "Arabah road."

The port of al-Wajh was known as the "Port of Hegra

(and maritime?) routes in and between the Egyptian and Arabian shores of the northern Red Sea in the Roman period," in *Networked Spaces: The Spatiality of Networks in the Red Sea and Western Indian Ocean* (Lyon: MOM Éditions, 2022), 513-28, DOI: https://doi.org/10.4000/books.momeditions.16486.

[72] In Num 33:34 the group moves to "Jotbathah," which means "Pleasantness, Goodness," from the verb *yatab*, "to be or do good." Compare this to the land Lot chooses to move to in Gen 13:10 i.e., "well-watered" and like a garden (see "Joshua and Lot" in Chapter 1).

[73] *Sudan English-Arabic Vocabulary*, Sudan Government, 1925, 211.

[74] Sayyid Abdul Husayn Dastghaib Shirazi," Greater Sins - Volume 2," §"What Does 'Becoming A'arab After Hijrat' Mean?," www.al-islam.org.

and Dadan."[75] It is wise to recall that Nabonidus conquers Dadan during his wandering in Arabia (Royal Chronicle, v 1-24); I am sure he would not overlook its convenient access to a natural port on the Red Sea.

There is a famous handbook from the early 1st Century CE entitled *The Periplus of the Erythraean Sea: Travel and Trade in the Indian Ocean,*[76] which serves as a first-hand guide to merchant sailors traversing the somewhat treacherous but bountiful waters from Arabia to India and beyond. It describes market cities and smaller towns on the coastline, what they trade in, the perils of local sea conditions, winds, peoples, etc. Though dated a few centuries later than the era we are concerned with, it demonstrates the challenges but also the rewards that trade along the coastline of the Red Sea and the Indian Ocean could offer, and this bears uncanny resemblance to what we find in the HB.

The Periplus describes a busy trading post that many scholars identify as al-Wajh:

> Now to the left of Berenice, sailing for two or three days from Mussel Harbor eastward across the adjacent gulf, there is another harbor and fortified place, which is called White Village, from which there is a road to Petra,[77] which is subject to Malichas, King of the Nabataeans. It holds the position of a market-town for the small vessels sent there from Arabia; and so a centurion is stationed there as a collector of one-fourth of the merchandise imported, with an armed force, as a garrison.[78]

The recent archaeological expedition team states:

> ...[A]ncient Leuke Kome (White Village) might, in fact, have been located somewhere in a large bay located just south of al-Wajh. Strabo confirms that Leuke Kome was a natural harbour (*hormos*) and so the bay south of al-Wajh would have provided a sufficiently large anchorage to accommodate [a] fleet of 120 large cargo ships. ... al-Wajh is the optimal location for that ancient seaport.[79]

---

[75] "Ancient Ports in the Red Sea," 3684, www.ancientportsantiques .com.

[76] The Periplus of the Erythraean Sea: Travel and Trade in the Indian Ocean by a Merchant of the First Century, Wilfred Harvey Schoff, trans. (New York: Longmans, 1912).

[77] This could well be the same route mentioned in Num 33:35 and Deut 2:8.

[78] Periplus, 19.

[79] Fiema, 112.

Below this safe harbour, *The Periplus*, continues, "Navigation is dangerous along this whole coast of Arabia, which is without harbour, with bad anchorages, foul, inaccessible because of breakers and rocks, and terrible in every way."[80]

> *Jehoshaphat made ships of the Tarshish type*
> *to go to Ophir for gold;*
> *but they did not go, for the ships were*
> *wrecked at Ezion-geber.*
> 1 Kgs 22:48

So this really is the farthest south down the (knobbly) "backbone" (recall the etymology of the verb *asam*, above, and also the "body" reference to *geshem*, mentioned earlier) of Arabia one would set anchor before heading out into the open Sea (in this time period, i.e., Jeddah becomes a large port in the 7th Century CE). The site has everything Nabonidus (Solomon) could want for his fleet of ships.

With respect to the tree-related verb *asam* and/or the noun *atseh*, the words also pertain to "wood," e.g., for kindling (Josh 9:23); for building (Gen 6:14, 2 Kgs 12:13); and manufactured goods (Exod 7:19, Deut 19:5), even idols (Deut 4:28). This is why *Hitchcock's Dictionary of Bible Names* and *Easton's Bible Dictionary* both translate "Ezion-geber" as "The Wood of the Man." What happens when the group first reach the other side of the Red Sea ("Marah")? Moses throws *a piece of wood* into the water (see below). Thus, the name once again denotes the immediate action and thereby preserves the place location (in the context of the journey), a pattern that runs throughout the narrative. All the indications point to Ezion-geber being al-Wajh.

ELOTH

"Arabic names often preserve ancient topographic ones, not impacted by town renaming after political changes."[81] "Eloth"

---

[80] Periplus, 20.

[81] Danièle Michaux-Colombot, "Bronze Age Reed Boats of Magan and Magillum Boats of Meluḫḫa in Cuneiform Literature," in *Stories of Globalisation: The Red Sea and the Persian Gulf from Late Prehistory to*

is a perfect example of this practice. It means "protrusions, terebinths," etc., from the noun *ayil*, "protruder," stemming from the verb *alal*, "to protrude." There is also a strong allusion in the etymology (i.e., the assumed root *'wl*) to "foolishness" or "worthlessness," especially in connection with idol-worship; this reflects the HB's sentiment toward Nabonidus (predominantly at Tayma).

Eloth, which must be near Ezion-geber, has sea on one side, volcanic rock on the other, so terebinths, or trees, *seem* unlikely. What it does have, in fact, is a large area of mangroves; the entire archipelago that begins at al-Wajh and runs about 100 km south, is rich in ("abounding with") mangrove trees.[82] In Nabonidus' day these would have been much denser, probably, and quite a memorable sight, set against the starkness of the landscape beyond. "Eloth" is, therefore, the area just south of the harbour, i.e., the mangrove forest.

> Along the whole of the coast of the Red Sea, down in the deep, grow trees like the laurel and the olive, which at the ebb tides are wholly visible above the water but at the full tides are sometimes wholly covered; and while this is the case, the land that lies above the sea has no trees, and therefore the peculiarity is all the greater.
> Strabo 16.3.6

-End of extract-

The site of Aqaba seems almost too risky for fleets (of a hundred or more ships?), laden with riches from afar. It seems a perfect spot for piracy, for being ambushed and penned in by ships on the other (Red Sea) side of the very narrow entrance to the gulf. The entire environment seems fraught with dangers that even prove difficult for today's mariners, let alone for the ancient, broad, heavy cargo ships that were probably slow to manoeuvre.

The entrance into the Gulf of Aqaba is extremely narrow and constricted by both islands and coral reefs. At the mouth of the Gulf, called the straits of Tiran, are two fairly large islands—Tiran and

---

Early Modernity, Andrea Manzo, Chiara Zazzaro, and Diana Joyce De Falco, eds. (Leiden: Brill, 2019), 119-53, here 151.
[82] "Status of Mangroves in the Red Sea and Gulf of Aden," PERSGA Technical Series 11 (PERSGA, Jeddah: 2004), 26-7, www.cbd.int.

Sanafiri. From the Egyptian shore to the larger island of Tiran, the distance is only three miles. Coral formations further constrict the seaway into two channels. The western one, called Enterprise Passage, is only 1,300 yards wide, while the Eastern Channel, known as Grafton Passage, is a scant 900 yards wide.

Navigation inside the Gulf is complicated by sudden squalls which sweep down from the high mountains, often without warning.[83]

A harbour/port at al-Wajh would have provided not only trade-route access but a clear vista (to see trouble approaching) and enough space for other ships to come to the rescue if required. It also has the benefit of the dangerous archipelago protecting it from the south. So, if Ezion-geber is on the eastern shore of the Red Sea itself, it makes perfect sense for Hiram and Nabonidus to combine forces, in order to make the most of the trade routes in all directions, and to provide protection for one another in these (physically and politically) dangerous waters.

NAVAL ASPECTS

In the days of Necho II (610-595 BCE) and his ambition to create a navy for the Red Sea, Edomite and Sabaean traders were considered potential adversaries in these waters, providing a "more than satisfactory explanation for the only serious Egyptian naval commitment in the Red Sea in pre-Ptolemaic times."[84]

Herodotus writes:

> When he had desisted from the canal Necho turned his attention to military campaigns, and triremes were constructed, some for the Mediterranean and others in the Red Sea for operations in the Erythrian Ocean. The slipways of the latter are still to be seen. And these ships he to use when the need arose.
>
> *Hist.* 2.159

---

[83] Commander Malcolm W. Cagle, USN, "The Gulf Of Aqaba: Trigger For Conflict," Proceedings Vol. 85/1/671 January 1959, https://www.usni.org.
[84] Alan B. Lloyd, "Necho and the Red Sea: Some Considerations," *The Journal of Egyptian Archaeology* 63 (1977): 142-55, here 148. Reading a few sailing blogs concerning the Red Sea, it seems nothing has changed!

Triremes were for battle, not haulage, so they cannot form the basis of any later trading fleet, which seems to be the overwhelming focus of Solomon's ships. However, when you look a little closer, you find that a military presence *is* accounted for, not only in the etymology of the toponym "Ezion-geber" (as above), but also in the terminology of 1 Kings. That is, Solomon's fleet is referred to (1 Kgs 9:26; 10:22) as *"oni Tharshish,* i.e., *a navy (of ships) of* Tarshish."[85]

The name "Naukratis" *means* "naval command,"[86] and I think the "ships of Tarshish" once had a connotation of being not necessarily patrol boats, but certainly armed; once out of the safety-net of Egypt itself, travelling open water, they would have to be.

The Egyptians were rather a xenophobic, almost paranoid lot, it seems, for they put great resources into protecting their lands from all potential infiltration, from every possible avenue. They built great fortresses on the outskirts of the Nile Delta, and set up patrols and barricades on the Nile itself, to keep unwelcome visitors out. There was also a long tradition of providing physical protection for trading vessels both in the Eastern Mediterranean and on the Red Sea, and crews often doubled as sailors and soldiers, depending on the mission.[87] The main Egyptian fleet, or Navy, was based at Memphis, which makes it all the more probable that Hiram maintained a contingent of sailors there, too. They could easily get to Arsinoe, at the tip of the Gulf of Suez, or be transported to a more southerly port for rendezvousing with Nabonidus' ships from across the Sea (if they were to board his ships, rather than sail on their own vessels).

Tyrian ships and their sailors had a great reputation for their maritime prowess but Diakonoff argues that their naval reputation possibly outweighed that for their trading, and claims that Ezek 27:5-11 describes Tyre's *military* forces.[88] Nabonidus, on the other hand, after losing his title as King and therefore his right to procure the services of the Babylonian troops at Gaza (for instance), and never really having any interest in war (so I have claimed, i.e., his early

---

[85] James Orr, ed., "Ships and Boats," *International Standard Bible Encyclopedia* (1915), https://www.biblestudytools.com. Also Strong's Concordance #590.

[86] Philip Chrysopoulos, "Naucratis: The First Ancient Greek Colony in Egypt," February 11, 2024, https://greekreporter.com.

[87] Gilbert, 104.

[88] Diakonoff, 171-81.

inscriptions sound like political 'spin' and propaganda, but his later words speak more of dreams, personal experiences, and the gods), was seemingly more concerned with accumulating wealth, leaving the 'protection' business to someone else. He reveals this side of his nature in the exodus narratives.

We must remember that Nabonidus and Hiram have both been powerful kings. Hiram was *still* a (vassal) king and had strong links to Egypt. Nabonidus was, as far as the exodus narratives demonstrate, an admirer of almost everything Egyptian, so it would not be surprising that his fleet at Ezion-geber was both designed on the basis of the Egyptian trade ships, but also, that it served as a flagship, i.e., as propaganda, showing his prestige and wealth to the world (as "Solomon"). He had commandeered the best spot on the eastern shore of the Red Sea, and was in cahoots with the region's best and most successful traders whose knowledge of the Sea meant that a once lucrative but long neglected trade route was potentially salvaged, i.e., the three-yearly run to Ophir (see below).

Nabonidus' contacts in Arabia over the years must have been quite an attractive incentive even for the Tyrians, whose links in the Mediterranean and Egypt were stronger. Most of the new trading prospects were emerging along the African coast and southern Arabia, and Nabonidus was probably acquainted with everyone worth knowing on the Peninsula, especially once his own trading empire grew at Tayma after the Sinai years.

It is evident that sometimes Hiram sent trained sailors/soldiers to work on Nabonidus' ships (1 Kgs 9:27-8; 10:22); sometimes he sent both sailors *and ships* (2 Chr 8:18); at other times the two fleets travelled side by side (1 Kgs 10:22). If Nabonidus was trading in and out of Naukratis/Thonis, his ships would need the skills of Hiram's sailors to guide the Tarshish boats across the rough Red Sea and into the Nile's 'conveyer belt' system into the port, much as pilot-boats do today. Sailing across the Sea was difficult at certain times of the year, with monsoon winds and the prospect of running aground on the many reefs and other hidden dangers; Tibbetts suggests that true "navigators" (e.g., Hiram's sailors) would mostly sail in the centre of the Sea to avoid the dangers of the coastline, turning to shore only as they approached a port, but that inexperienced sailors (such as the crew leaving Egypt with Nabonidus/"Moses," I have claimed) would make shorter trips from island to island, reef to reef, but would run the risk of being wrecked (like Jehoshaphat's ships).[89]

For such a relatively local trip, Nabonidus' modified cargo vessels sufficed, but perhaps it was for the voyage to Ophir that Hiram would send his own ships, as well as sailors, for this trip was clearly more extensive and would thus, necessarily, involve traversing the more dangerous waters of the southern Red Sea. Wherever Ophir was, it had to lay beyond the archipelago at "Eloth" and that would require much greater navigational skills than Nabonidus' crews might have been able to muster; they needed support vessels with experienced hands. Besides, the riches of Ophir would be the goal for Hiram, too, not just Nabonidus (Solomon). More on this below.

SILVER OF TARSHISH

Returning to the ostracon and the "silver of Tarshish" mentioned therein, given the potential for a two-hundred-year margin of error for purely palaeographic sources, rather than being restricted to the 7th Century BCE it may have its provenance anywhere between the 9/8th and the 6/5th Centuries BCE. Conventional dating for Solomon is the only way this object can find legitimization *before* the 6th Century BCE, but the conventional dating is erroneous. Therefore, I argue that either the ostracon is a fake or it belongs to a later period. If we assume a later date, and err on the side of generosity, there may be a rational explanation for the "silver of Tarshish" that requires no forgery or wrongly assumed chronology.

In the Bible, Tarshish is seen as the source *for* silver (e.g., Ezek 27:12); this silver is but one of several metals and other items to be obtained at the Tarshish marketplace; it is not described as silver mined or even smelted specifically in Tarshish, e.g., "Silver spread into plates is brought from Tarshish" (Jer 10:9).

If we take an earlier date for the ostracon, the silver being brought into the trading hub of Thonis-Heracleion and Naukratis would be imported from a variety of places (e.g., Africa, Ireland, by the Celts via Tartessos, etc.) and beaten into similarly-sized "plates" for transportation. Due to the link to Naukratis, it is possible to suggest that

---

[89] G. R. Tibbetts, "Arab Navigation in the Red Sea," *The Geographical Journal* 127.3 (1961): 322-34, here 323-5.

this commodity, "silver of Tarshish," that seems to be in high demand at the temple, pertains to a specific type of silver coinage.

The use of silver in pharaonic Egypt was limited because of the scarcity of the metal. Its value for hundreds of years was many times that of gold but with the changing political sphere, the improvements in maritime technology, etc., the balance between gold and silver eventually evened out, then settled at a gold/silver ratio of about 2:1. It wasn't "until the 4th Century BCE that Egypt's silver to gold ratio started to be more in line with the historical average ratio of approximately 13:1."[90]

At Naukratis, however, where the Greek mercenaries/soldiers were concentrated, there appears to have been a growing preference for payment via metals, rather than gifts of land or other "in kind" payments, which had previously been the norm. This began with the advent of the Ptolemaic Period (305-30 BCE): "A large amount of salaried mercenaries needing to be paid in coin was a tremendous drain on the treasury, especially considering that some of them insisted on being paid with coinage they were familiar with, as seen by the discovery of silver tetradrachms that were Athenian in type but minted in Egypt."[91] According to Meadows, analysing coins found at Thonis-Heracleion revealed seventy per cent of all the identifiable coins were Ptolemaic.[92]

Having said that, there is some evidence for silver coins being introduced during the reign of Pharaoh Nectanebo I (380-362) BCE of Dynasty 30, which takes us back almost a century closer to the time of Nabonidus. The single coin discovered bears the head of Athena and two owls, making it very Greek, but it also bears hieroglyphics which are translated as " 'all good [silver] or perhaps as 'good for all [purposes]'." [93] Essentially, the silver was 'hallmarked', attesting to its

---

[90] Joel Bauman, "Ancient Egypt: Silver to Gold Ratio of 1:1," January 29, 2020, https://schiffgold.com.

[91] Naphtali Lewis, *Greeks in Ptolemaic Egypt* (Oakville, CT, USA: The David Brown Book Company, 1986), 21.

[92] Andrew Meadows, "Coin circulation and coin production at Thonis-Heracleion and in the Delta region in the Late Period," in *Thonis Heracleion in Context,* Damian Robinson and Franck Goddio, eds. (Oxford Centre for Maritime Archaeology, 2015), 121-36, here 123.

[93] James W. Curtis. "Coinage of Pharaonic Egypt." *The Journal of Egyptian Archaeology* 43 (1957): 71-76, here 72-3.

purity. This is where I think the story might lead back to the "silver of Tarshish" phrase on the ostracon (if authentic).

The ostracon, I suggest, dates to a time when a) the second temple at Jerusalem was extant, and b) the use of silver became widespread as currency, not just as a means of trade.

For the first proviso, the problem lies in the accepted chronology, as even within the Jewish community there are radically different opinions as to when this temple was completed and sanctified for use. On one hand is the more prevalent theory that that it was completed in 520-515 BCE,[94] while on the other, the date is pushed forward to 349 BCE: "In 353 BCE, exactly seventy years after the destruction of the First Temple, the Jews began building again…. (under Ezra and Nehemiah)".[95] With the scarcity of archaeological evidence, all we can muster is an educated guess, of course, but within this timeframe, hallmarked silver coinage became extant in Egypt. While "coinage" is a contested term, it suits the purpose of this simple argument, i.e., that the reason anyone would want "silver of Tarshish," as opposed to other types of silver being traded, is because of this guarantee of its purity. This is potentially why the Greeks preferred to be paid in their own coinage, later, as silver could be so easily debased and its value diminished. They knew where they were with the Greek tetradrachms, and these became the foundation of the silver-standard used for international trade.[96]

Milne suggests that

> silver could have been, and probably was, shipped to Egypt as readily under the Twentieth Dynasty as under the Twenty-sixth, and there are no circumstances known which would suggest any alteration in its value between the two periods. Nor would the Persian conquest change the situation to any material extent: Persian *sigloi* and Phoenician silver coins are found in Egypt,

---

[94] Lawrence H. Schiffman, *From Text to Tradition: A History of Second Temple and Rabbinic Judaism* (Hoboken: Ktav Publishing House, 1991), 44-5.

[95] "The Second Temple is Built," https://www.chabad.org/library/article_cdo /aid/144773/.

[96] Joel Bauman, "Ancient Egypt: Silver to Gold Ratio of 1:1," January 29, 2020, https://schiffgold.com.

but, like the archaic Greek coins, under conditions which clearly suggest that they were regarded as bullion.[97]

He goes on to say that "in the hands of the Ptolemies, the purity of the coinage was fairly well maintained; and it was the mint at Alexandria, i.e., just west of Thonis, that dictated the standards. So even in this much later time, the implication of "Tarshish" as the Nile Delta region still applies, only now the locus of the silver standard is Alexandria, rather than Thonis/Naukratis.[98]

When silver coinage in the ancient world first became widespread in the 4th Century BCE, there was a need for specialists to be able to attest to the purity of the coins, as many forgeries quickly flooded the market. Most people, therefore, desired the newest coins, without any defacement or ware, for these would have the greatest weight of silver and probably be the purest (they had not been tampered with), etc.[99]

The ostracon would seem to date no earlier than to the 4th Century BCE. "Tarshish" could still be the colloquial (Hebrew) name for Thonis-Heracleion, and thus to its 'hallmarked' silver, preferred (by the Jews) to the Hellenistic tetradrachm. "Silver of Tarshish" thus suggests the purest, preferably 'hallmarked' silver coinage that was fit for the temple (i.e., for the priests of the temple). It may be that this special type of silver was relatively short-lived, or valued all the more as a means of 'saving' because of its scarcity, which might help explain so few archaeological examples.

In addition, we should recognise that the Jews of this period are still the inheritors of a Babylonian culture. They had lived and worked there for several generations. That is hard to disavow. In Babylonian society, silver was similarly deemed of great worth but it was also used as a monetary tool, not just as a basis for estimating the value of goods. The exiled Jews would have handled silver, if not in coin form,

---

[97] J. G. Milne, "Ptolemaic Coinage in Egypt," *Journal Of Egyptian Archaeology* 15.3/4 (1929): 150-3, here 150.

[98] Milne, 152.

[99] Peter G. van Alfen, "The 'Owls' from the 1989 Syria Hoard, with a Review of Pre-Macedonian Coinage in Egypt," *American Journal of Numismatics* 14 (2002): 1-57, here, 6-7 and n. 10.

certainly as 'money' (whatever the shape);[100] the tangible metal, pure as possible, must have provided a potential for personal wealth. In Egypt, however, the mentality was strikingly different:

> The palace and the temples … held most of the metals … and did not use them for financial purposes. When royal inscriptions list treasures captured or donated they account for items without expressing their value in gold, silver, or copper/bronze. Those metals appear with their weights recorded when they were part of the collections described as unworked materials.[101]

The Mesopotamian mind-set was, perhaps, more geared toward encouraging entrepreneurship than the state-run economy of Egypt; this in turn led to private investors, contracts, loans, etc., even the dawn of the dreaded "interest".[102] This would *have* to have influenced the industrious Jewish businessmen who first took a chance on leaving the security of Babylon, to start a new venture in Canaan. When an ostracon supposedly declares that a certain *type* of silver is demanded 'by God', you can be assured the (final) recipient of that silver is fiscally erudite.

OPHIR

The discussion concerning Ophir as a foreign location where fleets of ships went every three years inevitably includes the question of how

---

[100] "Small pieces of electrum, a naturally occurring amalgam of silver and gold, were stamped with the king's seal to officially designate them as 'money'. As the first 'world currency', staters circulated widely in a flourishing, sea-going trade linking Greek ports with those in Carthage, Egypt, Syria, Italy, and other remarkably distant realms" (Ancient Trade Route Collection International Monetary Fund, https://www.imf.org/external/np/exr/center/events/ancientr.htm). Sullivan notes the modern name of *Hacksilber* for these money-tokens (Benjamin M. Sullivan, "Paying Archaic Greek Mercenaries: Views From Egypt and the Near East," *The Classical Journal*, 107.1 [October-November 2011]: 31-61, here 35-6).

[101] Marc Van De Mieroop, "Financial Tool in Ancient Egypt and Mesopotamia," in *Explaining Monetary and Financial Innovation*, Financial and Monetary Policy Studies 39, P. Bernholz and R. Vaubel, eds., 17-29, here 21. DOI: 10.1007/978-3-319-06109-2_2.

[102] Van De Mieroop, 26.

far sea travel had advanced; this, however, must depend on the dating of the Solomon narratives. As I argue for a 6th Century BCE identification with Nabonidus, there is wider scope for pinpointing where Ophir might be.

Sources of Gold

Discussions on Ophir focus on the "gold" much like Tarshish is commonly linked to "silver"; there was another place, however, that also proved to be a significant source for gold, i.e., Uphaz/Eliphaz, which was a lot closer to home for Nabonidus.

In Dan 10:5 the vision of the fiery, shining man that comes to the author includes reference to this figure wearing a "belt of gold from Uphaz." The name "Uphaz" appears also in Jer 10:9, again linked with gold imports (and also silver from Tarshish). Uphaz is thought by some to be "Ophir," where the famed "King Solomon's Mines" were claimed to have been found in 1977, i.e., between Medina and Mecca.[103] Heck, however, places the richest gold resources in the Tabuk region, i.e., where Tayma is located.[104]

In the genealogies of Gen 36:9-19, Esau's firstborn is Eliphaz whose name means "God is gold," from *el* (Elohim/God) and the verb *pazaz*, meaning "to be agile or supple," and *Strong's* adds, "to solidify (as if by refining)," suggesting metallurgy; another verb *pazaz* means, more plainly, "to refine, best," suggesting goldsmithing. Eliphaz's firstborn is Teman, i.e., Tayma. Reuel is Eliphaz's brother, i.e., Jethro; the family base is in the territory of Seir. i.e., the Harraat region of Edom (Ezek 25:13). Thus, Eliphaz is most certainly representative of a location in Northwestern Arabia. If this is "Ophir," why would Solomon require ships to get there? It was in the desert. If it is in the desert, the list of toponyms in Deuteronomy 1 are all contiguous, and Moses doesn't suddenly jump on a ship and head to some distant place to continue his "words" to the Israelites!

So Uphaz pertains to a region in Nabonidus' Arabia. It possibly served as the *first* source for gold, before an alternative, i.e., Ophir, was

---

[103] Lois Berkowitz, "Has the U.S. Geological Survey Found King Solomon's Gold Mines?" *Biblical Archaeological Review* (September 1977), https://library .biblicalarchaeology.org/.

[104] Gene W. Heck, "Gold Mining in Arabia and the Rise of the Islamic State," *Journal of the Economic and Social History of the Orient* 42.3 (1999): 364-95, here 367-8

discovered/accessible. After all, Deuteronomy seems to be a reasonably contemporaneous text (to the exodus itself, in the 6th Century BCE), and Nabonidus' later career as an international trader would not necessarily be known at the time of composition. The name "Ophir" may well allude, phonetically/etymologically, to Uphaz/Eliphaz via the verb *'wh*, "to desire or draw near," and, Abarim suggests Ophir may mean "Coast of Riches, Gathering Mark of Wealth" (potentially from a derivative of the root *'wh*, *i.e.*, *'i*, meaning "coast," and the verb *'wh*, which means "to desire, covet"). This is steering us back into the Nabonidus world I see in the exodus narratives, the Solomon narratives, and Daniel; the once King of Babylonia is depicted in terms of being strongly driven by the accumulation of wealth, and this is not looked upon with favour by the early Jews.

The Maritime Situation

I suggest in *Arabian Sinai* that Nabonidus visited the Nile Delta (as "Moses") in 522 BCE (potentially confirmed by a subtle allusion to a lunar eclipse). This is the year Cambyses died; Darius I would follow, bringing with him rapid changes.

Although Pharaoh Necho II had begun work on a canal to link the Nile with the (current) Red Sea (*Hist.* 2.158), the task was allegedly abandoned when the pharaoh received an ominous omen. Sometime later, Necho supposedly hired the Phoenicians to explore the coastline of Africa. According to Herodotus (*Hist.* 4.42) they succeeded, though the historian himself had his doubts. They went, apparently, through the Red Sea to the Arabian Sea and onwards around the continent. Even today, this trip is downplayed or dismissed as being too immense an achievement for the period. However, an experimental voyage in a replica Phoenician ship in 2008 by Philip Beale, a former Royal Navy officer, proved the journey was possible, and that it took just about the same time as Necho's expedition.[105] According to the historian (*Hist.* 4.42) the Phoenicians, after a 19,000 mile round trip, arrived back where they started sometime in the earlier part of the "third year," while Beale's voyage lasted 2 years and two months; the former included stays on land to grow crops and load goods, etc., while the modern attempt changed the route slightly to take advantage of certain weather

---

[105] James Beresford, "Sailing Close to the Wind: The Phoenician Circumnavigation of Africa," *Minerva: The International Review of Ancient Art & Archaeology* (2013):34-7.

patterns (something Beale suggests the Phoenicians probably didn't do, i.e., they would have stayed closer to shore). The most significant aspect, for this current investigation, however, is the timing: The fleet returned in the third year—just as Solomon's famed ships.

So, on one hand it would seem *possible* that the reason 1 Kgs 10 mentions this three-year period is because the circumnavigation of Africa had been accomplished relatively recently and this was widely known. This would suggest that the riches mentioned were traded from the coastal markets along the journey; gold, ivory, monkeys, etc., could have come from a wholly African sojourn.

However, it seems to me that a pharaoh who had discovered the first complete route around Africa would have hailed it from the rooftops. There would have been great celebrations, boasting inscriptions set up around the land, etc. But there is no hint, anywhere, other than this legend from Herodotus. Have we simply not discovered the relevant inscriptions? And there is still the issue of the "peacocks."

Darius I seems to have been inspired by Necho II, in that he took up the challenge of the canal and he did boast about it; four stelae preserve an account of his achievement, which he claimed was intended to show that he had conquered Egypt and had constant access to it from Persia.[106] He was also intent on his own circumnavigation project that began with discovering the mouth of the Indus River (*Hist.* 4.44). Sending an expedition down the River to the Indian Ocean, the trip, including the return voyage around the Arabian Peninsula and back up to Egypt via the Red Sea (roughly 3000 miles), took *thirty* months. Clearly a long, arduous task, though a fraction of the distance to sail around Africa, we still are reminded of the three-year reference in Kings and Chronicles.

This was soon followed (ca. 518 BCE) by the conquest of major regions of northern India.[107] The trade links between Mesopotamia and the Indus regions was ancient even by Darius' time but having discovered the "southern" or Erythraean Sea (the Indian Ocean) was accessible, and with the canal linking the Red Sea to the Nile, there was *potential* for a truly international maritime trade route to the south and east, linking with the Mediterranean to the north.

It is during this rapid expanse in territory, trade, and probably shipping technology, that I think Nabonidus' own empire, back in

---

[106] Henry Colburn, "King Darius' Red Sea Canal," FEZANA 4.35 (2021):27-30.
[107] "Achaemenid conquest of the Indus Valley," https://dbpedia.org.

Tayma, flourished enough for him to have become the flamboyant, wealthy, famous "Solomon."[108] And I think it was this more localised *periplus* around the Arabian peninsula that created the means for one of Nabonidus' favourite things—reviving ancient traditions.

I suggest "Ophir" is Punt. This is not a novel idea, by any means, as various comparisons have been drawn between Solomon's enterprise and accounts of Pharaoh Hatshepsut, whose trading jaunts down the Red Sea to the south-eastern coast of Africa were highly publicised and boasted similar goods (e.g., gold, silver, monkeys, etc.).

It has also been argued that there is no evidence for direct trade between Egypt and Mesopotamia via a sea route around the Arabian Peninsula in the 10th Century BCE,[109] but I think this is precisely the route we need to be looking at in the 6th. I suggest that Ophir is the Hebrew commission name for Punt (which was apparently still called "Punt" even in the days of Cleopatra[110]). The controversial inclusion of the "peacocks" is key not only to the location of Ophir but also to the dating of the trips to procure them.

Peacocks

There are many who argue against the translation of *tukkiyyim* in 1 Kgs 10:22 and 2 Chr 9:21 as "peacocks," suggesting, for instance it is "an attempted translation of [a] Hebrew ... word not known from anywhere else," and pointing out that the Septuagint translates it as, "turned and carved stones."[111] When you are looking at the 1 Kings/2 Chronicles pericopes from a Nabonidus-perspective, however, the inclusion of "peacocks" may just prove highly significant, but only if the story of Nabonidus in Arabia *and* in the exodus are familiar. If we retain "peacocks" as the translation, we find not only a confirmation that Ophir and India are linked (but not identical) but also, a reaffirmation

---

[108] My previous work on Nabonidus suggests the name "Solomon" was coined by the author of the Song of Solomon, who was actually Nabonidus' second-wife. The Song was a very early composition, already known by the time of the fall of Babylon. Nabonidus was never the "King of Israel" in Jerusalem, but his reputation followed him, and the stigma of being "Solomon" persisted.

[109] Gilbert, 83.

[110] Mills, 2.

[111] Donald Keith Mills, "Ophir and Punt," *SIS Chronology and Catastrophim Review* (2019): 1-12, here 6.

of one of the strangest legends pertaining to "Moses" that includes highly unusual birds.

Mills relates a theory that *tukkiyyim* is derived from the Tamil term *Tokai* (*tôkei/tôkai*), which "is used in Tamil poetry to signify the bird by naming its most prominent attribute"; the word suggests "anything hanging down," referring (obliquely to my mind) to its tail, though it is, he admits, a very rare use of the word.[112] A peacock's tail is hardly renowned for being dragged on the ground; it is resplendent when raised and displayed proudly. Mills, rejecting this theory, asks: "Why should Tamil traders have used a 'very rare', 'poetical' word when dealing with traders from a foreign land? The lack of contemporary (1,000 BC) attestation of the word outside of the Bible … further weaken(s) the case."[113]

My response: They didn't, i.e., the term is *not* related to *tôkei/tôkai*.

Clark argues against the "peacocks" translation and sums up by saying that if *tukkiyym* is correct, "and if the comparison with Dravidian *tokei* is valid, the verses may have been added to the Hebrew text sometime after the sixth century B.C., when the peacock was known in Palestine."[114] Nabonidus as the inspiration for the tales of Solomon resolves this issue (and many more!).

The Indian (Sanskrit) word for peacock is *mayūra* (in Tamil, *mayil*), which sounds nothing like *tukkiyym*. I searched a Tamil dictionary for words containing "*tukki*"; there were two, i.e., *vayar̲koṭukki*, the herbaceous plant *Heliotropium ovalifolium* (or *tēṭkoṭukki, Helotropium indicum*), and *tiṭukkiṭu*, "to be surprised, startled, alarmed, frightened."[115]

Peacocks have a long history of serving as guard birds in India (and elsewhere today), for they make shrill calls when they sense danger:

> Peacocks are both territorial and curious, and an entire flock acting as a unit will investigate trespassers. They threaten

---

[112] Mills, 11-12.

[113] Mills, 11.

[114] Walter Eugene Clark, "The Sandalwood and Peacocks of Ophir," *The American Journal of Semitic Languages and Literatures* (1920):103-19, here 118. See also 108-11.

[115] Tamil Dictionary, https://agarathi.com.

unfamiliar humans, animals, or things by charging at perceived predators while screaming and can attack with sharp spurs called "kicking thorns" on their feet. The eerie peacock alarm-call sounds like a terrified woman or child fleeing assault, crying, "Help! He-lp! He-lp!" Carrying up to seven miles, it can make a grown man's hair stand on end and wake the sleeping and the dead. The birds give a less alarming call, "May-aw!" when planes fly over or cars drive by as well as to announce arrival of both dawn and dusk.[116]

The term *tukkiyyim*, I suggest, might well have derived from a colloquial name for the birds early traders encountered on the trade run to Ophir. The Indian traders might have referred to the bird, as Mills' scholar suggests, in terms of its most significant trait, i.e., *to the Indians*, the peacock's *protective nature*. That it was also beautiful was merely a bonus. The 'salesmen' probably promoted the peacock as the perfect guard animal for those with riches to protect, etc. This would have attracted Nabonidus, whose inscriptions tell of him constructing protective statues for his temples (including a vicious bird; see The Verse Account of Nabonidus, i 6-7). A peacock was therefore known as the "bird that is easily startled." Compare the cuneiform *tuk₄, tuku₄* "to tremble, quake, shiver, be angry." One only has to watch a peacock 'shivering' its tail feathers when agitated, to understand this allusion. There is also *tukku*: "an alarm, a warning, a voice from heaven."[117]

Actually, peacocks appear as royal-palace birds in the ancient Sumerian tale of Enki and the New World Order. Blessing various lands where trade has proven bountiful for Sumer, Enki says: "May your birds all be peacocks! May their cries grace royal palaces!" (ETCSL 1.1.3, 221-37) Notice how Enki does not mention the beauty of the tail, but the *noise* the bird makes. With the shifting political and environmental situation at Ur (especially), the trade between India (the Indus Valley) and Sumer also shifted; the rise of the Dilmun region as the chief negotiator in trade with Ur[118] possibly ended the influx of peacocks and they fell into obscurity for a long time. Even the

---

[116] Lucile Bayon Hume, "Avian Alarm System: A Peacock in the Yard is Worth Two Police on Patrol," December 22, 2016. https://countryroads magazine.com/outdoors/knowing-nature /avian-alarm-system/.

[117] "Tukku," https://www.assyrianlanguages.org.

[118] S. R. Rao, "Shipping and Maritime Trade of the Indus People," *Expedition* (Spring, 1965): 30-7, here, 36-7.

Assyrians show no iconography of peacocks, which might suggest they were being traded *after* the Neo-Assyrian period). Then it wouldn't be until Darius' conquest of the Indian regions, perhaps, that the peacock was re-discovered, with faster/farther trips by sea and the chances of survival increased. It is very possible Nabonidus was one of the first to purchase, display, and trade such creatures, and why they suddenly appear in Palestine around the same time (i.e., via Hiram III, who took the same traded goods to the Levant).

As for the peacocks relating to Moses (Nabonidus), Diodorus writes:

> Thus, for these reasons Moses was loved by the masses, and being deemed worthy of divine honour by the priest, he was called Hermes because of his ability to interpret [*hermeneia*] the sacred writing (*Praep. Ev.* 9.27.6).[119]

Immediately, the idea of Nabonidus being a lover of wisdom and sacred writings should resonate with the man I have been presenting in my analyses. He exhibits his passion for arcane wisdom constantly, throughout the Song of Solomon *and* the exodus narratives. In *Arabian Sinai* I attempt to explain this strange association with Thoth-Hermes further by reference to Herodotus' misunderstanding surrounding the nature of the ibis, which is the animal representation of Thoth. Again, I offer a snippet from the book to clarify:[120]

-Start of excerpt-

> Herodotus' remark on the "winged serpents" that travel from Arabia to Egypt and are thwarted by hungry ibis (*Hist.* 2.75-6) has been interpreted by some as a sighting of snake-like (i.e., salamander) fossils in a specific area of the Negev desert, 85 km south of (the conventional) Beersheba.[121]

---

[119] Caterina Moro, "Hero and Villain: An Outline of the Exodus' Pharaoh in Artapanus,") in *Israel's Exodus in Transdisciplinary Perspective: Text, Archaeology, Culture, and Geoscience*, T. E. Levy, T. Schneider, W. H. C. Propp, B. C. Sparks, eds. (Heidelberg: Springer 2015), 365-76, here, 368.
[120] Tyson, *Arabian Sinai*, 271-2.
[121] Karen Radner, "The Winged Snakes of Arabia and the Fossil Site of Makhtesh Ramon in the Negev," *WZKM* 97 (2007): 353-65, here 365.

Herodotus' description of piles of bare bones *might* suggest fossils, and the hostile landscape reveals a predominance of ammonites, etc.[122] The illustrations used to support the argument for winged-snake fossils, however, are somewhat unconvincing and would have to be witnessed *very* closely, i.e., not easily noted by passers-by.[123] For there to be piles of these all visible on the surface and considered by travellers to be recently devoured prey doesn't seem to tally. I think Herodotus is, once again, inventing connections between snippets of information he deems too good to ignore but for which he has no concrete explanation.

Herodotus' Arabian flying serpents come straight from the legends of Moses. If the ark, as I suggest, has winged serpents on the top, and it is carried in procession everywhere the Israelites go, many people would see it. With the later Philistine debacle, its notoriety as a powerful object would be enhanced. Herodotus might have heard stories about the winged serpents that came from Arabia (i.e., on the ark, from Sinai/Qurayyah), in the context of a dangerous and sometimes lethal phenomenon that had 'something' to do with Egypt, i.e., knowing that the winged serpent is familiar in Egyptian iconography. He also links the serpents with the ibis, suggesting this is why the Egyptians consider the birds sacred, i.e., they eat the snakes before they reach Egypt (*Hist.* 2.76).[124]

Ibis seldom, if ever, eat snakes, according to ornithologists; they feed on small crustaceans, worms, insects, etc., and sometimes other birds' or reptiles' eggs. A fourteen-year scientific study of the Sacred Ibis states "regurgitations in nests underestimate some rare cases of killed but non-swallowed vertebrates, possibly by a few

---

[122] Fossilised ammonites "were thought to be petrified coiled snakes, and were called snakestones. They were thought to have magical powers in Medieval times" (https://en.wikipedia .org/List_of_mythological_objects) but a coiled snake does not suggest a winged snake.

[123] Radner, 365, Figs. 4a and 4b.

[124] In *Hist.* 3.107, Herodotus suggests that Arabian frankincense is protected by these creatures, further linking the serpents to Nabonidus' world of incense, trade, etc.

specialized individuals,"[125] thereby confirming that a union of snake and ibis is very rare indeed (and may only occur when a snake attempts to attack eggs in a nest?).

In the early 19th Century, French archaeologists opened several mummified ibis and did find snakes in the abdominal cavities. However, "Jules-César Savigny, who investigated the habits of the ibis, … noted that the embalmers had apparently been serving 'truths deeper than mere facts of natural history'," i.e., the embalmers were alluding to a symbolic connection by *placing* snakes in the birds *post-mortem*.[126]

Josephus (*A.J.* 2.10.2) tells the story of Moses' early years in Egypt and how he was sent to Ethiopia to stop an incursion into Egypt. Coming to a certain impasse filled with flying serpents, Moses unleashes baskets of ibis that hastily set to work devouring the creatures. He and his army are free to pass and arrive at their opponents' territory early enough to surprise and thereby conquer them. Earlier, I told of Moses being worshipped as Thoth-Hermes, and as being held responsible for the sanctity of the ibis; Thoth's zoomorphic form is the ibis. There seems to be a kernel of truth in both Herodotus' and Josephus' renderings of Moses' snake-eating birds, but if they weren't ibis, what were they?

-End of excerpt-

So, if the legend that took hold in the imagination was of Moses possessing (clearly unusual) birds that ate snakes, and this was in a context of 'protection', I posit these birds were peacocks, not ibis. Peacocks *do* eat snakes, in fact, the Sanskrit name *mayūra* translates as "killer of snakes"; "Indian folklore even went so far as to say that peafowl had the ability

---

[125] Loïc Marion, "Is the Sacred Ibis a Real Threat to Biodiversity? Long-term Study of its Diet in Non-native Areas Compared to Native Areas," *CRB* 336.4 (April 2013): 207-220, here (online version) §4.2.2, "In the native area," www.science direct.com.

[126] "Savigny and the Sacred Ibis," Napoleon and the Scientific Expedition to Egypt, https://napoleon.lindahall.org/sacred_ibis.shtml.

to hypnotize cobras and make it so the cobras eggs wouldn't hatch."[127]

Josephus' Moses is said to have these protective birds when he lived in "Ethiopia," i.e., Nubia, a clue that must not be overlooked. The Greeks called Kush "Ethiopia" (not to be mistaken for modern Ethiopia farther south); Kush was Upper Nubia and this region, it is thought, included the coast of the Red Sea down to modern Eritrea (Lower Nubia reached from the Red Sea to Libya and as far south as the second cataract of the Nile).[128]

Indian Traders

Josephus states that Ophir (Sophir) was later called "the *Aurea Chersonesus* ("Golden Land") which belongs to India (*A.J.* 6.4) but Clark suggests this was too conveniently timed to be taken seriously, as India had, in Josephus' time (1st Century CE), recently become heralded as the source of much gold.[129]

It is suggested that *direct* trade between Egypt and India did not really take off until the Roman Period, but "early navigation was apparently dominated by Arabs and Indians, with a certain degree of participation by Phoenician sailors."[130]

This is precisely the situation I envision in Nabonidus' later life, under Darius I's reign, i.e., when exploration is uncovering alternative routes and discovering new (perhaps old) trading partners. The once close relationship between Mesopotamia and India (Indus Valley), long forgotten, is revived but in a different form. This time, the focus is on sea trade, on Arabia and Egypt. There would come a point, however, when common sense would kick in, and someone would realise that there was little point for the Indian traders to sail all the way from India to the Nile Delta, and little reason for the Egyptians, or Nabonidus/Hiram, to travel all the way to India. They would meet somewhere in the middle, i.e., Punt.[131]

---

[127] Gordon Ramel, "Do Peacocks Eat Snakes and How Do They Kill Them?" July 11, 2023, https://earthlife.net/do-peacocks-eat-snakes/.

[128] "Nubia," Britannica, https://www.britannica.com/place/Nubia.

[129] Walter E. Clark, "The Sandalwood and Peacocks of Ophir," *The American Journal of Semitic Languages and Literatures* 36.2 (1920): 103-19, here 112.

[130] "Indian Ocean textile trade: India to Egypt," § Early evidence for textile trade from India, Eastern Art Online, http://jameelcentre.ashmolean.org.

[131] This is what Nabonidus does for the Treaty of 549 BCE, where he meets the delegates from the three other nations at Tayma (I claim), a sort of halfway,

At the tip of the Horn of Africa, within modern-day Somalia, is a region known as Puntland. This is very probably a latter-day toponym, to provide status and significance to the place, in memory of the original Punt, which *may* point to this area being Hatshepsut's destination, at least in local lore. Most scholars today opt for Somalia as the location of Punt, perhaps for this reason.

The link to Nabonidus, as "Moses with his peacocks in Ethiopia/Nubia," makes it possible the original Punt lay on the shores of Upper Nubia (we cannot be certain of its ancient boundaries), or Eretria. In fact, since a forensic study conducted on mummified baboons in 2020 concluded that the apes found in Egypt came from the region of Eritrea, the chances of Punt being in this area have increased.[132] It was also tentatively concluded that Punt later became known as Aldus, a famed trading station in the Ptolemaic Period in just this area.

Even before this, however, there is evidence to suggest a potential revival of trading with Punt by the Egyptians in the time of Nabonidus:

> From the early first millennium BCE, there are no further records of Egyptians in Punt, or of Puntites visiting Egypt. There are, however, two incomplete inscriptions that mention Punt in a narrative context, and both are attributed to the 26th (Saite) Dynasty. One of these, the Defenneh stele, describes an expedition to Punt that was saved from dying thirst by unexpected rainfall on "the mountains of Punt" (Meeks, 2003). The Defenneh stele is a testament to the efforts of Saitic pharaohs to revive maritime commerce on the Red Sea, while also raising the possibility of renewed trade with Punt. It is perhaps no coincidence that the Saite dynasty (664-525 BCE) exists squarely within the radiometric date range of hamadryas baboons from Gabbanat el-Qurud.[133]

---

neutral point, that is commemorated by the name "Kiriath-arba" ("City of Four") in Gen 23:2 (Tyson, *Arabian Sinai*, 78).

[132] Nathaniel J Dominy, et al., "Mummified baboons reveal the far reach of early Egyptian mariners," eLife 2020;9:e60860. DOI: https://doi.org/10.7554/eLife.60860.

[133] Franziska Grathwol, et al., "Adulis and the transshipment of baboons during classical antiquity," 1-21, here, 16, https://www.biorxiv.org/content/10.1101/2023.02.28.530428v1.full.pdf.

Nabonidus was not the kind of man to watch others getting rich; Punt would be so tantalisingly close. We have long underestimated Nabonidus, but the Bible reveals a powerful, well-connected, driven man; it may be that he became aware of this intended revival during Ahmose III's (his father-in-law's) reign and once resettled at Tayma, he secured a piece of the action.

Hatshepsut's port of departure was almost directly opposite al-Wajh (a little north),[134] so Nabonidus and Hiram would have followed the same, well-attested route (perhaps with more detailed navigational information than we have inherited). "Egypt seems to have been the only country to have known of Punt, and to refer to it";[135] until the days of Nabonidus and Hiram III, and the biblical narratives. They would

Figure 3: Potential routes to Punt by Indian traders and Nabonidus/Hiram (Image: Public Domain Map, author's adaptations)

have split the cargo, Nabonidus heading for al-Wajh (Ezion-geber), Hiram taking the rest, including his share, to a more northern port, and

---

[134] "Ancient Ports in the Red Sea," #3544: "Philoteras portus, Philotere, (city founded by Satyros), port of Aennus, archaic Saww, Sww used during 12th Dynasty for expeditions to Land of Punt," https://www.ancientportsantiques .com/the-catalogue/red-sea/.

[135] Mills, 2.

sending the rest up the Nile to Naukratis/Thonis for international distribution.

The age of the Babylon-India intermediary, Dilmun, was followed by the rise of the great trading port of Gerrha, on the eastern shores of Arabia, perhaps even in the same location (ca. 690 BCE).[136] Nabonidus, as King of Babylon, would have had access to Indian merchandise from Gerrha and it is possible he had peacocks in Babylon. He would see Punt as a means of cutting out the middle-man, sending his own ships to reap the rewards of the newly discovered sea-route from India (instead of having goods travel across the desert, which would incur greater losses of live animals). With Punt not even as far as the Bab-el-Mandeb (Gate of Lamentation, Grief or Tears), the onus of navigating this dangerous strait would fall to the Indian traders who had been brave enough to venture so far on the Indian Ocean.

Therefore, the three-year period mentioned in Kings and Chronicles may simply refer to the schedule of the intrepid Indian traders, who made this trip from India to Punt only every third year. Nabonidus could get his "*algum*" wood from the same region,[137] gold would have come in from Africa *and* India, and the peacocks would have enjoyed a *relatively* comfortable journey from India and would be shipped to al-Wajh and Hiram's port comparatively quickly. [138]

Ophir as Omen

That is the geographical theory for the *place* "Ophir" within the context of Nabonidus' (Solomon's) trading empire. It is clear from my years of working with the symbolic etymology of the Bible that things are seldom so straightforward. There is another side to "Ophir" and one that is profoundly significant, for it tallies with every other allusion to Nabonidus in the HB: An alternative translation is "reducing to ashes," from *epher*, "ashes."

---

[136] "Gerrha," Arabia and the Arabs: The Making of an Ethnos, March 17, 2007, https://brown.edu.

[137] For a discussion of this wood being ebony from Eritrea and south-eastern Sudan, see Mills, 3-5.

[138] There is a native African peacock, i.e., the Congo Peacock. It is less decorative and, as in the case of the Indian peacocks, would probably die on the journey from the deepest Congo, overland. The retention of the Tamil word forces us to address the creature as an Indian import.

I was confused by this at first but gradually it made sense, for ashes are a sign of mourning but also of the most dire situations, of doom, and an inevitable fate (e.g., Ezek 28:18 ; Isa 44:20 ; Job 13:12, etc.)

This is precisely the perception of Nabonidus evidenced by the authors of the HB. At the end of the Song, his fate is sealed as being a direct, one-way trip to Sheol; in Exodus, Nabonidus is depicted as a deleterious character who meets his end without honour; in Daniel, he is given warnings and opportunities to change, but fails to do so, earning him the reputation that has overshadowed everything else he stood for, i.e., as the 'mad' king.

Thus, "ashes" become synonymous with inevitable doom. "Ophir" is a symbolic commission name to identify the land of riches, Punt, which bolstered Solomon's (Nabonidus') wealth and prestige but, in the end, was (according to early Judaism) one of three things that brought him low in God's eyes: "Apart from having married a Gentile … the king transgressed two other biblical laws. He kept many horses, which a Jewish king ought not to do, and, what the law holds in equal abhorrence, he amassed much silver and gold."[139]

I therefore think it cannot be a coincidence that immediately prior to the use of *tukkiyyim* ("peacocks") in 1 Kings and 2 Chronicles (a *hapax legomenon* used to draw attention to itself), 1 Kgs 10:14-1 has been describing the incredible wealth of Solomon; these verses in 1 Kings relate to Daniel's tale of the "golden statue" (Daniel 3), revealing a symbolic connection to "the beast" with the number "666"!

Those who argue that Ophir is a place in Arabia because it is listed as one of Joktan's sons in Genesis 10, are only seeing half the evidence. It is certainly linked to Arabia, in that it is associated with Nabonidus, but it is located on the south-eastern coast of Africa. It is so placed in the 'genealogies' because it could not be placed anywhere else, being a Nabonidus-specific toponym of import.

"Joktan" represents Nabonidus.[140] The name stems from the verb *qaton*, "to be small or insignificant" and is translated by *Strong's* as "he will be made little." In the Brown–Driver–Briggs Lexicon, "Joktan" is said to mean, in Arabic tradition, "strike, beat"; this is the most damning action in Exodus, i.e., Moses "strikes/beats" not just the Nile,

---

[139] "The Marriage of Solomon," *Legends of the Jews*, 4.5, (22), https://www.sefaria.org /Legends_of_the_Jews.4.5.105?lang=bi.
[140] See my paper, "Nabonidus and the Arabian Genealogies (Genesis 10 and 11)."

not just 'a rock', but a person; this one act supposedly precludes him from entering the Promised Land.

CONCLUDING REMARKS

My aim for this paper was to reassess the "ships of Tarshish," and by extension the mysterious land of "Ophir," in terms of a 6th Century BCE Nabonidus-based paradigm for the "Solomon" narratives in the HB.

It is clear that an understanding of "Tarshish" must incorporate a broader sphere of reference including, most importantly, the relationship between Nabonidus (in Arabia) and Egypt. Everything from trading routes, types of boats, payment of local workers, and the conquests of other kings come into play, resulting in a plausible and cohesive evolution of the name and its usage.

The "ships of Tarshish" were not exclusive to Nabonidus/ "Solomon" but because some of the early Jews experienced them first hand (i.e., those who remained at Tayma and were probably serving as Nabonidus' crew), and commemorated them in the chronicles of their time with Nabonidus in Arabia, they became associated with this group of people. Others, such as the Cypriots, the Tyrians, etc., also had Tarshish boats—boats that traded through Thonis/Naukratis—but they had names for them in their own language; it was the Hebrew-speaking Jews who took an existing Assyrian toponym and gave it their own twist.

Nabonidus and his peacocks, traded from the Indian ships that docked at Punt, would become the inspiration for Moses and his wondrous ibis, the latter a nod to the Egyptian element of the man's postexilic interests.

Importantly, the very language of the HB needs to be revisited with a stronger focus on the etymology of toponyms, and the context of a 6th Century BCE world employed to reveal the hidden connections between those toponyms. Therein lies the original meaning and intention of that which has confounded us for centuries.

BIBLIOGRAPHY

"Achaemenid conquest of the Indus Valley." https://dbpedia.org.

"Ancient Ports in the Red Sea." www.ancientportsantiques.com.

"Egyptian Alabaster Stone." https://egyptianmarble granite.com.

"Egyptian Navy." https://naval-encyclopedia.com.

"Gerrha." Arabia and the Arabs: The Making of an Ethnos. March 17, 2007. https://brown.edu.

"Indian Ocean textile trade: India to Egypt." Eastern Art Online. http://jameelcentre .ashmolean.org.

"Javan." Jewish Virtual Library. https://www.jewishvirtuallibrary.org.

"Nubia." Britannica. https://www.britannica.com.

"Phoenician Mining." https://phoenicia.org.

"Savigny and the Sacred Ibis." Napoleon and the Scientific Expedition to Egypt. https://napoleon.lindahall.org/sacred_ibis.shtml.

"Status of Mangroves in the Red Sea and Gulf of Aden." PERSGA Technical Series 11. PERSGA, Jeddah: 2004. www.cbd.int.

"Tarshish." https://www.abarim-publications.com.

"Tarshish." Jewish Virtual Library. https://www.jewishvirtuallibrary.org.

"The Marriage of Solomon." *Legends of the Jews.* https://www.sefaria.org.

"The Second Temple is Built." https://www.chabad.org.

Abudanah, Fawzi, Saad Twaissi, et al. "The Legend of the King's Highway: The Archaeological Evidence." *Zeitschrift für Orient-Archäologie,* Band 8 (2015): 156-187.

Akkadian Dictionary. https://www.assyrianlanguages.org.

Albright, W. F. "New Light on the Early History of Phoenician Colonization." *Bulletin of the American Schools of Oriental Research* 83 (1941):14-22.

Alfen, Peter G. van. "The 'Owls' from the 1989 Syria Hoard, with a Review of Pre-Macedonian Coinage in Egypt." *American Journal of Numismatics* 14 (2002): 1-57.

Bauman, Joel. "Ancient Egypt: Silver to Gold Ratio of 1:1." January 29, 2020. https:// schiffgold.com.

Beitzel, Barry J. "Was There a Joint Nautical Venture on the Mediterranean Sea by Tyrian Phoenicians and Early Israelites?" *Bulletin of the American Schools of Oriental Research* 360 (2010): 37-66, here 47, n. 26; "The city of Opis is where the Assyrian king Sennacherib famously had Syrian-built ships dragged overland on rollers from the Tigris River to the Euphrates River in 694 (BCE)" (W&N, 11 n. 100).

Belov, Alexander. "Archaeological Evidence for the Egyptian *baris* (Herodotus *Historiae* 2.96)" Pages 195-210 in *Thonis Heracleion in Context*. Edited by Damian Robinson and Franck Goddio. Oxford Centre for Maritime Archaeology, 2015.

Beresford, James. "Sailing Close to the Wind: The Phoenician Circumnavigation of Africa." *Minerva: The International Review of Ancient Art & Archaeology* (2013):34-7.

Berkowitz, Lois. "Has the U.S. Geological Survey Found King Solomon's Gold Mines?" Biblical Archaeological Review (September 1977), http Lois s://library.biblical archaeology.org/.

Bomhard, Anne-Sophie von. *The Decree of Saïs: The Stelae of Thonis-Heracleion and Naukratis*. Oxford Centre for Maritime Archaeology: Monograph 7. Oxford: University of Oxford, 2012.

Bosch-Gimpera, P. B. "The Phokaians in the Far West: An Historical Reconstruction." *The Classical Quarterly* 38.1/2 (1944): 53-9.

Cagle, Commander Malcolm W., USN. "The Gulf Of Aqaba: Trigger For Conflict." Proceedings Vol. 85/1/671. January 1959. https://www .usni.org.

Chrysopoulos, Philip. "Naucratis: The First Ancient Greek Colony in Egypt." February 11, 2024. https://greekreporter.com.

Clark, Walter Eugene. "The Sandalwood and Peacocks of Ophir." *The American Journal of Semitic Languages and Literatures* 36.2 (1920): 103-19.

Colburn, Henry. "King Darius' Red Sea Canal." FEZANA 4.35 (2021):27-30.

Covey-Crump, W. W. "The Situation of Tarshish." *The Journal of Theological Studies* 17.67 (1916): 280-90.

Cross, Frank Moore. "An Interpretation of the Nora Stone." *Bulletin of the American Schools of Oriental Research* 208 (1972): 13-19.

Curtis, James W. "Coinage of Pharaonic Egypt." *The Journal of Egyptian Archaeology* 43 (1957): 71-76.

Diakonoff, I. M. "The Naval Power and Trade of Tyre." *Israel Exploration Journal* 42.3/4 (1992): 168-93.

Dominy, Nathaniel J., et al. "Mummified baboons reveal the far reach of early Egyptian mariners." eLife 2020;9:e60860. DOI: https://doi.org /10.7554/eLife.60860.

Esposito, Serena. "Riverboats and Seagoing Ships: Lexicographical Analysis of Nautical Terms from the Sources of the Old Kingdom." Pages 32-41 in *Stories of Globalisation: The Red Sea and the Persian Gulf from Late Prehistory to Early Modernity*. Edited by Andrea Manzo, Chiara Zazzaro, and Diana Joyce De Falco. Leiden: Brill, 2018.

Fiema, Zbigniew T. et al. "The al-ʿUlā–al-Wajh Survey Project: 2013 Reconnaissance Season." ATLAL: *Journal of Saudi Arabian Archaeology* 28.2 (2020): 109-31, https://hal.science/hal-03064753 /document.

Flavius Josephus. *The Works of Flavius Josephus*. Translated by William Whiston. London, 1737, 1895

Freeman, Philip M. "Ancient References to Tartessos." Pages 303-34 in *Celtic from the West: Alternative Perspectives from Archaeology, Genetics, Language and Literature*. Edited by Barry Cunliffe and John T. Koch. Oxford: Oxbow Books, 2012.

George, A. "Babylonian and Assyrian: A History of Akkadian." SOAS Research Online (2007): 31-71.

Gilbert, Gregory P. *Ancient Egyptian Sea Power and the Origin of Maritime Forces*. Canberra: Sea Power Centre, Australia, 2008.

Grathwol, Franziska, et al. "Adulis and the transshipment of baboons during classical antiquity." 1-21. https://www.biorxiv.org/content/10.1101 /2023.02.28.530428 v1.full.pdf.

Heck, Gene W. "Gold Mining in Arabia and the Rise of the Islamic State." *Journal of the Economic and Social History of the Orient* 42.3 (1999): 364-95.

Heller, André. "Why the Greeks Know so Little about Assyrian and Babylonian History." Pages 331-48 in *Melammu 7: Mesopotamia in the Ancient World*. Proceedings of the Seventh Symposium of the Melammu Project Held in Obergurgl, Austria, November 4–8, 2013. Edited by Robert Rollinger and Erik van Dongen. Ugarit-Verlag, 2015.

Herodotus. *Histories*. Edited by Tom Griffith. Hertfordshire: Wordsworth, 1996.

Hoenig, Sidney B. "Tarshish." *The Jewish Quarterly Review* 69.3 (1979): 181-2.

Hume, Lucile Bayon. "Avian Alarm System: A Peacock in the Yard is Worth Two Police on Patrol." December 22, 2016. https://countryroads magazine.com/ outdoors /knowing-nature/avian-alarm-system/.

Koch, John T. "Paradigm Shift? Interpreting Tartessian as Celtic." Pages 185-302 in *Celtic from the West: Alternative Perspectives from Archaeology, Genetics, Language and Literature*. Edited by Barry Cunliffe and John T. Koch. Oxford: Oxbow Books, 2012.

Leichty, Erle. *The Royal Inscriptions of Esarhaddon, King of Assyria (680-669 BC)*. Royal Inscriptions of the Neo-Assyrian Period, Vol. 4. Edited by Grant Frame, Jamie Novotny. Winona Lake: Eisenbrauns, 2011.

Lewis, Naphtali. *Greeks in Ptolemaic Egypt*. Oakville, CT, USA: David Brown Book Company, 1986.

Lipinski, Edward. "Epigraphy in Crisis: Dating Ancient Semitic Inscriptions.

Biblical Archaeological Review (July/August, 1990). https://library .biblicalarchaeology.org/.

Lloyd, Alan B. "Necho and the Red Sea: Some Considerations." *The Journal of Egyptian Archaeology* 63 (1977): 142-55.

López-Ruiz, Carolina. "Tarshish and Tartessos Revisited: Textual Problems and Historical Implications." Pages 255-80 in *Colonial Encounters in Ancient Iberia: Phoenician, Greek, and Indigenous Relations.* Edited by Michael Dietler and Carolina Lopez-Ruiz. Chicago Scholarship Online (2009). DOI: 10.7208/chicago/9780226148489.001.0001.

Lora, Sebastiano. "A religious building complex in the ancient settlement of Tayma (North-West Arabia) during the Nabataean period: changes and transformations." *Dossier : Archéologie des rituels dans le monde nabatéen* 94 (2017): 17-39. DOI: https://doi.org/10.4000/syria.5766.

Macdonald, Michael C. A. "Arabians, Arabia, and the Greeks: Contact and Perceptions." 1-33. https://www.academia.edu/4593009.

Marion, Loïc. "Is the Sacred Ibis a Real Threat to Biodiversity? Long-term Study of its Diet in Non-native Areas Compared to Native Areas." *Comptes Rendus Biologies* 336.4 (April 2013): 207-220. www.science direct.com.

Masson-Berghoff, Aurélia, et al. "(Re)sources: Origins of metals in Late Period Egypt." *Journal of Archaeological Science: Reports* 21 (2018): 318-33.

Meadows, Andrew. "Coin circulation and coin production at Thonis-Heracleion and in the Delta region in the Late Period." in *Thonis Heracleion in Context*, Damian Robinson and Franck Goddio, eds. (Oxford Centre for Maritime Archaeology, 2015), 121-36.

Michaux-Colombot, Danièle. "Bronze Age Reed Boats of Magan and Magillum Boats of Meluḫḫa in Cuneiform Literature." Pages 119-53 in *Stories of Globalisation: The Red Sea and the Persian Gulf from Late Prehistory to Early Modernity.* Edited by Andrea Manzo, Chiara Zazzaro, and Diana Joyce De Falco. Leiden: Brill, 2019.

Mills, Donald Keith, "Ophir and Punt." *SIS Chronology and Catastrophim Review* (2019): 1-12.

Milne, J. G. "Ptolemaic Coinage in Egypt." *Journal Of Egyptian Archaeology* 15.3/4 (1929): 150-3.

Möller, Astrid. "Naukratis as Port-of-Trade Revisited." *Topoi. Orient-Occident* 12.13.1 (2005): 183-192.

______. *Naukratis: Trade in Archaic Greece.* Oxford: Oxford University Press, 2000.

Moro, Caterina. "Hero and Villain: An Outline of the Exodus' Pharaoh in Artapanus." Pages 365-76 in *Israel's Exodus in Transdisciplinary Perspective: Text,*

Archaeology, Culture, and Geoscience. Edited by T. E. Levy, T. Schneider, W. H. C. Propp, B. C. Sparks. Heidelberg: Springer 2015.

Muhly, J. D. "Copper, Tin, Silver and Iron: The Search for Metallic Ores as an Incentive for Foreign Expansion." Pages 314-29 in *Mediterranean Peoples in Transition, Thirteenth to Early Tenth Centuries BCE.* Edited by S. Gitin, A. Mazar, E. Stern. Jerusalem: 1998.

Nehmé, Laïla. "Land (and maritime?) routes in and between the Egyptian and Arabian shores of the northern Red Sea in the Roman period." Pages 513-28 in *Networked Spaces: The Spatiality of Networks in the Red Sea and Western Indian Ocean* (Lyon: MOM Éditions, 2022), DOI: https://doi.org/10. 4000/books.momeditions.16486.

Novotny, Jamie. "Tarsisi" (2020). A Pleiades Name Resource. https://pleiades .stoa.org.

Orr, James. "Ships and Boats." *International Standard Bible Encyclopedia* (1915). https://www.biblestudytools.com.

Pfeiffer, Stephan. "Egypt and Greece before Alexander." *UCLA Encyclopedia of Egyptology* (2013): 1-12. http://escholarship.org/uc/item/833528zm.

Pilkington, Nathan. "A Note on Nora and the Nora Stone." *Bulletin of the American Schools of Oriental Research* 365 (2012): 45-51.

Radner, Karen. "Šubria, a safe haven in the mountains." *Assyrian Empire Builders*, University College London, 2012. http://www.ucl.ac.uk /sargon /essentials /countries/ubria/.

_____. "The Winged Snakes of Arabia and the Fossil Site of Makhtesh Ramon in the Negev." *Wiener Zeitschrift Für Die Kunde Des Morgenlandes* 97 (2007): 353-65.

Ramel, Gordon. "Do Peacocks Eat Snakes and How Do They Kill Them?" July 11, 2023. https://earthlife.net/do-peacocks-eat-snakes/.

Rao, S. R. "Shipping and Maritime Trade of the Indus People." *Expedition* (Spring, 1965): 30-7.

Schaudig, Hanspeter. "Edom in the Nabonidus Chronicle: A Land Conquered or a Vassal Defended? A Reappraisal of the Annexation of North Arabia by the Late Babylonian Empire." Pages 251-64 in *About Edom and Idumea in the Persian Period: Recent Research and Approaches from Archaeology, Hebrew Bible Studies, and Ancient Near East Studies.* Edited by B. Hensel, E. Ben Zvi, and D. V. Edelman. Sheffield: Equinox 2022.

Schiffman, Lawrence H. *From Text to Tradition: A History of Second Temple and Rabbinic Judaism.* Hoboken: Ktav Publishing House, 1991.

Schwarzwald, Ora (Rodrigue). "Stress Assignment in Words with -i Suffix in Hebrew." Bar-Ilan University, Israel, http://www.skase.sk/Volumes

/JTL38/pdf_doc /06.pdf.

Shea, William H. "The Dedication on the Nora Stone." *Vetus Testamentum* 41.2 (1991): 241-45.

Shirazi, Sayyid Abdul Husayn Dastghaib. "Greater Sins – Vol. 2." § "What Does 'Becoming A'arab After Hijrat' Mean?." www.al-islam.org.

Speiser, Ephraim Avigdor. "The Pronunciation of Hebrew Based Chiefly on the Transliterations in the Hexapla (Continued)." *The Jewish Quarterly Review* 23.3 (1933): 233-65.

State Archives of Assyria. https://oracc.museum.upenn.edu/saao/corpus.

Sudan English-Arabic Vocabulary. Sudan Government, 1925.

Sullivan, Benjamin M. "Paying Archaic Greek Mercenaries: Views From Egypt and the Near East." *The Classical Journal* 107.1 (October-November 201)1: 31-61.

Tamil Dictionary. https://agarathi.com.

The Periplus of the Erythraean Sea: Travel and Trade in the Indian Ocean by a Merchant of the First Century. Translated by Wilfred Harvey Schoff. New York: Longmans, 1912.

Tibbetts, G. R. "Arab Navigation in the Red Sea." *The Geographical Journal* 127.3 (1961): 322-34.

Tyson, Janet. *Arabian Sinai: Nabonidus and the Exodus.* Norwich: Pirištu Books, 2024.

_____. *She Brought the Art of Women: A Song of Solomon, Nabonidus, and the Goddess* Norwich: Pirištu Books, 2023.

Van De Mieroop, Marc. "Financial Tool in Ancient Egypt and Mesopotamia." Pages 17-29 in *Explaining Monetary and Financial Innovation*, Financial and Monetary Policy Studies 39. Edited by P. Bernholz and R. Vaubel. DOI: 10.1007/978-3-319-06109-2_2.

Weiershäuser, Frauke, and J. Novotny. *The Royal Inscriptions of Amēl-Marduk (561-560 BC), Neriglissar (559-556 BC), and Nabonidus (555-539 BC), Kings of Babylon.* The Royal Inscriptions of the Neo-Babylonian Empire, Vol. 2. University Park: Eisenbrauns, 2020.

Whitcomb, Donald. "Aqaba." Pages 14-17 in *Oriental Institute 1994-1995 Annual Report.* Edited by William M. Sumner. Chicago: Oriental Institute, 1995.

Wilkie, J. M. "Nabonidus and the Later Jewish Exiles." *Journal of Theological Studies* 2.1 (1951): 36-44.

Zorea, Carlos. "Spain in the Bible: From 'Tarshish' to 'Sefarad'." POLIS. *Revista de ideas y formas políticas de la Antigüedad* 28 (2016): 157-188.

4

NABONIDUS AND THE ARABIAN GENEALOGIES
(GENESIS 10 AND 11)

This is an analysis of the Genesis 10 and 11 genealogies as they pertain to the postexilic world of Nabonidus, King of Babylon (556-539 BCE) and the early Jews I expound in my works. In the Song of Solomon, he is "Solomon," in Genesis, he is "Abraham," and in Exodus he is "Moses." These are invented names to suit the narrative context but in each instance, the name is a pseudonym, for the king's historical name was never to be mentioned.

Whilst researching for my paper, "Nabonidus, Tarshish, and Ophir," I was drawn to the Genesis list because of the name "Ophir," not expecting to find what I did. I *should* have expected it, however, as I have been working with etymology and gematria (i.e., the numerical value and symbolic significance attributed to letters, words, phrases) for years and in every single case, I have found significant meaning pertaining to my claims about Nabonidus. It is uncanny. Because it is such fun discovering things that support your ideas, I simply ran with it, and wish to share my findings with anyone who is interested and/or who has read my work. It is all interconnected. If you take this paper in isolation from my previous theories concerning Nabonidus, the 6th Century BCE exodus from Babylonia, and what happens in the Song of Solomon, it may not make much sense, but I am posting it for those who are following the trail along with me, or who wish to apply the process to their own investigations.

I will keep this more informal than usual, just get the idea across, i.e., that biblical etymology is far more than merely determining a root verb, or a related noun; it is a scribal tool employed by the authors of the Bible to encapsulate several layers of meaning. Sometimes a name/toponym might reveal thematic links to another person/place; sometimes there may be a secret meaning that only the immediate context, or perhaps a broader pattern, can reveal.

What strikes me is the level of attention given to the Arabian nations, tribes, etc. (Gen 10:21-31). Why would so much effort be put into the preservation of this lineage, when it is so clear that the two

109

factions (the early Jews and the Arabian peoples) were not wholly compatible. Why bother to make such a detailed account (twice)? Why is it *these* sections of the genealogies that use the imagery of a father begetting a son, when the previous lists are generalities, nations, peoples, "descendants," "families," etc.?

It also becomes evident, very quickly, that hidden within these superficially simplistic genealogies are many examples of animosity and resentment, but also a true desire to encapsulate the actual history of the events (of the exodus). Every name has multiple subliminal meanings that anticipate what the subsequent texts reveal about Nabonidus (as Abraham, Moses, *and* Solomon).

What I present, below, is an illustration of how the etymology works by building a definite *pattern* of meanings and allusions. In addition, I include the gematria provided for the names in Genesis 11, as this is another tool used by the Hebrew scribes for even further encoding of vital information. On their own, the names may seem to us odd and arcane, but together, especially when understood in light of the Nabonidus-related theories I have already presented, they reveal a concerted effort to connect Genesis with Exodus, Exodus with the Song of Solomon, and all the way through are snippets of scribal magic. Once 'you', as a 6th Century BCE Jew, recognised that, you would have understood that everything that happens thenceforth must be 'God's will', because these names predict, or anticipate what has yet to be told. In reality, of course, the entire story is already known to the authors; most of them, or their parents, lived through the events that make up the Pentateuch. They write retrospectively, sometimes in riddles, sometimes so cleverly I have burst out laughing with joy. They truly were impressive wordsmiths.

Genesis 10 and 11 (and 25) should be assessed together, though I suspect they were written by different people, with different elements of import they wished to convey. The addition of lifespans/ages in Genesis 11 is a boon, for they provide further confirmation of the proposed meaning of the names. There isn't a single one that fails to fit the pattern of being an encoded account of the exodus (i.e., the 6th Century BCE exodus from Babylon). Of course, many of the names in Genesis 10 do not need to be explained here, as I am only interested (for now) with the ones that seem to be directly related to Nabonidus' influence on the early Jews.

The first pattern I noticed is the triad of Noah's sons, Shem, Ham, and Japheth (Gen 10:1). This is also how the analysis in *Arabian Sinai* begins,[1] i.e., with a symbolic patriarch and three sons, i.e., Terah, who has Abram, Nahor, and Haran (the latter being immediately replaced by Sarah). By the time of the exodus the triad is represented by Aaron, Moses, and Miriam. It is a vital pattern for understanding the arcane theological nuances of the exodus narratives.

The next important pattern to note is the "two brothers" setup. In Genesis 10 we have Peleg and Joktan, the two sons of Eber, while in the exodus narratives we find Aaron and Moses, sons of Mamre. The first pair, via the etymology of their names, anticipate the second pair's actions in the subsequent texts. Genesis 10 focuses more on Joktan's lineage, while Genesis 11 is more concerned with Peleg's.

GENESIS 10

Peleg

Means "division, cleft," from *palag*, to split or divide," for "in his day the earth was divided." I suggest this relates to Aaron, who is gradually separated from his original role in the Sinai mission; he is cut off, demoted, and eventually succumbs to his fate on Mount Hor. Throughout the tale of Sinai, Aaron is a divisive character, siding with the calf-worshippers, gossiping with Miriam, and winning his own supporters. A schism is created when Moses demands to know who is loyal to whom.

Joktan

This is Nabonidus (Moses). The name means "he will be made little," from *qaton*, "to be small." In my first book on Nabonidus, *She Brought the Art of Women*,[2] I claimed there are two curses in the Song, one against Nabonidus ("Solomon") and the other against Nitocris (his Egyptian wife). For Solomon, the author encodes a phrase akin to: "his name is worthless." This is why we cannot read Nabonidus' name anywhere in the Bible. It was considered anathema. So, "Joktan" becomes yet another

---

[1] Janet Tyson, *Arabian Sinai: Nabonidus and the Exodus* (Norwich: Pirištu Books, 2024).

[2] Janet Tyson, *She Brought the Art of Women: A Song of Solomon, Nabonidus and the Goddess* (Norwich: Pirištu Books, 2023).

slur on the ex-king, anticipating several biblical texts and their attempt to bring low, humiliate, and otherwise "make little" the once arrogant and very much disliked Nabonidus (e.g., Exodus, Numbers, Song of Solomon, Daniel). More amazingly, perhaps, in the Arabic tradition, "Joktan" means "to strike or beat"; this is what Moses is known for, i.e., in Exodus he strikes an Egyptian, the Nile, etc., but in Numbers, he strikes a very special "rock" (in Arabia) and it is because of this act he is denied the 'right' to enter Canaan.

Joktan's "sons" are even more fascinating. Each name pertains to a concept, place, event, character, etc., that will become part of the exodus narratives and, as such, they anticipate everything to follow, suggesting Genesis was written after the events of the exodus under Nabonidus. They are *not* biological offspring; such a genealogy would not be condoned for Nabonidus in the Hebrews' recorded history. I'm still working on one or two of these, but here is what I have so far :

Almodad
Abarim Publications suggests "immeasurable; not measured; God is beloved, the measure of God," from *el*, God, or particle of negation + either *madad*, "to measure," or *dod*, "beloved." *Dod* is a key word in the Song of Solomon, and has to do with Nabonidus' initiation into Nitocris' religion, where Nabonidus (Solomon) is *dodi*, i.e., "the beloved." If "particle of negation" + *dod* is correct then this might suit a Song allusion, i.e., Nabonidus is *not* the "beloved" (anymore). Though this may sound rather vague, the exodus narratives allude to just this notion, where Nabonidus is told some home truths and is brought down a peg or two by the one person the thought would never betray him. Then there is the idea of the "measure" of Nabonidus in Dan 3:27, playing with the Osirian 'weighing of the soul' ritual, suggesting a post-Sinai perspective on what Nabonidus was up to after leaving Babylon.

Sheleph
Means "drawn out," from *shalap*, "to draw out, to extract." This reminds us of Moses being drawn, or extracted from the marshes. This idea would then link not only to the birth-legend of Moses, but to the significance of the two marshlands in the exodus narratives, i.e., one in Babylonia, one in Egypt.

Hazarmaveth

This means "enclosure of death," from *chatser*, "enclosure," and *mawet*, "death." This is a great name, alluding to one of the most obscure yet satisfying etymological finds so far in my research. In *Arabian Sinai* I reveal that there is a place mentioned in Numbers relating, very specifically, to avenues of ancient graves especially near Khaybar, known to us today as "keyhole" or "pendant" graves. Many over twenty feet in length, they were once thought to be animal enclosures but have since been confirmed as burials. What else is a grave if not an "enclosure of death"? There is also an entire region that is synonymous with 'death', i.e., the Harraat (volcanoes and lava fields of Northwestern Arabia). Khaybar is the most notorious region of the Harraat (for travellers).

Jerah

A little obscure, even for me, this means "honeycomb," from *ya'ra*, "honeycomb." There is a symbolic use of honey/honeycomb in the Song (and in the Joseph and Asenath legend), but I have yet to figure out how it relates to a location/person/event relevant to the exodus narratives. It must do, so I will persist. It may be an allusion to the "sweetness" of the manna, which is said to be like cakes baked with honey, so this would, according to my research thus far, suggest Tayma's salt-flats.

Hadoram

Most emphatically, this is Sinai. The name means (according to Abarim Publications), "thunder on high, noble generation, glory on high, esteemed snake-charmer," possibly from one of: *hdd*, "to thunder," *dor*, "generation"; *hadar*, "glory" *hada*, "to snake-charm," and *rum*, "to be high." Each of these has an uncanny bearing on the Sinai experience I describe in the book, "thunder" and "glory" being the most obvious, but the allusion to snakes is brilliant, as this is a profound theme in the tales of Sinai.

Uzal

Means "going away," from *azal*, "to go about or away." Brown-Driver-Briggs suggests "pointed, sharp." Both possible translations pertain to one woman in the exodus narratives, and suggest either Beersheba or Peor, near/at the Sinai region.

Diklah

Means "palm grove" (by consensus). The oasis of Tayma is referred to by several toponyms in the HB, the most important is "Elim," also linked to palm trees (see my related paper, "Nabonidus, Tarshish, and Ophir").

Obal

The name is also rendered "Ebal," which has meanings that include "stone/stony," "bare mountain," "stripped bare," and "ancient heaps" (from various biblical dictionaries) and "heaps of barrenness" from Abarim Publications. The latter is said to stem from the use of the verb *awa*, "to bend or twist" (with the underlying insinuation of guilt, ruin, iniquity, etc.) and perhaps *bala*, "to become old or worn out" (suggesting something that has become useless, worthless, and is thus destroyed). The noun *ballaha* means "terror or calamity." Ebel is a "Horite," a descendant of Seir, from the land of Edom (Gen 36:21).

In *Arabian Sinai* I reinterpret the origins and death of Aaron based partly on the etymology associated with him and his alleged relatives. Aaron comes from the region of the Harraat, the volcanic peaks between Tayma and the Red Sea. He dies there, on Mount Hor (one of the peaks). The Harraat, which lies on the southern border of Edom, I have interpreted as "Seir"; it is notorious for being a deadly place. Vivid descriptions of the terrain from early Western explorers include many terms such as "terror, fearful, dreaded," etc. The lava offers little room for growth of vegetation and the hills do, indeed, look stripped bare. This lava, in places, has the appearance of wavy, twisted hair; in Gen 36:23, Ebal's father is Shobal; "Shobal" means "flowing, wavy."

However, the scene of Aaron's death includes him being stripped of his garments before he 'dies'; I claim (in my book) he is killed because Nabonidus had enough of his defiance (and was jealous); his death is laced with insinuations of guilt, ruin, iniquity (on both sides).

Abimael

Meaning, perhaps, "*el* is father," from *el*, "a god" and *ab*, "father." Several times in the HB Nabonidus is accused of deifying himself; if the "father" of Abimael is Joktan, and Joktan is Nabonidus, this would relate to Tayma (where he did deify himself, I argue) and/or Sinai (where others thought he was deifying himself, but they simply got the wrong end of the stick).

On the other hand, I like to see *ab* ("father") and *mael* ("chief, prince"), i.e., "father of the prince." In the book I show that Nabonidus' son, Belshazzar is on the exodus with him (incognito). He is the final link to Babylon for the Israelites, and he seems to follow in his father's footsteps in Arabia.

Sheba

This will have to await *Nabonidus and the Queen of Sheba*.

Ophir

See my paper "Nabonidus, Tarshish, and Ophir."

Havilah

This name suggests "bear, make to bring forth, dance, drive away, fall grievously with pain," possibly from the verb *hul* "to be strong" (*hayil* means "might"); or from another *hul*, "to whirl (dance)"; or the noun *hil* ("pain"). This would relate to Miriam's musical outburst after crossing the Sea, in Exodus 15; Miriam dies (violently) in Kadesh.

It is one of the borders of Ishmaelite territory (Gen 25:18), and also the place where Saul fights the Amalekites (1 Sam 15:7). The place where Joshua battles Amalek in Exodus 17, is "Rephidim," which I claim is, or is linked to "Kadesh," south-west of Tayma, roughly in the same spot a Nabonidus inscription was recently discovered.

Jobab

The name means, "to call shrilly," from *yabab*, "cry or call shrilly." This plays directly on the etymology of two figures in Exodus, linking one to the metallurgical skills of the Qenites, and also linking them both to each other. The name suggests Midianites.

Looking at the territory of the Joktanites, two toponyms are provided:

Mesha

Meaning "saving, salvation," from *yasha'*, "to save." Both Ptolemy (Geo. l. 6. c. 7) and Pliny (Nat. Hist. l. 6. c. 23) claim Mesha was a port on the Red Sea. This name plays with the etymology of a 'secret' figure in the exodus narratives, who is also linked to Ezion-geber, Nabonidus' port on the Red Sea.

Sephar
Commonly defined as "enumeration, census," from *seper*, "a record," or from *sepher*, "a missive, document, writing, book."

Together, Mesha and Sephar mark the boundaries of the Arabian landscape of Moses' mission (cf. Deut 1:1-2, which I discuss in detail in *Arabian Sinai*). In the Hebrew text, we read: "from Mesha toward Sephar, the mountain of the east," that is, "from Ezion-geber to Sinai," which is exactly what we see in the exodus narratives. The "east" is a known term to signify Arabia (Judg 6:3) and, although my first thought was to identify the "hill country" of the NRSV as being the Harraat (east of Ezion-geber), the HB specifies "*the* mountain," singular. This can only be Sinai, in the location I have suggested in my book. Sinai is the place where the laws are 'enumerated', where "the book" is written, where the final draft is 'recorded' (in stone).

GENESIS 11

Then there is the gematria of the ages provided in Gen 11:10-26. The following examples include terms that have the same numerical values. Naturally, there may be hundreds of potential matches but with a biblical text you are dealing with a very specific, immediate context for each name, age, etc. Gematria is something you cannot make up or manipulate; it is indelible, effectively written into the very words themselves.[3] I am not fluent in Hebrew, so I rely on others' translations, which limits my palette of ideas to work with but it is enough to prove a point and it is fascinating.

The 'lifespans' are broken up into two parts, i.e., the age at which the character supposedly has the first son, then the age at death. This is not historically 'true' but a way of showing us that gematria is being used and which way the author expects us to interpret it. For instance, if you do what I did, at first, and add the most obvious constituents of

---

[3] Most examples are taken from Bill Heidrick, "Hebrew Gematria," https://www.billheidrick.com. Some from "Letters of Light," https://www.chabad.org.

the total, e.g., $438 = 400 + 38$, you get a slightly different interpretation. The authors are handing it to us on a plate, so we will go with their breakdown but include the total in the overall understanding.

The ages descend from a 500-base to a 400-base, to 200-base, to 100-base, to "threescore and ten" (the traditional age of a human, Ps 90:10). They decrease in value as we travel from what is myth to what is real life; from ages that are obviously not human-based, to the final level, i.e., the transition from a symbolic past, to a historical context. Shem represents the ancient past; Terah is the turning point. Everyone up to and including Nahor (I) have "other sons and daughters" but Terah, representing the 'lunar father' (see his entry below) of the postexilic triad, has only the three vital children, i.e., representing the Moon, Sun, and Stars; these are fully human, historical figures who are later depicted as Moses, Aaron, and Miriam.

Name	Lived for (Years)	Gematria provided
Shem	600	100 + 500
Arpachshad	438	35 + 403
Shelah	433	30 + 403
Eber	464	34 + 430
Peleg	239	30 + 209
Reu	239	32 + 207
Serug	230	30 + 200
Nahor (I)	148	29 + 119
Terah	70	70

1. In the Beginning, 500-base

Shem

The "father of all the children of Eber" (Gen 10:21) has a name that simply means "Name," but a name is the essence, the 'truth' of a thing, place, person, or people. Shem stands alone as the ancient ancestor beyond time, beyond the alphabet for gematria (which ends at 400, though you can add numbers together, etc.); but immediately we see how the rest of the genealogy of Genesis 11 is going to be laced with negative inferences. The very first number is negative:

100: the letter *kuf*, meaning "monkey; baseness"; death; negative thought, speech and action; ungodliness; moral/intellectual baseness.
500: to burn, blaze; to be burned; to bind; to fetter; a writing, a poem; to hide or secrete; to keep secret; shoulder-piece of the high priest's ephod; the congregation of Yahweh.
600: "Splendour"; exaltation; settling of water

Shem's gematria provides a potted synopsis of what is soon to follow in the exodus narratives: The exiles were once bound and fettered (and perhaps still are on the exodus, figuratively); there is emphasis on the writing of the law(s), and the Song (poem) of Solomon foundation; there will be secrets and even a hidden body; the congregation of Yahweh is comprised of the Qenites and (some of) the Israelites; splendour and exaltation are synonymous with their worship; the high priest/priesthood is the culminating 'takeaway' from Sinai (for the Jews). One might suggest "Shem" encapsulates the entire Pentateuch.

The reference to "two years after the flood" (Gen 11:10, i.e., the 'settling of the waters') intrigues me further, as the period of two years is related to Nabonidus' first influential lunar eclipse, in his second regnal year (554 BCE). Just a thought: If we consider this a play on words, and that the "flood" here is actually a reference to the flooding of the Nile, when Nabonidus is there in Exodus, this would indicate a calendrical clue, for I have argued that scene takes place in 522 BCE (based partly on another lunar eclipse), so two years before that would be ca. 524 BCE. It is the death of Ahmose III (526 BCE) that inspires Nabonidus to go to Egypt the second time. Two years before the 'flood' in this context would allude to the 'birth' of Nabonidus 'great idea' and his planning for the Egypt visit (i.e., this may pertain to the sacrifice of Isaac episode I link to this sudden realisation, in my book).

2. From Ur to the Desert, 400-base

Arpachshad
This is not an individual, per se, either, but already the transition from pure myth to elements of history are beginning to show, for this name is imbued with allusions to both a nation/conglomerate, and a person (a figurehead).

Brown-Driver-Briggs suggests the name "Arpachshad" is a combination of *'rp* (in cognate languages), i.e., "extent, border," and *Chesed*, "Chaldeans." Therefore, something like "extent or boundary of the Chaldeans." To me, this suggests a delineation, a cutting off point, i.e., where the Babylonian sphere is taken over by the Arabian sphere, a transition from the exile in Babylon, to Abraham/Moses and the exodus itself through the desert.

The 400-base, represented by the letter *tav* (the last letter of Hebrew alphabet), suggests "Truth," "Life," "Death." This tells us that everything to follow will be the 'truth' (as seen through the eyes of the authors); it is a historical tale of Life and Death. So far so good.

The gematria of Arpachshad is:

35: NOTHING; to be tottering; to shear away/shave off; to set as a boundary
403: Fortified cities; he shall startle many nations; to snatch away; wine press
438: To bind, surround; to spread out; clothed in splendid array; closing of womb/barrenness

Arpachshad (the nation) is denoted by fortified cities and the ability to make many nations tremble. This is certainly Babylonia.

A more direct allusion to the ex-king is the 'snatching away' of two people in the exodus narratives, and the idea of "NOTHING" (relating to a curse on Nabonidus' name in the Song of Solomon). Strikingly, an allusion to "wine press" is relevant to both the Song and the exodus tales (i.e., as a euphemism for "blood"). Shearing, or shaving off, relates to "Samson," i.e., another avatar of Nabonidus.

Nabonidus stands for everything the Israelites hate and he has a more direct avatar in "Joktan" (not mentioned again in this list, note) but "Arpachshad" should be seen as a *precursor* to Nabonidus himself, i.e., a negative archetypal Babylonia.

438 alludes to the exile, perhaps, under royal command, but then it also allows for a personal quip again, by potentially alluding to the other curse in the Song of Solomon, i.e., Nabonidus' Egyptian wife is cursed to have a barren womb.

Shelah

Represents the Ishmaelite connection. Strong's suggests potential links to *shelach, Shiloach,* and/or *shalach*; *shelach* means "weapon, missile," *Shiloach* means "a well, reservoir, fountain," and *shalach* means "to send": All three pertain to the story of Ishmael, who is sent away, is discovered near the well at Beersheba, and who is said to become a great archer.

The associated noun *shalal* means "plunder, or booty"; this relates to the "kidnapping" of Lot, i.e., I interpret the 'kidnapping' as a tale of an attempted raid on Nabonidus' ships at Ezion-geber (on the Red Sea coast of Arabia), i.e., "booty" is taken and Abraham and Lot (pseudonyms, as I explain in *Arabian Sinai*) retrieve it. Another *shalal* means "extracted, pulled out"; this pertains to Isaac, who is plucked (by God in the story) from certain death at the hands of his father. I discuss the filial connection between Lot and Isaac in my book.

The gematria is:

30: beater, chastiser; staff, declaration or solution (of a riddle); "Brother/ Friend of Yah"; deceit, falsehood; "Deceptive"; to pound, strike; "Renown of Yah"; to be weary, feeble; to pierce, to wound; to destroy;
403: note how this echoes the 403 in the previous name
433: a carrying away; captivity, captives; exile, exiles; a family, race, people or nation; a tribe.

This signifies Nabonidus, according to the general assessment of Nabonidus-Moses I present in my book.

The number '30' gives quite a lot away, in fact: Nabonidus beats/strikes several things in the HB; he chastises many; he carries the famous staff; as "Solomon" Nabonidus loves a riddle, as Moses he makes declarations; Moses is called a "Friend of God"; to the Jews he is deceitful; in the scene in Exodus where Moses goes up the hill and has to have his arms held up, he reveals a weakness; he is a violent ex-king and many are killed, including someone significant, who is "pierced" through at his command.

The number 433 speaks for itself.

Although this name "Shelah" strongly suggests Nabonidus, we are still to see this as a broad perspective on his influence on the Arabian peoples; the allusions to Ishmael's story remind us that it is

Nabonidus' family and supporters who settle in Arabia (not in Canaan). These people are generally understood to be the Ishmaelites.

Eber

Means "region beyond," or "one who passes over," from the verb *abar*, "to pass over, through, etc., to travel," i.e., Eber is the land of Arabia. The Israelites have two potential "pass overs"; the first one comes before the death of the firstborn, of course, in Exodus, but the second comes after the Sinai days, when they make their final 'crossing over' into Canaanite land. The caravan journey through the Arabian Desert qualifies as travelling in the 'region beyond'. "Eber" becomes synonymous with Heber, who is a character we meet in 1 Chronicles 4 and Judges 4; he is the son of a Qenite, an Arabian nomad (one who travels through the Arabian Desert).

34: to roll or flow in waves; to well(up) with dew; "Brother of Renown"; a dashing (to pieces)/breakers; moving; "Roaming"; "Yah is Gracious"; to be strong, powerful; strength; wound, hurt; to cover up, envelop; "Strife."
430: "God Judges"; to be about to be smashed; to be destroyed; to be refreshed; the vital or animate principle, life/soul in the blood; seat of hunger, thirst, weariness.
464: pleasant; "Two Cisterns," a sighing, a cry for pity

"Rolling" refers to the landscape of 'rolling sand dunes', just as *negev* (the Negeb), which although commonly defined as stemming from *negeb*, "to be dry," some suggest also, the root verb *gabab* ("to be convex or concave"). It simply suggests "the desert." The dew welling up might pertain to the appearance of the manna (explained in my book); dashing to pieces echoes the scenario of Jehoshaphat and his ships of Tarshish (see my paper on that topic); roaming is self-evident, I think; the idea that God is gracious stems from the constant references to things like water when everyone is thirsty, food when they are hungry, etc.; the emphasis on power and strength alludes to the battle with Amalek; to wound/hurt has multiple echoes in the narratives; to cover, envelop links directly to the etymology of Lot, who is a multi-faceted character and ends up at Tayma; strife is another broad allusion but may link to the water-from-the-rock scenarios in Exodus and Numbers.

The same sorts of things are related by 430: God acts as judge throughout the exodus narratives; Moses inaugurates "the judges" at Sinai; smashing might pertain to the destruction of the golden calf; the blood sacrifice is vital to the rites at Sinai; the desert is a place of hunger, thirst, and weariness.

464 gives us Hagar's crying to God for pity on her thirsty son; the "pleasantness" of Lot's new lands, once he leaves the company of Abraham (he heads into Arabia); but the best one, for me and my work, is "Two Cisterns," which refers to "Dothan" of Gen 37:17. A Persian noun, *data*, is suspected to be the root word, here, meaning "decree or law" but, Abarim Publications notes, the Chaldean word *doth*, means "well or fountain." This dual concept is uncanny, for there is a place with a well, which has a pseudonym in the HB that reveals a significant event in history took place there, involving a 'decree' of sorts (that is in my book, too). Dothan is where Joseph is sold to the Ishmaelites, meaning the latter are in their own territory, i.e., Northwestern Arabia (around the Tayma region). "Joseph" is critical to understanding much of what Nabonidus does at Sinai, i.e., he retrieves "Joseph's bones" from Egypt.

By the way, if we just look at 64 (400 + 64), we learn that the following phrases are linked: complaint; to move to and fro; to incline oneself, to rest, to settle down; to repose; place of judgement; to be slack, weak, languish; to be warm, heated; to be in (sexual) heat; to rut; to conceive; to traverse; to go around, to encompass; to besiege, to surround; to turn or change, to become like.

The Israelites complain *all the time*!; they to move to and fro between Tayma and Sinai; Nabonidus' group remain with him at Tayma for many years; it is at Sinai the new judicial system is inaugurated; at Rephidim/Kadesh is the battle with Amalek, where Moses proves too weak to keep his arms up; the sexual reputation of Tayma and the idea of conception stem from the Song of Solomon; the group have to "skirt around" the Harraat in order to get from Tayma to Sinai; with the acceptance of the covenant entered into with the locals at Tayma, Nabonidus and his entourage become 'like' the Arabians.

3. At Tayma and Sinai, 200-base

The 200-base is represented by the letter *resh*; it means "poor" or "evil." The Talmud (Nedarim 41a) suggests the only true poverty is a lack of wisdom. One who deemed "a reish" is considered to act in defiance of God and is therefore evil (Shabbos 104a).

Sinai is where Nabonidus introduces the solar aspect of the new deity, "I AM," and in my book I discuss the strong connection to Hiram of Tyre, so it is remarkable that "Lord of Heat" (another name for Baal, which is used as a pseudonym for Nabonidus more than once) should have this gematria, i.e., he was the Phoenician Sun god.

Other terms for 200 include: to turn or wind, to twist or pervert; to pour out; to cast (metal); a people or nation, aggregation or community; to awake; to be angry; "Anger"; to lick, to suck; to swallow down, to consume greedily.

Twisting, turning, etc., brings to mind the etymology of Aaron's name and his depiction in the narrative; he is a metalworker/smith (with links to snakes, which also 'twist and bend'); of course, Aaron creates a molten golden calf (casting); the community is that of the Qenites; the 'awakening' is rather complex but I presume it would apply to what Nabonidus attempts to do (symbolically) at Sinai (with Joseph's bones), but it also ties in with the 'awakening' aspect of discovering hidden wisdom (a theme running through the Song and the exodus narratives); the anger issue is both Moses' (Nabonidus') and someone else's, i.e., one of the women on the journey; the licking, swallowing, and being greedy pertains to Nabonidus at Tayma in the earlier years – this relates to the Song of Solomon's hidden tale of blood rites.

Thus, the 200-base provides a very specific and definite foundation for a negative perception of the Nabonidus-crowd down in Arabia. The early Jews have no time for them. But, because they are an undeniable part of the history of the new Israel/Judaism, their story must be told, however obscured and through gritted teeth.

This is the context into which the next character is introduced.

Peleg

A representation of Aaron. The Arabian Desert ("Eber") is his father, figuratively, but in a sense this is perfect for the Aaron we see between the lines of the exodus accounts.

The gematria:

30: to pound, strike; "Brother/Friend of Yah"; falsehood, deceit; "Deceptive"

209: to travel, journey; wayfarer; "Wanderer"; manner of life; lot/destiny; to shine, gleam; to be glorious

239: Iron; tool; sceptre; to cast lots; inheritance; "a wind-driven leaf"

The metallurgy of the Qenites is clear, i.e., striking metal, making metal tools, etc.; Aaron is an itinerant smith; a leaf blowing in the wind suggests a nomadic lifestyle, a wanderer, etc.; as a Qenite, Aaron, though not specifically mentioned as such, is to be considered a "friend of Yah(weh)" (e.g., he also 'met' "I AM" on Sinai) just as Reuel is (the meaning of this name is "Friend of God" and Reuel is Jethro, the Qenite); Sinai is where lots are cast; it is the site of the divine "glory" but also where Aaron was meant to be Nabonidus' representative for the solar aspect of his deity (shining, etc.), before he had a 'better' idea; Num 36 makes an odd but profound statement about inheritance (at Sinai), possibly linked to Aaron; the alleged deception/deceit of the Midianites (Qenites) leads to Moses' war with them.

Reu

Meaning "friend, companion, fellow, etc.," from *rea'*, "friend or associate") is a shortened version of Reuel from Exodus 2, whose name means "friend of God" and which I argue is a commission name for Jethro, in his role as intermediary between Nabonidus and the Qenites' "Yahweh." The verb *ra'a* means "to pasture or feed"; the participle *ra'a* denotes a "shepherd." However, the noun *ra'* means "evil"; the verb *ra'a'* suggests "to be bad or evil, to be offensive," etc. Although Peleg and Reu have the same overall gematria of 239 (the same number means a direct connection), this is divided differently for each.

32: to be or make pure; faultless; divine glory

207: a flame or blaze; region of light, the east; light of faith; revelation; to light, to kindle; to make bright, to lighten; to illuminate or enlighten (the mind); the Sun, dawn, east

239: Iron; tool; sceptre; to cast lots; inheritance; "a wind-driven leaf"

Rulers and leaders were considered "shepherds" of their people; when Moses first goes to Midian, he meets the daughters of Reuel (Jethro) and marries one (Zipporah); they are pasturing sheep; Moses serves as a shepherd to Jethro's flock (metaphorically); the same 239 phrases make Reu a Qenite, too; Jethro and Amminadab (Exod 6:23) are the same person (the latter name means "my kinsman is noble/generous," from the noun *am*, "kinsman or people," and the verb *nadab*, "to willingly give"); Jethro fits the definition for "Amminadab" in that he is of high rank ("noble") and is willing to "give" or share his religious wisdom (the name is also in Song 6:12 as two words usually translated as "my noble people"); the Qenites use fire for worship, they know how to bring the "glory" at Sinai; as metalworkers they refine metals; they provide much new knowledge for Nabonidus in his religious quest. Jethro is, at least in the beginning, considered a wise, 'faultless' leader (but then things go wrong). The Sun at dawn is a symbolic image pertaining to Moses at Sinai during a special event potentially orchestrated by Jethro.

Serug

Represents Nabonidus; this character is to be equated with Genesis 10's "Joktan." The name means "branch" from the noun *sarig*, "branch or tendril"; from *sarag*, "to be intertwined." It alludes to a 'branching off' from the mainstream (typical Nabonidus) but also the twisting, winding nature of snakes, a profound theme for Moses/Nabonidus.

30: to pound, strike; "Brother/Friend of Yah"; falsehood, deceit; "Deceptive"

200: The letter *resh*, "poor in wisdom; evil"; "Lord of Heat" (Phoenician Sun god, Baal); to pour out; to cast (metal) to turn or wind, to twist; to awake; to pervert; to swallow down, to consume greedily; to lick, to suck; new wine (trodden out); a bough or branch

230: "King of Kings," i.e., official title of the King of Babylon; to lick up or lap up; to strike or beat; to cut down or fell; to destroy utterly; "Perverse"

When you see the exodus narratives as being a tale of Nabonidus and a handful of Jews on an exodus from Babylonia to Tayma, via Canaan, all of this hits the mark. He was, indeed, the King of Kings; the licking, swallowing greedily, and wine references all have to do with the tale in the Song of Solomon, about Nabonidus and the Elixir Rubeus rite (and this is hinted at again in Exodus); beating, striking, and cutting down/destroying allude to his numerous violent actions and the consequences of his bad temper. He is considered a bough/branch of the Qenites, in that he adopts them as his 'family' and is initiated into their cult (perhaps an allusion to his staff?); he is heavily influenced by the Tyrians. He is remembered for declaring himself wise but everyone else seemed to think he was 'mad' and thus perverse, deceitful, and even evil.

The number 30 links him with Peleg, just as "Joktan" was in Genesis 10.

4. Setting the Scene for the Exodus, 100-base

The 100-base is symbolised by the letter *kuf*, which means "Monkey" (in terms of an inferior intellect, etc.); Chabad.org describes the *kuf* thus:

> … its three lines represent unholy thoughts, profane speech and evil actions. These negative qualities are illustrated within the actual form of the *kuf*. Its long left leg plunges beneath the letter's baseline. It represents one who ventures below the acceptable, an individual who violates the circumscribed boundaries of the Torah.

There is only one name with the 100-base gematria:

Nahor

At first, I found this very odd, as the name recurs very quickly, as a 'grandson'; it is the only name in the genealogies to be repeated, so there must be a reason for this (i.e., we can't simply suggest a grandson is often named after his grandfather, as no other instances are mentioned in these Genesis genealogies). I do have a theory, which I shall explain below.

"Nahor" means "to snort, scorched," from *nhr*, "to snort vigorously," which Abarim suggests may relate to the root *harar*, "to be a central hub of heat." I offer another snippet from my book, *Arabian Sinai* suggesting a metallurgical understanding of the etymology:

-Start of excerpt-

> As for the "snorting" aspect, I have my own interpretation. In Gen 2:7, Yahweh breathes into his creation, into Adam, to bring him to life. The verb used to describe this "blowing" is *naphach*,

("to inflate, blow hard, scatter, kindle," etc.). Dougherty writes that Yahweh blows into the nostrils of Adam to give life, much as a smith would use a blowpipe to stir the fire in the furnace – the root of the word *naphach* "is the exact equivalent of the Babylonian root *napâḫu* which refers primarily to the activities of a smith in kindling fire by means of blowing."[4] Thus, the "snorting" idea is just a variation on the puffing or blowing of the smith, and the ultimate inspiration (in the literal sense) of the deity.

The "*hor*" element brings to mind Mount Hor; the "scorched" element of "Nahor" comes into play in this capacity, but the discussion must await the section on Seir, later. This aspect is key to linking Aaron and Nahor.

-End of excerpt-

The gematria is:

29: to crush, break; to tread to pieces, tread down. "Leader"; to bind together; to combine; to lie; a liar; a lie, falsehood
119: a decree, account, edict; to grow small, diminish; to be slight or trivial; errors or wrongs
148: "Portion of Yah"; salted; brightness; to shine or gleam; to be splendid or illustrious; to anoint; to appoint; to bind, to hold, stick together; clay, potter's clay, earthenware; to strip, peel off; insight, wisdom; wise teachers; "Double Camp" (Mahanaim); to cut or smite through; to cast or hurl down

Nahor (II), the 'grandson', is Aaron. In the exodus narratives he is first considered to be the perfect choice for one aspect of the tripartite deity Nabonidus envisions, i.e., the solar aspect; the etymology of his name reflects that (from *'or*, "to be or become light"). Shining, gleaming, splendour, etc., all echo this perception. This makes "Portion of Yah" applicable but in a different sense than in the context of the name "Hilkiah"; it suggests he is one portion *of* the deity ("I AM").

For a short while he is considered (appointed) one of the "leaders." As things change, however, we find his significance is decreased when Nabonidus has what he thinks is a better idea. Aaron

---

[4] Raymond P. Dougherty, *The Sealand of Ancient Arabia*, Yale Oriental Series 29 (New Haven: Yale University Press, 1932), 180.

is side-lined, diminished, 'trodden down' by Nabonidus. Aaron is seen to be in cahoots with a woman later seen as a liar, and although he "sins" the same "sin" as Miriam (gossiping about the Cushite wife), he is not immediately punished. His fate is postponed. The 'binding together' idea is reflected in the etymology of "Levite" (from *lawa*, "to join or connect").

Aaron is the one who has the wisdom of magic; he teaches Moses, he speaks (utterances) for Moses. He is the one who inscribes the tablets that relate Moses' 'decree'.

The clay is interesting, as this crops up a few times in my analysis (*Arabian Sinai*). My suggestion of where Sinai is located is known for its unique pottery, a valuable commodity in Nabonidus' day. But there is another, symbolic, aspect to "clay" that is used elsewhere in the HB, confirming not only this location, but also the link to Nabonidus himself.

The idea of being "salted" also alludes to the Arabian environment, where the "covenant of salt" is one of the first things Nabonidus ensures on his return to Tayma. Not exclusively to do with Aaron, it simply affirms the geographical/ethnic milieu.

"Double Camp" (Mahanaim) has two potential connections: 1) it appears in the Song of Solomon, which is the tale of Nabonidus and Nitocris at Tayma, and 2) it alludes to the "Double" aspect of Nabonidus and Pharaoh Ahmose III, which I reveal in *Arabian Sinai* (one might suggest Aaron is Moses' "double" at first, but this isn't a strong enough theme in the HB to warrant an allusion in the gematria).

Finally, there is the idea of cutting/hurling down, i.e., killing. Aaron, I claim, is killed on Nabonidus' orders. He is unceremoniously "stripped bare" and left, unburied on the mountain (I explain this in more detail in the book, of course). Aaron is deemed, by God in the HB, to be just as guilty as Nabonidus; both are denied entry into the Promised Land for their respective sins. I do have a suspicion that perhaps Aaron is killed elsewhere in the exodus narratives and that this described action is purely symbolic.

Obal/Ebal from Genesis 10 is a Horite, so is Nahor of Genesis 11; both are avatars of Aaron, whose home is in the Harraat, west of Tayma, where Mount Hor is to be found.

5. The Mirror, "threescore and ten"

Terah

The very next stage in this overall symbolic retrogression from the 500-base of an archaic "Shem," all the way down to the humans of Exodus, is the *transitional* figure, "Terah." In *Arabian Sinai*, I explain how the tale of Abraham and Moses are 'mirror images' of each other in many ways. Abraham's story tells the tale of the first exiles to leave Babylonia with Nabonidus, via the Euphrates and down through Canaan, being dropped off along the way at various sites. Nabonidus (Abraham) then continues on, doing his own thing, first visiting Egypt on a very personal quest, then returning to Tayma with those of the Israelites (and others) who hedge their bets and think an ex-king will probably give them a better life (which many seem to regret). Then the Moses narratives relate what happens later, when Nabonidus gets this 'brilliant new idea' and heads back into Egypt to retrieve "Joseph's bones."

So, "Terah" is used as a literary device, a pivot within the genealogies, to turn us, the audience, around so we are no longer looking to the ancient past, but to the 'present day' (or life-experience, to the authors). He is the "mirror" that allows for this profoundly sophisticated 'mirroring' scribal technique. He his neither myth nor person.

This is why "Nahor" is the only name to be repeated:

"Terah" is a representation of the lunar deity Sîn, Nabonidus' favourite god; the name is echoed in "Ter/Teri," or "Ilteri," the lunar cognate in Tayma. In his inscriptions, he tells of Sîn demanding certain things of him, such as a dagger for his idol, and the dedication of a daughter to the temple at Ur. Nabonidus has many dreams that guide his actions; he scrutinizes omens and plans things to land on auspicious days, so I see "Terah" as the (Genesis) author's way of inferring that the sudden, unexplained departure of Nabonidus from Babylonia was 'an act of god' (actually, it was the invasion of the Persians), and that he was somehow inspired by, or 'told' by Sîn to make this journey (home, to Tayma). That Moses is said to remain in Harran for five(?) years before actually leaving for Canaan, suggests another strong Sîn connection, Harran being one of the two centres of Sîn worship (the other being Ur).

This is where the exodus story begins, creating a cyclical pattern that shifts from Arabia (the Arabian genealogies of Genesis 10 and 11) to Mesopotamia (Ur of the Chaldees), then back to Arabia (Tayma/Sinai). This is fate at work, destiny; this is where Nabonidus belonged all the time (i.e., his own story is basically rooted in Tayma, as he spent so little time in Babylonia; then he returned to Babylon a few years before Cyrus invaded; then he left again, i.e., I claim he went back to Tayma, via Canaan). The cyclical movement mirrors that of the two exodus stories (Abraham's and Moses').

Terah, with the gematria of **70**, becomes the "father" to humans at the age by which a human lifespan is reckoned (Ps 90:10, "threescore and ten"). The number also suggests: goings, progress; processions; ways; caravans, companies of travellers (i.e., the exodus); night; by night (the lunar aspect, which Nabonidus himself represents in the new symbolic amalgamation of Sun, Moon, and Stars).

CONCLUDING REMARKS

This has been an informal exercise in symbolic etymology and gematria, to reveal the consistency of the HB's allusions to Nabonidus and his dealings with the Israelites in the geographical context of Arabia. It was not a history they relished but it was their own; they had the presence of mind to record the bad and uncomfortable with the good and the empowering elements, which helps us comprehend the otherwise (but as usual) biased history. The Israelites under Nabonidus either loathed him or exploited his connections and authority; those under "Abraham" retained a more positive account because they got what they wanted, i.e., they were settled in Canaan. Those who stuck with him in Tayma had a hard time and this is profoundly evident when you assess the exodus narratives with Nabonidus as "Moses."

In my forthcoming book, *Nabonidus and the Queen of Sheba*, I look further into the Genesis genealogy lists, specifically Cush's immediate ('sons') descendants (Genesis 10), and those of Abraham and Keturah, in Genesis 25. One of the main discoveries there is that the exodus narrative concerning the striking of the rock to procure "water" is of prime importance as at least five names allude directly to this scenario. Every name in these two lists pertains, or alludes to a specific aspect of the exodus tale, be it a location, an event, or a personal trait of a character.

The Hebrew scribes were skilled and imaginative, playing with words like they were moulding clay. I never cease to be amazed. I hope this short paper inspires you to delve into this type of analysis for your own area of study. I always prioritize the etymology over any conventional interpretation, as names were always considered the essence of the thing being named. A name was imbued with specific meaning at the time of its first use. We need to respect that. If the etymology seems so arcane and unconnected to my own idea of what something 'means', I know it is *my* shortcoming that needs to be rectified., i.e., I'm looking in the wrong place, there's something I haven't understood, etc. The meaning *is* there.

5

THE THREE NAAMAHS
(NABONIDUS AND NITOCRIS)

The last five years or so I have been researching and writing about the patterns I am discovering within the Hebrew Bible (HB) that seem to illustrate an intense focus on Nabonidus, King of Babylon (556-539 BCE) and his Egyptian wife, Nitocris II. In *She Brought the Art of Women*,[1] I argued that the Song of Solomon preserves the tale of their stormy marriage and occult shenanigans at Tayma, Arabia; in *Arabian Sinai*,[2] I demonstrated that the exodus narratives themselves are *centred* on Nabonidus after the fall of Babylon. The evidence I have been presenting to bolster my claim that much of the HB is inspired by the exiles' experiences both during Nabonidus' reign and after, when he went back to Tayma with a handful of "Israelites," seems inexhaustible, as every time I finish one topic, another reveals itself, and I am almost overwhelmed with the data and with the necessity of presenting the information in a manner that does it justice.

Here, I want to demonstrate what happens when you accept this Nabonidus-based premise and assess the etymology and contexts associated with "Naamah," a name that jumped out at me during the writing of the Queen of Sheba book, for not only is this the name of one of the wives of Solomon (and thus Nabonidus), it is also the name of a demon.[3]

If you haven't been following my arguments on this topic, this analysis may sound a bit confusing, so I apologise, but this is an entirely new paradigm and so much needs to be related before anything resembling a brief explanation (i.e., a "soundbite" for convenience) can

---

[1] Janet Tyson, *She Brought the Art of Women: A Song of Solomon, Nabonidus and the Goddess* (Norwich: Pirištu Books, 2023).

[2] Janet Tyson, *Arabian Sinai: Nabonidus and the Exodus* (Norwich: Pirištu Books, 2024).

[3] This paper deals with the biblical references to the name, not the later folklore; for this, see Janet Tyson, *Nabonidus and the Queen of Sheba: Roots of a Legend* (Norwich: Pirištu Books, 2024), 85-88.

be provided. At this stage, it is much like attempting to follow a stream-of-consciousness narrative without familiar anchors; everything is different, seemingly haphazard, until you become conversant with the patterns, the repetitions, and the consistent allusions.

There are three "Naamahs" mentioned in the Hebrew Bible, i.e., in Gen 4:22; 1 Kgs 14:21; and Josh 15:41.

Gen 4:22

In the last generation of descendants of Cain, Naamah is the daughter of Lamech and Zilla.

"Lamech" is said to mean "strong man," from an "unused root that means "to be strong and robust."[4] It also potentially stems from the verb *muk*, "to be low," or, as Abarim puts it, "for humiliation" (to be brought low). This corresponds, almost uncannily, with one of Nabonidus' pseudonyms, "Joktan," in Gen 10:25, which means "to be small" and thus reiterates the scribes' consistent desire to humiliate and 'bring low' Nabonidus.[5]

In other discussions I have claimed that Genesis is a relatively pro-Nabonidus text, in that its version of the Abraham story (which constitutes the first wave of the exodus from Babylon) is more affirmative than Exodus' tale of Moses (the second phase of the exodus narrative). I posit there were several authors of Genesis (as with most biblical texts) and that each had a subjective agendum for including certain allusions and references. While the tale of Abraham is a positive one, other parts of Genesis, especially the genealogies, reveal what has now become, to me, a familiar tactic of preserving the disdain for Nabonidus that began with the Song of Solomon and its curses (for more on this, please read *She Brought the Art of Women*, available to download online).

Lamech, echoing another familiar pattern (echoing Nabonidus, of course) , has *two* wives, Ada and Zillah.

"Zillah" can mean either "bell" or "shadow," stemming from the verb *salal*, meaning "to ring" and/or "to be dark." She is the mother of Tubal-cain, the original smith, and of course, of Naamah. Zilla is Lamech's second wife.

---

[4] Abarim Publications, "Lamech," www.abarim-publications.com.

[5] See my paper, "Nabonidus and the Arabian Genealogies: (Genesis 10 and 11)," 3.

Other terms linked to *salal* include the noun *silsal*, which can denote a strange sound, such as a buzzing, perhaps "ringing noise," or a form of "spear"; *mesilla*, "bell"; and *selselim/mesiltayim*, "percussion instruments." This is most telling, if you have been following the research, for it describes one person we already know, i.e., Jehudijah. She is Nabonidus' second-wife; she is a songstress/poet who is accompanied by a musician; her daughter, Ennigaldi-Nanna ("Miriam") plays a percussion instrument; the notion of a bell and perhaps the noise it makes, ties in with etymology of "Aaron," who is a smith, and whose work with metal results in 'ringing' sounds (he is also potentially a musician). The "spear" allusion is profoundly apt, for this is how both Jehudijah and Aaron die (I have argued), i.e., at the end of the spear hurled by Phinehas in Num 25:14-17.[6] As for "shadow," throughout the Song of Solomon, Jehudijah is a character in the shadows, i.e., in the shadow of the exotic, illustrious, powerful Nitocris, and this led to much resentment, which is noticeable in both the Song and the exodus narratives. So, for my money, "Zillah" is an avatar of Jehudijah.

"Adah" on the other hand, represents Nitocris. The name means "ornament," from *adah*, to ornament," or "to ornament oneself." The noun *iddah* (from the assumed root of *'dd*) is used only once in the HB, in Isa 64:6, i.e., "our righteous deeds are like a *filthy* cloth." The word *ed* ("filthy") means "menstruation," from the idea of being ritually unclean. This term seems to be alluded to in the etymology of "Gilead" in Song 4:1, in the context of Nitocris' womb-blood.[7] Just to support this idea, the etymology of Adah's two sons, "Jabal" and "Jubal" (and note the veritable twinning of the names, which is an element of other Genesis genealogies, and which relates to the naming of "Massah and Meribah" in Exodus 17, i.e., this pattern is *directly* associated with Nabonidus[8]) reiterates a menses allusion. "Jabal" means "a conduit," or "something that flows," from the verb *yabal*, "to flow; to bring (especially with pomp)," which might suggest ritual, as in the Elixir Rubeus rite; the noun *yabal* means "conduit." "Jubal" has the same etymology but the two are distinguished by their respective associations within the text (Gen 4:20-1): Jabal represents those who

---

[6] Tyson, *Arabian Sinai*, 355-62.

[7] Tyson, *She Brought*, 94. Hence the word *niddah* and the laws pertaining to purity and especially in the context of menstruation and other bodily fluids.

[8] Tyson, *Queen of Sheba*, 13; 41, 45.

live in tents, and Jubal represents musicians. With their half-brother Tubal-cain, the maker of "bronze and iron tools" (a smith), this triad (another symbolic motif throughout the exodus narratives) denotes the peoples of the Hijaz, i.e., the nomadic tribes and the metallurgical/musical society that eventually bring us Aaron, Jethro, and Jehudijah (the Qenites).

Keeping an eye on the translation of "to flow," associated words include *yubal,* or *ubal,* "stream" or "river." In the Song, Nitocris' blood, her menses, is her most valuable possession, trait, commodity. It is her identity and her prime responsibility in her sacerdotal life. She avoids pregnancy at the risk of being disowned, perhaps even killed, or sent back to Egypt in disgrace. She never has Nabonidus' children, and elsewhere I have shown how the HB deals with this using very subtle wordplay.[9] So, I argue that these two names, intentionally following the twinning pattern to point to a direct link with Nabonidus, are mentioned to refer to this aspect of Nitocris' life; they represent her "flow"; this is what defines her, from the Song, to the exodus tales, to the Queen of Sheba legend. In Song 4:15, "flowing streams" appear in the verses pertaining to the induced miscarriage that ends Nitocris' prospective role as a "birth mother."[10] Just hinting at her menses is enough to identify her, as her name must never be mentioned.

"Jabal" and "Jubal" are, like many other HB names, symbolic constructs to serve a purpose in the narrative; they are not actual people, nor literal ancestors. Once you start following the etymological clues, this becomes strikingly clear.

So, we see, *yet again*, the familiar patterns of wordplay and etymology, telling a story on multiple levels, with a superficial sense of a timespan (i.e., by using the genealogy format), but in fact, reiterating a central theme that is repeated over and over throughout the HB: Nabonidus and Nitocris and their 'sordid' life at Tayma, and to an extent Jehudijah's constant presence, are at the root of the HB itself. They permeate Genesis, Exodus, Numbers, Deuteronomy (I have not worked on Leviticus), Kings/Chronicles, the Song of Solomon, Ecclesiastes, Daniel, etc. One "generation" begets another, each with its own element of *the same tale*, all anticipating textual references that have yet to be written, if conventional dating of the HB is accepted. How can this be explained, other than to suggest Genesis was written

---

[9] Tyson, *She Brought*, 213.
[10] Tyson, *She Brought*, 116.

much later than the entire exodus narratives (at least)?

"Naamah" in Genesis, then, is the *product* of Nabonidus and Jehudijah … how does this work? I see this as an allusion to the Song of Solomon and the account of the 'triad' in Tayma. Without Jehudijah's Song, nothing would be known of Nitocris and the effect she had on Nabonidus. Without Jehudijah's previous infatuation with Nabonidus, the entire scenario depicted in the Song would never have happened. And we must remember that Jehudijah was also one of Nabonidus' wives and *did* bear him children, so taking all this into consideration, I read "Naamah's" genealogy as a direct acknowledgement of *Jehudijah's* importance to the early Jewish history (and this crops up several times in my research; she had many followers). In effect, on might say Lamech/Nabonidus and Zillah/Jehudijah "beget" Naamah/Nitocris because it is their memories of her live that on in the biblical texts.

Naamah is called an "Ammonite." The noun *am* simply means "people." The ancestor of the Ammonites, according to Gen 19:38, is "Ben-ammi," the incestuous son of Lot. Now, this in itself is rather inflammatory, for it suggests that "Naamah" is the product of incest; this is one of the subtle allegations in the Song, when Nitocris first comes to Tayma and has to defend herself to the "daughters of Jerusalem" (i.e., the women of the harem) because her sacerdotal role back in Egypt had been a highly sexual one, i.e., as "God's Hand" (so I argue).[11] There is also a subtle intimation of incest in the exodus narratives, concerning Nabonidus and his own daughter, Ennigaldi-Nanna ("Miriam").[12]
However, there is another way of understanding this term, "Ammonite," that links directly to Nitocris II, or at least one of the main allusions to her identity, i.e., the fact that she was of Libyan descent. "Ammonite" can suggest a person *from* "Ammon," or a worshipper *of* "Ammon." The deity Ammon was a Libyan god who became assimilated into the Egyptian Amun, but retained much of its non-Egyptian characteristics.[13] Nitocris, of course, as First Prophet of Amun-Ra, is a worshipper of Amun and is thus an "Ammonite" by

---

[11] Tyson, *She Brought*, 10-13, et al.
[12] Tyson, *Arabian Sinai*, 11 and Note 31; 70, Note 84.
[13] "Ammon," https://www.worldhistory.org.

virtue of her faith (remember that all allusions to both Nitocris and Nabonidus in the HB are intentionally skewed; those who already knew who the allusion was pointing to could see the connection immediately – it is only we, far removed from that world, who find it difficult).

The site of Ammon worship in Libya was centred at the oasis of Siwa, about 500 km west of Memphis; the name of the oasis in ancient times was "Ammon," so anyone coming from this region might be called an "Ammonite." What is doubly intriguing, for this discussion, is that the site was given special attention by Ahmose III, Nitocris' father, as he built a shrine there. Scholars suggest this was merely a political "thank you" for the Libyan support during his accession, but I suspect there is more to it.

Herodotus tells the tale of Ahmose marrying a woman from Cyrene (on the coast of Libya), "Ladice" (*Hist.* 2:181), and I have elsewhere argued that this is a reference to Ankhnesneferibre, which Herodotus probably did not realise at the time he heard the 'legend'.[14]

The Libyan connection, with respect to Nitocris, is subtly hinted at here and there in my research, but the most obvious link is to a rabbinical claim that many, even now, consider a mere aberration, i.e., they claimed Solomon (Nabonidus) married into Necho II's dynasty, which had its roots in Libya.[15] I have suggested that Ahmose married Necho's granddaughter, Ankhnesneferibre, and Solomon/Nabonidus married Necho's great-granddaughter, Nitocris II. At the Siwa shrine, the Libyan ruler and Ahmose are depicted as equals,[16] perhaps in honour of his wife's people.

So, the reference to Naamah being an "Ammonite" may well be another preservation of the Nitocris/Libyan motif.

---

[14] Tyson, *Arabian Sinai*, 157-9. Many of Herodotus' "histories" have fallen short of being accurate by modern analyses using the historical record. He admits many times to having several versions of a tale, or to not believing what he has been told, etc. His mishmash story of the wedding of Nitetis (*Hist.* 3.1-3) is one of the foundations of the Nabonidus/Nitocris hypothesis I am presenting (though its value is far surpassed by the biblical evidence).

[15] "Libya" at that time, of course, was a broad term to describe a great swath of territory west of the Nile, with the African continent basically divided into Libya and Ethiopia (to the south).

[16] "Ammon," https://www.worldhistory.org.

1 Kgs 14:21

In 1 Kgs 14:21, Naamah is introduced as the "mother" of Rehoboam, Solomon's eldest son.[17] She is not referred to as Solomon's "wife," which *might* suggest either she was a concubine, or for some reason the authors did not wish to identify her with the 'honour' of being a "wife."

Nitocris was not Belshazzar's biological mother, but she *did* become his step-mother; he was possibly about thirty or so when his father remarried. Interestingly, though, Herodotus makes a similar assumption, in that he suggests the son of Labynetus (Nabonidus) was also Nitocris' son (*Hist.* 1.74; 1.188), and even I have speculated that rumours might have circulated concerning a possible 'alliance' between Nitocris and Belshazzar that might have been misconstrued as a sexual liaison, further fuelling the notion that their relationship was a lot closer than appears on the surface,[18] but it was not one of (biological) mother-son. Perhaps the later biblical authors were not so cognisant of the facts and just assumed the family connection, or perhaps they never really intended it to be so black and white. "Son of" so many other applications, besides biological lineage, so why not in this instance, too? He was Nitocris' step-son, perhaps co-conspirator/friend.

The name "Naamah" means "pleasant, sweet," from the verb *naem*, "to be pleasant, sweet, delightful, beautiful," etc.; these epithets remind us of the gushing praise from the king in the Song of Solomon, when Nitocris is first at court, and when he believes her to be pregnant, but the term *naem* is only used in the Song to describe Nitocris' *blood* (Song 7:6). Egyptian emissaries visit Nitocris just before she takes possession of Jehudijah's child and while she is feigning her second pregnancy; these men prove to be aggressive and threatening, demanding she return with them to Egypt, or face the consequences of them revealing her secret to the king.[19] They speak of her "delectable, delightful, sweet, etc." womb-blood as a delicacy they yearn for and will *take*, if necessary. The term *naem* thus has negative (salacious) connotations in this context, despite its translation. In effect, "Naamah" in 1 Kings gives us *the* most concise but potent and significant allusion to Nitocris there is, and one that follows through into the "Queen of

---

[17] For more on Rehoboam see my paper, "Shishak and Rehoboam in a Nabonidus-based Paradigm."

[18] Tyson, *She Brought*, 245-7.

[19] Tyson, *She Brought*, 177.

Sheba" pericope, i.e., her blood-rite, the Elixir Rubeus.[20]

Josh 15:41

This one is a little more obscure, and a fuller analysis is beyond the scope of this paper, but I will offer up what I have thus far.

The name "Naamah" appears in a long list of cities defeated by the Jews under Joshua. In *Arabian Sinai*, I suggest two things that may be germane to this current discussion, i.e., 1) Joshua's first attack on Jericho was a symbolic gesture to show that he was willing to actively demonstrate against his father's oppressive rule over the Jews (as seen from the perspective of the Jewish authors, naturally);[21] and 2) allusions to the Nabonidus/Nitocris legacy are sometimes hidden deep within a text, purposefully obscured to all but the most dogged (e.g., women are depicted in an all-male context, or a single name is inserted nonchalantly, but with specific connotations).

In this instance, we have three intriguing names that might easily be passed over as just other names in a relatively boring list; in fact, they allude to our royal couple: "Jokthe-el (Josh 15:38)," "Naamah," and "Makkedah" (both in 15:41). Previously, I argued that "Jok-" names tend to be associated with Nabonidus.[22] "Jokthe-el" is said to mean "God subdued"; it appears in 2 Kgs 14:7 as a toponym supposedly created by King Amaziah after his conquest of Sela/Petra, i.e., the same Sela/Petra where Nabonidus left a large rock inscription.[23] "God subdued" may well refer to the demise of "Moses," for this is the farthest he goes with the Israelites and from there, supposedly gives up the ghost (not being allowed to continue because of something he did that 'angered God'[24]). "Jokthe-el" first appears in the HB, however, here in Josh 15:38 as a territory allotted to Judah. So for now, let's just acknowledge that an allusion to Nabonidus is being made via the connection to Sela.

"Naamah," we now know, relates to Nitocris. It is no different

---

[20] Tyson, *Queen of Sheba*, 1-16.

[21] Tyson, *Arabian Sinai*, 384.

[22] Tyson, *Queen of Sheba*, 43-51.

[23] Nab. 55 (Frauke Weiershäuser and J. Novotny, *The Royal Inscriptions of Amēl-Marduk (561-560 BC), Neriglissar (559-556 BC), and Nabonidus (555-539 BC), Kings of Babylon*, The Royal Inscriptions of the Neo-Babylonian Empire, Vol. 2 (University Park: Eisenbrauns, 2020). See also Tyson, *Arabian Sinai*, 368-9.

[24] For the explanation of this see Tyson, *Arabian Sinai*, 163-73.

here. This is one of those woman-amidst-the-men examples; just because it is here a toponym, most assume it is just a coincidence and don't look any deeper.

What unites these two people-based toponyms, and gives them significance in this context, is the name "Makkedah" or "Maqqedah." This is traditionally translated as "the place of shepherds," which doesn't seem to make any sense at first. The suggested etymology Strong's states is "from the same as *naqod* in the denominative sense of herding," hence the idea of "shepherds." The noun *noqed* means "shepherd" and is used only twice in the HB: 2 Kgs 3:4, where Mesha, King of Moab is called a "sheep breeder," and Amos 1:1, where Amos is said to be "among the shepherds." Without lengthy analysis, I can't see any *direct* allusions in these two contexts to our current discussion (2 Kings is another episode where there are multiple kings together in battle, and there are a few subtle parallels to the exodus narratives, such as the long march 'around Edom', bloody rivers, and miraculous water in a parched land; this is not significant to our present discussion). On the other hand, the associated adjective *naqod*, means "speckled." The play on these terms in the name "Maqqedah," I suggest, alludes to Genesis 30-31 and the story of Jacob, Rachel, Leah, Laban, and the speckled sheep, which is another rendition of the Nabonidus/Nitocris/Jehudijah love-triangle narrative, complete with the one loved-but-barren wife, another who is fertile but 'in the shadows', a hidden agreement between the two women, and the ultimate, miraculous reversal of barrenness so that a special, symbolic child may be born. In the Genesis parallel, Rachel is to be understood as another avatar of Nitocris; as "Sarah" in Genesis, Nitocris has a pregnancy thrust upon her, i.e., "Isaac."[25] Rachel's "son" is Joseph. *This* is the point of the subtle allusion to the sheep/shepherds, i.e., to get us to "Joseph." Hold that thought for a moment.

The name "Maqqedah," however, can be assessed differently, by breaking it down into *maq* and *qedah*. The noun *maq* means "decay, rottenness, stench," from *maqaq*; "properly, a melting, i.e. putridity; to decay, rot, fester, pine away" (Strong's). The verb *qedah* (Aramaic) means "kindle"; *qadaha* (Arabic) means "strike fire."[26]

---

25 Tyson, *Arabian Sinai*, 12-13;

26 Shahenaz Issa and Ayman Yasin, "Religious Conflict Between Israeli and Hamas: Naming of Weapons and Battles," *International Journal of Religion* 5.2 (2024): 198-212, here 202. There is also "Kadesh," meaning "sacred place,

We know that Nabonidus is associated with "fire" because he is "Sheshbazzar," the "fire worshipper" of Ezra 1:8-11; 5:14-16.[27] Much of what occurs, ritualistically at Sinai is set in the context of fire, heat, and light, emphasising the concentration on the solar aspects of his mission. At the very centre of all of this is "Joseph," or rather, "Joseph's bones." You will have to read about that separately, as it is quite a complex discussion in *Arabian Sinai*, but for our purposes here, all that is required is the knowledge that Joseph's bones represent the solar deity at Sinai, and that there is evidence to suggest Nabonidus retrieves the bones stealthily (i.e., he steals them), and that he has a pre-arranged resting (hiding?) place for them, once he has performed the necessary rites and rituals at Sinai. This place is called the "Cave of Machpelah," the very same site Abraham supposedly purchases as the burial spot for Sarah, in Genesis 23.[28]

The "Cave of Maqqedah" is where Joshua (Belshazzar) supposedly traps the "five kings" and holds them captive until he is ready to kill them (Josh 10:16-28). Reflecting his father's harsh military tactics, e.g., massacres, exposing the dead on "stakes," etc.,[29] Belshazzar is depicted as the ultimate warrior, fearing no one, killing all who stand in his way. It seems the returning Jews quite liked Babylonian might when it suited them! The Cave had been meant as a hiding place for the kings but in the end, it turns into a tomb, for once the five are killed and hung in trees for a day, their bodies are hurled back into the Cave and the entrance is sealed up. They are left to rot.

I suggest this is an intentional play on the "Cave of Machpelah" (Gen 23:17). Even the "trees" (upon which Joshua will hang the five kings) are explicitly mentioned to ensure the connection will be made (recall that I argue for Genesis being written *after* the exodus narratives). This is another demonstration of Belshazzar's alleged defiance of his father, i.e., just as "Jericho" represented his apparent rejection of Nabonidus, so this symbolic negation of Sarah's Cave is understood to be a rejection of "Sarah" herself (i.e., Nitocris, who is,

---

sanctuary," from the verb *qadash*, "to be holy or consecrated" but this may also be a play on the nouns *qadesh* and *qadesha*, referring to religious prostitutes (male and female, respectively). This gives more fuel to a scathing epithet from the Jewish writers' perspective.

[27] Tyson, *Arabian Sinai*, 201-2.

[28] Tyson, *Arabian Sinai*, 75-81.

[29] Tyson, *Arabian Sinai*, 355; 359.

several times, subtly depicted in the HB in terms of not being allowed to enjoy her peace in the afterlife).

It is inferred in the subtext of the exodus narratives that Nabonidus uses "Joseph's bones" as a representation of the solar aspect of the triad of deities (Sun, Moon, and Stars) that he wishes to amalgamate; "Joseph's bones" are actually the remains of Nitocris' father, Ahmose III.[30] Nabonidus intends to store the ossuary (or *aron*) in the Cave he had purchased from Ephron (Gen 23:1-20). So, by depicting the denigration of the Cave, it must be assumed that the "bones" of Ahmose III, are similarly (symbolically) desecrated and their alleged "holy" status nullified.[31]

The degradation of the site, by alluding to it as decayed and stinking, reiterates Jehudijah's original employment of the tired, broken old Jerusalem for Nabonidus' kingdom, in the Song. Just as in Exodus, with Moses standing at the bloody Nile, and the scribes playing with the notion of menstruation and the laws of *niddah*,[32] Nabonidus' pride, his hubris, and his outlandish plans are brought low by a simple pun, an etymological shift that changes everything. The place where Nitocris and the solar-deity avatar are laid to rest becomes a decaying, smelly place, a tomb for *enemies*. Its destruction at the hands of Nabonidus' own flesh and blood, Belshazzar (so the Jewish authors would have us believe), fulfils the prophetic symbolism of the very first "plague," i.e., that Nabonidus' antics would eventually bring about the destruction of his own gods (and kingdom).

<h2 style="text-align:center">SUMMARY</h2>

All three instances of the name "Naamah" in the Hebrew Bible can be consistently interpreted within the Nabonidus-paradigm I am arguing for. From the genealogy in Genesis, we are presented with the original, core story, i.e., the Libyan roots of the Egyptian Nitocris, hints of the significance of her menstrual blood, and the rivalry between her and Nabonidus' second-wife, Jehudijah. In 1 Kings we learn of the misconstrued relationship between Nabonidus' son Belshazzar and

---

[30] Tyson, *Arabian Sinai*, 224-65

[31] Which brings to mind Herodotus tale (*Hist.* 3.17). of the desecration of Ahmose III's tomb.

[32] Tyson, *Arabian Sinai*, 120-2.

Nitocris, but more importantly, Nitocris' blood-rite, the Elixir Rubeus, in a potential allusion to the Song of Solomon. In Joshua, we see this "son," allegedly nullifying the effects of Nabonidus *and* Nitocris on the new generation of Jews. So much information, so many connections and allusions, with just one name!

I am sure there are elements I have not mentioned; I would be thrilled to think someone reading this might already know of another Nabonidus detail to link these three references. My goal is only to promote an alternative perspective which, for me, has been relentlessly insightful. I truly think we need to be seeing the Hebrew Bible in terms of a 6th Century BCE foundation. It resolves so many nagging questions.

BIBLIOGRAPHY

Abarim Publications. www.abarim-publications.com.

"Ammon," https://www.worldhistory.org.

Herodotus, *Histories*. Edited by Tom Griffith. Hertfordshire: Wordsworth, 1996.

Issa, Shahenaz and Ayman Yasin. "Religious Conflict Between Israeli and Hamas: Naming of Weapons and Battles." *International Journal of Religion* 5.2 (2024): 198-212.

Tyson, Janet. *Arabian Sinai: Nabonidus and the Exodus*. Norwich: Pirištu Books, 2024.

____. *Nabonidus and the Queen of Sheba: Roots of a Legend*. Norwich: Pirištu Books, 2024.

____. *She Brought the Art of Women: A Song of Solomon, Nabonidus and the Goddess*. Norwich: Pirištu Books, 2023.

Weiershäuser, Frauke, and J. Novotny. *The Royal Inscriptions of Amēl-Marduk (561-560 BC), Neriglissar (559-556 BC), and Nabonidus (555-539 BC), Kings of Babylon*. The Royal Inscriptions of the Neo-Babylonian Empire, Vol. 2. University Park: Eisenbrauns, 2020.

6

SHISHAK AND REHOBOAM
IN A NABONIDUS-BASED PARADIGM

This is a demonstration of how the name "Shishak" can be interpreted to harmonise with the Nabonidus-inspired version of the HB texts I am proposing. Once you shift the Abraham/Moses/Solomon paradigms from their conventionally assigned dates to the 6th Century BCE, so many conundrums find potential resolution.

Obviously, over time, the significance of Nabonidus the *man* faded, recollections of the details of his reign turned into obscure legends and the original, highly detailed etymological, numerological, and symbolic scribal techniques that preserved his story melded into the cacophony of "my interpretation is true, yours is not" that has obscured the *history* of much of the HB since it was written. My goal is to provide as many potential examples as possible of this 'original' story, rediscovered within the etymology of names and toponyms, gematria, and wordplay.

You will get more from these papers if you have read at least my book on the Song of Solomon, i.e., *She Brought the Art of Women* (available for free download online).[1] It will give you the background information for understanding the relationship between Nabonidus and Nitocris, and why this was of such interest to the early Jewish scribes and the subsequent rabbis. *Arabian Sinai* focuses on the exodus narratives, with Nabonidus as the characters "Abraham" and "Moses." I provide citations for references to this earlier material, so you can get to the information quickly.

The sooner the use of commission names can be accepted (i.e., that characters in the Bible can have more than one name), the easier it will be to follow the logic of the patterns they make, etymologically. This opens a text up, as if it has been crouched in a dark corner for centuries, just waiting for the light to be switched on! I may wax poetical, but it has truly been a cathartic experience for me, and I want

---

[1] Janet Tyson, *She Brought the Art of Women: A Song of Solomon, Nabonidus, and the Goddess* (Norwich: Pirištu Books, 2024).

you to see how it can work for *any* biblical text. It's just a case of a little imagination, some lateral thinking, and a lot of time looking for patterns. It really is worth the effort.

"SHISHAK"

In *She Brought the Art of Women*, I argued that Nabonidus is the inspiration for "Solomon" in the HB, this means Solomon's son, "Rehoboam," must be Belshazzar, the crown prince. Nabonidus, by the way, reigned as King of Babylon for *seventeen* years; this might be one of many HB instances of the "son" echoing the actions/traits of the "father."

Rehoboam is said to have succeeded to Solomon at the age of forty-one. As I claim all HB ages are to be interpreted symbolically (whether understood as literal or not), i.e., using gematria, I posit that "41" in this instance is *possibly* an allusion to *ayil*, "a strong ram or buck; stag, hart; to knit or twist together; to be strong, mighty; mighty or foremost man; great or strong tree, oak, terebinth, palm; power or force."[2] Of course, there might be a different word with the same numerical value, but this one really does fit Belshazzar. He is the young 'buck' (by biblical standards!), the up and coming generation; he is a strong military man, following in the footsteps of his father (in the Song, Nabonidus is depicted as both a stag and a strong, mature tree); might/power/force is a given (even the "twisting together" and "palm" references are apropos, being allusions to the Qenites' metallurgy[3] and the Arabian oases, respectively).

Historically, we know that Nabonidus began his reign in 556 BCE and that in his third year (553), soon after an ominous lunar eclipse in 554, he left Babylon for Arabia (Verse Account 2.5-7). For the next ten years he was predominantly absent from Babylon, spending the first three years "wandering" about, conquering cities, etc., before settling down in Tayma (I claim), where he spent the next seven years.[4] While he was away, he left his son, Belshazzar, in charge of things back in Babylonia, to the point where many have argued he was, de facto, "King" but there is no evidence to suggest he received

---

[2] Bill Heidrick, Hebrew Gematria, www.billheidrick.com.

[3] Janet Tyson, *Arabian Sinai: Nabonidus and the Exodus* (Norwich: Pirištu Books, 2024), 14; 24-6; 283; 367.

[4] This corresponds to the seven years' penance prescribed in Daniel 4:19-27.

that title officially; there are several indications that he remained the crown prince, even in his diplomatic/governmental position.[5] He was one of several children, as he is referred to as "the eldest" in inscriptions, and thus came from a previous marriage (there is no information on who this wife might have been).

1 Kgs 14:25 claims that in Rehoboam's "fifth year," "Shishak of Egypt came against Jerusalem."

"Shishak" is traditionally identified with Pharaoh Shoshenq I (945-925 BCE), a suggestion of Jean François Champollion, the early 19th Century Egyptologist. Listed on the Bubastite Portal relief at Karnak are the names of about a hundred and fifty cities Shoshenq conquered in the Levant; Jerusalem is conspicuous by its absence. Jerusalem in 549 BCE was (still) a rundown, ramshackle, provincial little place, left in the hands of the locals after the elite were taken into exile forty years previously; it would not have been worthy of a formal Egyptian invasion, and there is no archaeological or historical evidence to the contrary (and this applies also to the conventional 10th Century BCE timeframe for "Solomon"). Despite this identification never really 'working' in the real world, it has been promulgated for nearly two centuries.[6] Once again, change the paradigm, just for a moment, and you can see that convention has been holding us back, binding us to an outmoded way of reading the HB. It is, perhaps, time to shift gear and try a new route.

Bimson bravely states:

> The identification of Shoshenq I with biblical Shishak ... soon became a firm link between Egyptian and Hebrew chronologies, and has kept the two in step through major and minor adjustments to both. Severing that link, or at least recognising it as purely hypothetical and therefore provisional, would have

---

[5] Paul-Alain Beaulieu, *The Reign of Nabonidus King of Babylon 556–539 B.C.* (New Haven: Yale, University Press, 1989), 90-2.

[6] For a concise discussion see Aidan Dodson, "Shoshenq I: A Conventional(ish) View" in *Solomon and Shishak: Current Perspectives from Archaeology, Epigraphy, History and Chronology*, Proceedings of the Third BICANE Colloquium held at Sidney Sussex College, Cambridge 26-27 March, 2011, Peter James and Peter G. van der Veen, eds. (Oxford: BAR International Series 2732, 2015), 10-16.

considerable benefits. It would allow serious consideration to be given to radical adjustments to Egyptian chronology, which a growing number of scholars believe to be necessary.[7]

If the HB's Nabonidus foundation is consistent (which I argue to be the case), the "Shishak" pericopes *must* have some logical connection to the history of Nabonidus and his son; I have never claimed to be able to figure all of this out by myself, and there are many gaps in the historical record, even for Nabonidus, who is relatively well-represented. There may be accounts of skirmishes, etc., that have not yet been discovered, or evidence laying in plain sight, obscured by traditional boundaries (for instance, I discovered a potential parallel between the 'kidnapping of Lot' scenario in Genesis and a historical account of Belshazzar in a very similar situation[8]). My experience thus far has shown me that what we find on the surface of the HB texts is often not the whole story; the truth of the matter, the crux of the issue, might lurk far beneath, in the little nooks and crannies of etymology and wordplay.

Firstly, unlike the English translations, the name "Shishak" is used *twice* in the Hebrew version of 1 Kgs 14:25, i.e., "Shishak, King Shishak of Egypt" (*me·leḵ šî·šaq šū·šaq*). For my work, I immediately take notice of anything that is repeated in quick succession; it invariably denotes hidden meaning. The first thing I did was look at any potential calendrical clues in the HB texts I had already analysed, and then compared the result with historical events within that timeframe. I think I have found "Shishak" just where he needs to be to support a Nabonidus-based paradigm for the HB.

"Rehoboam" is to be identified as Belshazzar and, as I have demonstrated elsewhere, he joined Nabonidus' caravan through Canaan, undercover as "Lot" and then as Joshua, the army general.[9] He

---

[7] John J. Bimson, "Shishak and Shoshenq: A Chronological Cornerstone or Stumbling-block?" in *Solomon and Shishak: Current Perspectives from Archaeology, Epigraphy, History and Chronology*, Proceedings of the Third BICANE Colloquium held at Sidney Sussex College, Cambridge 26-27 March, 2011, Peter James and Peter G. van der Veen, eds. (Oxford: BAR International Series 2732, 2015), 3-9, here 8.

[8] Tyson, *Arabian Sinai*, 140-1.

[9] Tyson, *Arabian Sinai*, 36-40.

was the Jews' "saviour," their hero, their leader. *They* perceived him as "King," just as they had known him (effectively) back in Babylon, even though he seems to have resided in Tayma and worked alongside his aging father to build up the trading empire there (there is a possibility he spent seventeen years toing and froing, from Tayma to Canaan, assisting with military excursions, etc., but I doubt *very much* he lived in Jerusalem).

So when did Rehoboam take over from Solomon? I have attempted to calculate the year Nabonidus died, and thus when his son would have come to the throne, using only the information provided in the HB. We have the following clues:

✴ Nabonidus leaves Ur (as Abraham) with the first wave of returning exiles in 538 BCE

✴ As Moses, he is in Egypt (with Aaron) at the age of 80 (Exod 7:7); there is a subtle allusion to a lunar eclipse that suggests this is 522 BCE[10]

✴ We are told Moses dies at the age of 120 (Deut 34:7)[11]

✴ 120 - 80 (years) is 40; 522 BCE plus "forty years" gives us 482 BCE

Now this is where things get interesting. 482/1 BCE is the year King Xerxes of Persia (486-465 BCE) sacked Babylon after two revolts subsequent to his accession in 486 BCE. In a revengeful series of events, Xerxes ransacked the temple Esagila in Babylon, removing of all things, a vast golden statue of a man, echoing the allegory of the golden statue in Daniel 3.[12] Herodotus describes other golden objects, such as altars, tables, and a "throne"; these would not have been left untouched, given that Xerxes apparently had the priestly guardian of the statue killed so he could remove it. This, I think, might be a calendrical clue in 1 Kings, i.e., it is a recorded invasion by an outsider,

---

[10] Tyson, *Arabian Sinai*, 110-14.

[11] No age is given for Solomon. I have elsewhere interpreted Moses' age in terms of gematria, and it seems "120" is Nabonidus' number (used twice more in his dealings with Hiram and the Queen of Sheba); it has a very specific meaning. See *Arabian Sinai*, 369-70.

[12] Tyson, *Arabian Sinai*, 344-9.

of a temple Nabonidus ("Solomon") had strong ties to, where much gold was stored and then stolen.

The gold in 1 Kgs 14:26 is in the form of "shields," rather than a statue; this is to echo the "shields" in 10:17, of course, but we must recognise these are not shields used in battle; gold is too malleable and costly to use for fighting.[13] Rather, they are understood as Solomon's conspicuous wealth, hanging on the walls not of the temple, but the "House of the Forest of Lebanon" i.e., part of his residential complex *in Tayma*. They become a symbol of decadence.

Now, Xerxes is known to have ruled with an iron rod, so to speak; he liked things done his way, and he made sure everyone knew it. In a way, he sounds a little like Nabonidus, except Xerxes took his might from his military prowess, while Nabonidus' might lay in his overwhelming *personal* 'authority'. One of the most significant aspects of Xerxes' reign is something seemingly inconsequential, but it supports the theory here, that "Shishak" is *this* Persian king ...

In 1 Kings 14, Shishak is called "King of Egypt"; he is not referred to as "Pharaoh." In all the other references to the "king of Egypt" in the Pentateuch, both titles are used interchangeably, e.g., Gen 41:46; Exod 1:8,11; Deut 11:3, etc. The interesting thing about Xerxes is that he was the only Persian king to *reject* the title of "Pharaoh." I think this is why we see, in the Hebrew text of 1 Kgs 14:25, the name "Shishak" *twice* in succession; the first one replaces the title of "Pharaoh." This is an idiosyncrasy, something that can be used to pinpoint a time and a person.

Xerxes took two actions which may reflect religious intolerance. First he confiscated the property of many temples. His second step was a break in the tradition of previous Achaemenid rulers, who had followed the practice of assuming the local title of king in conquered lands. Xerxes refused to call himself Pharaoh, perhaps because of religious connotations of the office.[14]

That "Shishak" is the first such king of Egypt to be given a name in the HB, suggests this is a historical anchor that dates the composition of 1 Kings. The authors of the HB had known about Ahmose III through Nabonidus, they knew of Cambyses from their experiences in Babylon and/or Egypt, but neither are given names in the HB, not even

---

[13] Compare Song of Solomon 4:4; 2 Sam 8:7-8; Ezekiel 38:4, 39:9.

[14] Muhammad Dandamaev, "Xerxes and the Esagila Temple in Babylon," *Bulletin of the Asia Institute* 7 (1993): 41-5, here 41.

pseudonyms (which I have argued is because of the way in which the texts are written, i.e., in retrospection, a technique that allows them to say anything they wish about their 'captors', rulers, etc., without risking reprisals, for their stories are all set in the past; all they have to do to avoid retribution for sedition is to say, "this is our *ancient* history … it's not about *you*"). Xerxes was beyond the scope of their insulated world since leaving Babylonia, so he *is* named, albeit symbolically (merely alluding to the invasion would be enough of a clue for people at the time to know who this was meant to be; this blatant reference to historical fact is not done with the HB renditions of Ahmose or Nabonidus, where everything is hidden under layers of wordplay, etc.).

Xerxes' effect on Babylon, where many Jews remained, must have had a huge impact that reverberated across geographical boundaries and sent shudders through the Jewish people as a whole. To later generations, it would have seemed as though Daniel's foreboding was vindicated, i.e., Nabonidus' kingdom, based on hedonism and greed, had indeed come to nothing. But this was Babylon; in the meantime Nabonidus had set up his new kingdom at Tayma, and that was apparently *quite* successful!

The *only* thing I have an issue with is Rehoboam's "fifth year." The events of 482/1 BCE take place in *Xerxes'* fifth year. For this to be a calendrical reference to Belshazzar's (perceived) reign, he would have to have succeeded Nabonidus in 487/6, at the same time as Xerxes succeeded his father, Darius.

When you work with the numbers in the Bible, the gematria, or the calculations, are usually quite straight forward, almost deceptively so, so I used only those numbers directly associated with Nabonidus' alleged age (as Abraham and Moses) and length of reign (as Solomon), as set out in the texts. This is all that *should* be needed. If the "fifth year" is inextricably associated with Rehoboam, I must be overlooking something.

I do, however (as usual) have a theory.

What if the authors of 1 Kings 14 are being very clever indeed, and have superimposed the historical account of Xerxes onto the account of Rehoboam/Belshazzar? We are supposed to see both, together. The depiction of this prince is one that echoes that of Nabonidus (Solomon); he is a bit of a bully (like Xerxes) and is seen as being complicit in the idolatry and fornication that Nabonidus was held responsible for. As "Joshua," in the account of the initial entry into Canaan and the march to Jerusalem, he was a hero-figure; there were even hints of his being the antithesis of his father, when he seemed to question Nabonidus' ways.[15] But as the evidence does seem to suggest that Belshazzar played a vital role in Tayma *after* the exodus, and was remembered by the locals as a forefather,[16] it would seem the later Jews, the writers of 1 Kings who had already written of the decline and fall of Solomon, now saw his son in terms of his father, i.e., an enemy to the Jews, *not* a hero. He had 'let them down' by returning to Arabia, by joining his father in making his fortune, rather than remaining in Canaan with them. They gave him the credit of "reigning over Judah" (1 Kgs 14:21) but his legacy was debauchery and profanity. Like father like son.

This, I think, provides us with the meaning of the "bronze shields"; they represent the Arabian aspect, the Qenite, metallurgical, Aaron/Jethro/Jehudijah world of Moses in Tayma and at Sinai. Bronze figures heavily in the building and furnishing of the temple of Solomon, which I claim was in Tayma, not Jerusalem, and it is plentiful in this region of copper mines and smiths. The Jewish authors use the demotion from gold to bronze shields as an *insult* to Rehoboam (Belshazzar), with the additional slur that he lacked the authority to keep the shields on his house walls, as his father had done, but had to surrender them to the guards every time he went out (to the temple). Just as the crown prince had been denied the authority of a king in Babylon, despite his responsibilities in his father's absence, so now he is impotent, a king in name at last, but not in nature or prowess.

So, by depicting the account of Shishak coming to plunder Jerusalem, the authors create an allegory of judgement and rejection, but also inevitability.

Back to the "five years" conundrum, then; if Belshazzar began his stint in Babylon as, let's call him the "regent," when Nabonidus first left for Arabia in 553 BCE, the fifth year of his perceived reign would be 549 BCE. This is precisely when everything 'kicks off' at Tayma. It is the year of the coalition between Egypt, Babylon, Samos, and Lydia against an advancing Cyrus; it is the same year Nabonidus enters into a conciliatory marriage with Nitocris II (so I claim), daughter of

---

[15] Tyson, *Arabian Sinai*, 182.
[16] Tyson, *Arabian Sinai*, 306-7.

Ahmose III; and the year in which she first arrives at the new royal court in Tayma, i.e., where the Song of Solomon begins. As Rehoboam is *twice* defined as the son of "Naamah, the Ammonite," whom I understand to be Nitocris (see my paper on this topic[17]), this aspect is important to the comprehension of the pericope.

It is also necessary to recall that in the Song of Solomon, "Jerusalem" is a pseudonym, a disparaging name given to Tayma during Nabonidus' seven-year residency;[18] being a rundown, meagre site at the time, it was a fitting setting for Jehudijah's tale of the deranged, doomed king and his sordid relationship with the 'sorceress', Nitocris.

A frequently used tool in the scribes' etymology box is the utilisation of both their Hebrew/Aramaic *and* their knowledge of Akkadian to construct symbolic names to suit the context. I refer to these as "commission names," as they are given to a character, or even a place, for the purposes of encoding certain pertinent information within a given scenario; they change as the situation changes. This technique I have uncovered in the New Testament, too.

We can never know what went through the minds of the authors as they made up these names, but the consistency of this potential linguistic hybridisation seems to substantiate a profoundly clever manipulation of two languages, in order to arrive at the precise meaning being presented. The names serve as mnemonics, in a way, reminding the audience of key traits or actions that will link the new name to an already known character.

For "Shishak," I looked at all the Akkadian and Hebrew *shush-* and *shish-* words and this is what I found:

šūšu - sixty (Solomon has sixty queens and sixty guards in the Song of Solomon)

šušippu - a towel ; 2) wool, linen : dirty, clean (cf. Isa 64:6, i.e., "our righteous deeds are like a filthy cloth"; an allusion to menses[19])

šuškallu (Sumerian origin) - 1) a battle-net for gods, figurative sense: an envelope (in the Song, Nitocris is frequently described in

---

[17] Janet Tyson, "The Three Naahmas (Nabonidus and Nitocris)."

[18] Tyson, She Brought, 147; Arabian Sinai, 307.

[19] Tyson, *She Brought*, 93-4.

terms of being one who attempts to 'ensnare' the king, and this is echoed elsewhere in the HB)

šušruḫu - (deity) glorified (Moses allusions, obviously: Sinai, self-deification, etc.)

šūšûtu - 1) an announcement, an edict, a decree (the edict of Cyrus)

šūšanu - lily, lotus (a clear allusion to the Song's "lily of the valley" who turns out to be *not* Nitocris, but Jehudijah!); cognate for the Egyptian *seshen/sšn*

In Hebrew we find:

shesh - something "bleached white"

shesh – six (one of the avatars of Nabonidus in the Bible is the "beast" with the number "666"[20]; Solomon's throne has six steps [1 Kgs 10:19], making the seat of the throne the seventh, echoing the great ziggurat Nabonidus himself designed in seven tiers; this is a sign of his hubris)

shishshim – sixty (as above)

shayish - alabaster/marble (appears in the Song as part of Nitocris' symbolic statue; allusion to Egypt)

shushan – lily (as above)

The term *shesh* also appears in the etymology of the names "Tarshish" and "Sheshbazzar," both inextricably linked to Nabonidus.[21]

There are two other Hebrew words which might have a bearing, if used as a form of assonance, or broken down and their suffixes employed for added meaning, i.e., *choshek*, meaning "the dark; hence (literally) darkness; figuratively, misery, destruction, death, ignorance, sorrow, wickedness:--dark(-ness), night, obscurity"; and *ashaq*, to oppress, wrong, extort. Both terms vividly reflect the mood, atmosphere, traits, etc., of both the Song of Solomon's sinister side, *and* the exodus narratives when seen with Nabonidus as Moses. In Exodus 10:21, the term *choshek* is used to describe the ninth "plague"

---

²⁰ Tyson, *Arabian Sinai*, 346-9.
[20] Tyson, *Arabian Sinai*, 346-9.
[21] For "Tarshish," see my paper "Nabonidus, Tarshish, and Ophir." For "Sheshbazzar," Tyson, *Arabian Sinai*, 201-2.

(darkness).

The "*-ak*" suffix may simply be a 'particle of affirmation' (*Strong's*, "surely, truly," etc.) but I like to think there could be more to it.

The name "Shisha" appears unceremoniously in 1 Kgs 4:3, as the (apparently Egyptian) father of two of Solomon's scribes. Might this be an intentional scribal clue to the unravelling of "Shishak" in its Nabonidus/Nitocris mode? "Shisha" would have the same etymology as provided above for "Shishak" but instead of the suffix being "*-ak*" it is just "*-k*"; this allows for two more direct allusions to Nitocris that otherwise wouldn't be possible.

1. The letter "k" in Hebrew is *kaf*, with a numerical value (gematria) of 20. Its shape is bent, curved, and this has led to the notion that it signifies submission "to a greater force."[22] The letter is said to have a meaning of "palm" or "crown," with the overall interpretation of something that submits to, or succumbs to, a forceful, higher authority (the Crown itself). In previous discussions, I have claimed Nitocris died at the hands of the Persians soon after Babylon was taken.[23] The number 20 is also a factor in the gematria of "Sarah's" age, and "Sarah" is a posthumous avatar of Nitocris.[24]

2. The meaning of "palm" is not a reference to the palm-tree but to the "hand" (though the tree gets its name from the palmate leaves, which themselves are likened to a hand). Though Nitocris is depicted in the Song of Solomon in terms of her avatar, Ishtar, whose iconography/epithets include the palm-tree, the more germane allusion is to Nitocris as God's Hand, which I claim is strongly hinted at in the Song, both linguistically and symbolically. I have argued that even if she was not officially God's Hand in Karnak (though I think she was), she *assumed* the role at Tayma, in order to function effectively in her sacerdotal role as the keeper of the Elixir Rubeus.[25]

---

[22] Chabad.org. "Kaf-Chaf," https://www.chabad.org/library/article_cdo/aid/137083/jewish/Kaf-Chaf.htm.

[23] Tyson, *She Brought*, 225-7.

[24] Tyson, *Arabian Sinai*, 76.

[25] This is also an element of the 'divine name' "Jedidiah," given to "Solomon" in 2 Sam 12:25 (Tyson, *She Brought*, 24); both are derogatory allusions.

There are, in the Song, frequent references to the sexual nature of Nabonidus' marriage to Nitocris, his liaisons with the other harem women, the Elixir Rubeus rite, etc.; in the exodus narratives this theme continues, from a potentially suppressed sexual encounter with his own daughter, to his ambivalence toward homosexuality, etc. Indeed, without the sexual aspect of Nabonidus' depiction in the HB, there would be much less 'evidence' to work with! It lies at the very core of the early Jews' abhorrence. With this in mind, then, I find the following comment about the potential Egyptian rendering of "Shishak" most intriguing:

> Finally, it should be noted that the root *šqq* does not mean 'attack' …or 'rush at', but rather 'to yearn' and, by extension, terms denoting the vocalization of intense desire, such as 'cry, groan, make a noise' …making it perhaps not quite as appropriate for a militant Egyptian king.[26]

Indeed; but it *is* appropriate for another allusion to Nabonidus/Nitocris, and the sentiments expressed in the Song of Solomon and the exodus narratives. Perhaps the scribes who wrote of "Shishak" knew of this Egyptian word and toyed with it.

Therefore, it seems to me that the 1 Kings scribes are playing with the name "Shishak" to illuminate several aspects of the Nabonidus/Nitocris legacy, while at the same time, using an actual, recent, historical event to both place the alleged reign of Solomon's son (Belshazzar) in context, and to highlight the overall outcome of this Babylonian father-son royal duo. That "Shishak came against Jerusalem" might be interpreted as the harrowing effect of Nabonidus and Nitocris on the Jewish people, where "Jerusalem" once again serves as a symbolic pseudonym (as it had in the Song), *not* the city itself, and "Shishak" becomes synonymous with the entire

---

[26] Troy Leiland Sagrillo, "Shoshenq I and Biblical Šîšaq: A Philological Defense of Their Traditional Equation," in *Solomon and Shishak: Current Perspectives from Archaeology, Epigraphy, History and Chronology*, Proceedings of the third BICANE colloquium held at Sidney Sussex College, Cambridge 26–27 March, 2011, Peter J. James, Peter G. van der Veen, Robert M. Porter, eds. (Oxford: Archaeopress, BAR International Series 2732, 2015), 61-81, here 67.

Nabonidus/Nitocris phenomenon; they were a profoundly traumatising experience for the Jews, who were disheartened when their once golden-boy, Belshazzar, followed suit.[27]

It might very well be from this allegory that the later rabbis would come up with their notion about the marriage of "Solomon and Pharaoh's daughter" (Nabonidus and Nitocris) being the instigation of the fall of Israel: At the moment the royal couple consummated their marriage, the rabbis suggested, an archangel descended with a reed in his hand, which he planted in the sea; around it grew a thickly forested island, upon which grew the seeds of the Roman Empire, which would eventually carry out God's revengeful plan (Avodah Zarah, 1:2, 39c). The early Jews perhaps reckoned Babylon falling to Cyrus a matter of politics; Babylon's holy sites falling to Xerxes must have seemed divine retribution and not something they wished to see happen in Jerusalem (hence the warning tale of "Shishak").

ADDENDUM

2 Chronicles 12 provides a slightly more elaborate account of Shishak's alleged invasion, including the number of chariots and the size of the cavalry; such numbers are propagandistic and should be investigated in terms of potential gematria. Because the Xerxes' invasion was actually on Babylonian soil, there would have been no historical record of this violent act on Jerusalem, and no communal memory of it. The authors of 2 Chronicles clearly had an issue with this, and provided a rationale for the extraordinary claim in 1 Kings.[28]

The justification, according to 2 Chronicles, was that the "bronze shields" were a sign of Rehoboam's humility (sort of along the same lines I have suggested, but in terms of him voluntarily making inferior

---

[27] Consider the scenario presented in 1 Kgs 12:6-19, in which Rehoboam (also Belshazzar) turns out to be not just an echo of his father (Nabonidus) but even worse!

[28] I am of the opinion that the authors of the Hebrew Bible were far more contemporaneous than we have imagined, i.e., dating of texts has rested heavily on the content *within* the texts, taken quite literally. I suggest many of the authors knew each other, or knew of each other's works. The potential for intertextuality research is greatly increased when this is considered, especially when augmented by an etymological approach to interpretation, as the patterns are not necessarily limited by textual boundaries.

shields, rather than having them intentionally suggesting an insult). As the wayward king seemed to have repented and "humbled himself" (2 Chr 12:12) in the nick of time, Jerusalem was *spared* Shishak's wrath. The "King of Egypt's" tirade was reconfigured as a divine tool, an omen warning of impending judgement and repercussions, but thwarted when Rehoboam miraculously 'saw the light'. As seen with certain other HB characters, Rehoboam is allegedly allowed to rest amongst his (Jewish, therefore imposed) ancestors in hallowed territory, but once you see what is going on behind the scenes, it is clear this is a tactic to preserve ownership of the past and to make it wholly Jewish; in the meantime, back in Arabia, other stories are being told to contradict these claims.[29]

(The last phrase of 1 Kgs 14:12, i.e., "conditions were good in Judah," seems to be an attempt to dispel the discrepancy 2 Chronicles would later rationalise; Judah was actually poor, meek, and relatively unimportant.)

BIBLIOGRAPHY

Beaulieu, Paul-Alain. *The Reign of Nabonidus King of Babylon 556–539 B.C.* New Haven: Yale, University Press, 1989.

Bimson, John J. "Shishak and Shoshenq: A Chronological Cornerstone or Stumbling-block?" Pages 3-9 in *Solomon and Shishak: Current Perspectives from Archaeology, Epigraphy, History and Chronology*. Proceedings of the Third BICANE Colloquium held at Sidney Sussex College, Cambridge 26-27 March, 2011. Edited by Peter James and Peter G. van der Veen. Oxford: BAR International Series 2732, 2015.

Chabad.org. "Kaf-Chaf." https://www.chabad.org/library/articlecdo/aid /137083/jewish/Kaf-Chaf.htm

Dandamaev, Muhammad. "Xerxes and the Esagila Temple in Babylon." *Bulletin of the Asia Institute* 7 (1993): 41-5.

Dodson, Aidan. "Shoshenq I: A Conventional(ish) View." Pages 10-16 in *Solomon and Shishak: Current Perspectives from Archaeology, Epigraphy, History and Chronology*. Proceedings of the Third BICANE Colloquium held at Sidney Sussex College, Cambridge 26-27 March, 2011. Edited by Peter James and Peter G. van der Veen. Oxford: BAR International Series 2732, 2015.

---

[29] E.g., see *Arabian Sinai*, Chapter 16.

Sagrillo, Troy Leiland. "Shoshenq I and Biblical Šîšaq: A Philological Defense of Their Traditional Equation." Pages 61-81 in *Solomon and Shishak: Current Perspectives from Archaeology, Epigraphy, History and Chronology*, Proceedings of the third BICANE colloquium held at Sidney Sussex College, Cambridge 26–27 March, 2011. Edited by Peter J. James, Peter G. van der Veen, Robert M. Porter. Oxford: Archaeopress, BAR International Series 2732, 2015.

Tyson, Janet. *Arabian Sinai: Nabonidus and the Exodus*. Norwich: Pirištu Books, 2024.

______. *She Brought the Art of Women: A Song of Solomon, Nabonidus and the Goddess*. Norwich: Pirištu Books, 2023.

7

SCORPION RISING
NABONIDUS AND THE ASCENT OF AKRABBIM

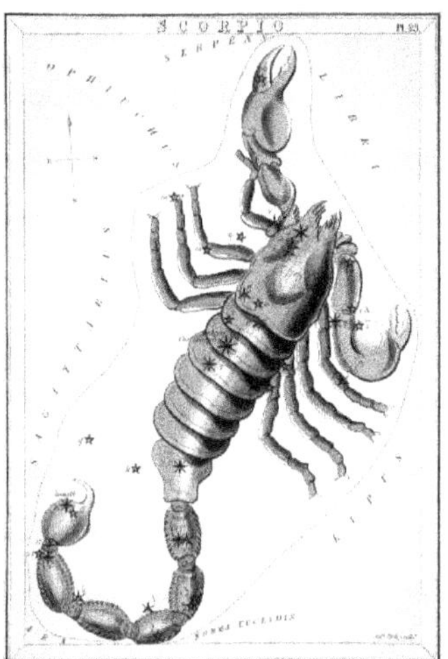

Figure 1: Constellations Scorpius and Orion, as depicted in Urania's Mirror: Or, A View of the Heavens, Sidney Hall and Jehoshaphat Aspin, 1824 (Public Domain)

The following is an analysis of the "Ascent of Akrabbim" within the context of a 6th Century BCE, Nabonidus-inspired exodus narrative, as discussed in the body of research I am hoping will provide some alternative interpretations of toponyms (at the very least) in the Bible. As with most of my papers on the topic of Nabonidus, it helps if you follow the story somewhat chronologically, beginning with *She Brought the Art of Women*, which is available free online.[1] This introduces us to Nabonidus, from the pen of a first-hand witness to the goings on at Tayma, Arabia. *Arabian Sinai* then focuses on the "exodus" years, from the fall of Babylon to Sinai and beyond.[2]

In *Arabian Sinai*, I have argued that Nabonidus is the historical

---

[1] Janet Tyson, *She Brought the Art of Women: A Song of Solomon, Nabonidus, and the Goddess* (Norwich: Pirištu Books, 2023).

[2] Janet Tyson, *Arabian Sinai: Nabonidus and the Exodus* (Norwich: Pirištu Books, 2024).

159

figure behind the character of "Moses," and that his son, Belshazzar, is the inspiration for "Joshua." The final push into Canaan, I suggest, was *not* from the northern tip of the Dead Sea, across the Jordan river; this was a symbolic notion to push Jewish, rather than Nabonidus' Arabian-based agenda.

The entire Arabian context of the exodus was expunged, with toponyms appropriated by the Jews who settled in Canaan; every significant location in the Hijaz was (figuratively) 'transferred' to their new territory in the Levant. The ceremonial crossing of the River Jordan was most certainly propaganda; the actual crossing from Edom/Moab into Canaan was at Sela, taking advantage of Nabonidus' familiarity with the route and exploiting his own royal inscription to 'inspire the troops'; he had passed this way before, as King.[3]

Much of what I have discovered about Nabonidus and the exodus from Babylonia in 538 BCE has proven to be esoteric in nature, heavily influenced by Egyptian solar ritual, and with hidden cosmological references. With this in mind, the "Ascent of Akrabbim" takes on a whole new meaning.

SELA

The division of territories by Joshua includes this demarcation for the southern boundary of the land of Judah:

> And their south boundary ran from the Dead Sea, from the bay that faces southward; it goes out southward of the ascent of Akrabbim, passes along to Zin, and goes up south of Kadesh-barnea ... and comes to its end at the sea (Josh 15:3-4).

The "bay that faces southward" is self-explanatory; the boundary then follows that trajectory south of the "ascent of Akrabbim," to Kadesh-barnea. It then heads into the wilderness, and here, the word used is *abar*, "to pass over, through, or by, pass on," i.e., *to "cross." This*, I suggest, is the location of the original crossing of Jordan, i.e., the *lower* Rift Valley, not the river[4]; the watery crossing in Joshua is to mirror,

---

[3] For a full description see Bradley L. Crowell, "Nabonidus, as-Sila', and the Beginning of the End of Edom," *BASOR* 348 (2007): 75-88.
[4] For "Jordan" as a toponym see Tyson, *Arabian Sinai*, 384-5.

160

symbolically, Moses' (and the Israelites') crossing of *Yam Suph* (i.e., "In ancient battle accounts, a military engagement officially commences when a belligerent crosses a waterway"[5]).

The boundary of Judah is shared with that of the Amorites; both have as their starting point, Sela: "from the ascent of Akrabbim, from Sela and upward" (Judg 1:36).

In *Arabian Sinai* I suggest that Kadesh-barnea is Sela and that the name reflects a dual association with both Sinai and Kadesh (in the Hijaz), i.e., Sela is twinned with the sacred site of Sinai *and* the profane, some might say 'unholy' site of Kadesh (due to associations with murder, battle, etc.).[6] The name "Sela" is thought to derive from the Arabic root *sl'* meaning "to cleave, split"; this alludes to it geological form, i.e., it has twin peaks, upon which are two high-places (sacred) and a fortress (profane). This structure also emulates the rock in the *horeb*, i.e., at Kadesh/Rephidim, which is split in two,[7] making the name "Kadesh-barnea" a perfect blend of the two sites.

The "Wilderness of Zin," I posit, is the Canaanite version of the Arabian Wilderness of Sîn, subtly altered to maintain the allusion of a wholly Israelite/Levantine exodus, whilst rejecting the Arabian/Nabonidus connection. Recognising the mirroring of toponyms is crucial in any effort to comprehend them. Zin borders Paran from the Canaanite perspective, just as Paran borders Sîn from the Arabian (see *Fig. 2*).

The "Ascent of Akrabbim" is mentioned in Joshua as though it were a familiar place, not simply some random location in a foreign land on the way into Canaan. Those chronicling the incursions would not list the local names of every village or valley they encountered, as these would mean nothing to anyone else; they create commission names (toponyms) for significant sites. The names are inextricably linked to the immediate context of the narrative; the same location might receive a different commission name when another event at that site is being discussed, or a different character is the centre of focus. Imagine someone has just come home from a battle in a foreign land and is trying to describe where they went, but you have no idea – you haven't been there. They might use descriptions like "the valley where

---

[5] Jacob L. Wright, *War, Memory, and National Identity in the Hebrew Bible* (Online Publication: Cambridge UniversAity Press, 2020), 55.
[6] Tyson, *Arabian Sinai*, 170-4.
[7] Tyson, *Arabian Sinai*, 161-2 and 181-2.

the soldiers died" or the "pass from which we could see the plain" etc.

Thus we see, for instance, the forty names listed in Numbers 33 that represent the "forty years" *before* the crossing into Canaan, each pertaining to an event or person in the exodus narratives.[8] While some were certainly locations where something of import happened, others might not have been physical locations at all, but simply narrative markers (i.e., the etymology of this sort of toponym usually reveals a character-based meaning, rather than a direct allusion to a geographical element such as a valley, river, cliff, etc.). Commission names shift according to context, but if several pertain to the same character or place, there will *always* be a clue within the etymology that connects them. It is a brilliant technique, and one that reveals much of the hidden narrative of the Bible.

The term used in Josh 15:3 for "Ascent" is *maaleh,* "an ascent" e.g., a slope, a rising pathway, a stairway, etc. This seems to point to a physical site, for at Sela, a mountain/hill isolated on all four sides from the surrounding terrain, there are multiple ancient stairways leading up to the summit. The description of the boundary of Judah (in Josh 15:3-4) though, does suggest the Ascent itself might be the steep slope of the wadi that leads from the Dead Sea to Sela (from that direction, one would have to ascend the walls of the valley to reach Sela; from Sela, one would have to descend into the valley to cross over).

"Akrabbim" is the plural of *aqrab,* "scorpion," ergo, the "Ascent of Scorpions." The simplistic argument suggests this means a steep passage made dangerous by scorpions but such creatures are commonplace in the desert, so unless the site was *unnaturally* inundated with scorpions, which one would think would put the group off using this route (or wishing to retain it within their territory), it isn't enough of a rationale for inventing a toponym based on scorpions.

Mythology/Astronomy

There are at least two other ways of interpreting the "Ascent of Akrabbim": 1) there is the relevant Babylonian mythology to consider, and 2) the link to cosmology needs addressing, as this reiterates some of the strongest symbolism in the story of Nabonidus at Sinai and how

---

[8] Tyson, *Arabian Sinai,* "Appendix 5," 381-5.

the Jews felt about what he was doing.[9]

1. Scorpion-men

In Babylonian myth there are the Aqrabuamelu, the descendants of the scorpion man created by Tiamat, the sea-serpent mother of the gods. The hybrid, half-human creatures became gatekeepers to the underworld, and specifically for the solar deity, Shamash, as he slumbered behind the mountain(s) of Mashu each night. Mashu was a *cleaved/split* mountain (twin-peaked), which provides a link to Sela, both in the etymology of "to split/cleave," and in Sela's dual high-places divided by a "gateway."[10]

In the Epic of Gilgamesh, the region beyond the Aqrabuamelu, beyond the gates to the realm of the resting Sun god, is dangerous and foreboding. To me, this highlights the last-post nature of Sela in Joshua, i.e., beyond there, in the direction of the rising Sun ("East"; Arabia) is the realm that must be forgotten, disavowed, where everything considered anathema dwells. This was where Moses deviated from his previous lunar-based devotions and seemed to worship the Sun. From the crossing of the Jordan Valley onward, only Canaan exists for the "Israelites"/Jews.

2. Scorpius

In keeping with the solar theme, there is a fitting cosmological allusion that might be exploited by the scribes here, involving the constellation of Scorpius.

I have previously claimed that Nabonidus was enamoured with his Egyptian pharaoh buddy and father-in-law, Ahmose III. Although they potentially had a falling out long before Ahmose died in 526 BCE, Nabonidus, I argue, was so fascinated with the Egyptian Osirian philosophy and rituals, he exploited his relationship with the pharaoh posthumously, using the solar-deity aspect of the king's identity as a

---

[9] The Egyptian goddess Selket is symbolised by a scorpion; her most common role is that of an antidote to snake bites; yet another subtle allusion to the Sinai years with Nabonidus? In Hellenistic times, the constellation became associated with the figure of the healer Asclepius, who used snakes. This is, biblically, a vital allusion to Moses and the 'brazen serpent' used to ward off snakes in the desert (but also to a much more profound serpentine connection, as you can read in *Arabian Sinai*).

[10] See photos on https://nabataea.net/explore/cities_and_sites/sela-1/.

symbol for the solar aspect of the new hybrid deity, "I AM."[11] The ensuing accounts of "Moses" on Mount Sinai are thus strongly imbued with Egyptian Osirian concepts as they relate to the mythology of the rebirth of the Sun god, Re. Once you recognise this pattern in the exodus narratives, the "Ascent of Akrabbim" and its scorpions suggests a potential connection to something astronomical, rather than geographical.

The constellation Scorpius is thought to be one of the oldest known in recorded history; it was bigger, originally, with the constellation we now know as Libra forming the claws of the beast. In Arabia, this constellation is known as Al 'Aḵrab.[12]

In Greek mythology, dating to at least the 9-8th Century BCE, the scorpion in the night sky was said to have been placed there by either Gaia or Artemis (depending on the version of the myth) in honour of the scorpion's success in defeating the legendary strongman, Orion. Orion, apparently, had been boasting about how strong he was, how nothing and no one could match his power and skill as a hunter. The goddess, annoyed with Orion's hubris, sent the scorpion to challenge him. The battle was doomed from the start, and the scorpion defeated the proud hunter with each attempt to crush him. Orion was taught a lesson in humility and as he fled for the final time from his omnipotent adversary, the scorpion stung his foot; he succumbed to the bite and died. The constellation of Scorpius seems to be chasing that of Orion over the hemisphere forever, for as it rises in the heavens, Orion dips below the horizon, apparently hiding until it is safe to return.

If you have read any of my other discussions concerning Nabonidus, you will know that his hubris lies at the bottom of just about everything. He was, as far as can be discerned from the biblical and some of the external, historical renditions of him, an arrogant man with delusions of grandeur. Yes, he was once King of Babylon – no delusion there – but after he handed Babylon to Cyrus and escaped the job he clearly never really wanted, he became a law unto himself and everyone under his control felt the weight of that hubris.

If the "Ascent of Akrabbim" alludes to the rising of Scorpius in the sky, this points to Sela as the final setting for "Moses" (Nabonidus) and his departure from the "Israelites" (Jews). Identified as the place

---

[11] Tyson, *Arabian Sinai*, 225-66.

[12] Richard Hinckley Allen, *Star Names: Their Lore and Meaning* (New York: Dover Publications, 1963, 1899), 362.

where Scorpius was first seen at its heliacal rising, Sela becomes synonymous with the heavenly pursuit of Orion by the scorpion; the latter wins and is granted the toponym in honour of its success, while the "fool" (see below) slips below the horizon, having fallen victim to his own conceit. In fact, Scorpius was a feared constellation, notorious for being linked to negative omens concerning harvests,[13] and even the royal household.[14] The final 'defeat' (i.e., rejection) of Nabonidus at Sela seems written in the night sky.

In the Hebrew Bible (HB), the name for Orion is *Chisel/Kisel* (Job 9:9, 38:31; Amos 5:8); this means "fool" (from *chasal/kasal*, "to be stupid"). How fitting! The Jews' memory of Nabonidus is a predominantly negative one; as I demonstrate throughout *Arabian Sinai*, the HB scribes never miss an opportunity to cast aspersions and paint him as a misguided madman. The Song of Solomon sets a precedent for this, with its all-embracing curse (i.e., "Your name is empty"[15]), and the entire depiction of Moses at the Nile is an effort (in hindsight) to ridicule his ambitions for a new deity.[16]

Interestingly, Abarim Publications suggests that the

verb כסל (*kasal*) is decidedly negative. Intellectually this root describes pareidolia: ... observations that are not related by any verifiable theoretic structure and only kept together by the insistent "belief" of the observer ....[17]

This couldn't be more apt, for Nabonidus is known for having strange ideas about things, e.g., he devised an idol of Sîn that nobody understood (Verse Account 1.7-8); he is depicted in Daniel 4-5 as having vivid dreams he believes are significant to his life but no one else comprehends them; he is referred to as "mad" with the insinuation that he was prone to "hallucinations"[18]; and as having one of these

---

[13] Michael Baigent, *Astrology in Ancient Mesopotamia: The Science of Omens and the Knowledge of the Heavens* (Toronto: Bear and Co., 1994), 130.
[14] Baigent, 145.
[15] Tyson, *She Brought*, 50-1.
[16] Tyson, *Arabian Sinai*, 116-22.
[17] Abarim Publications, "Chesil," https://www.abarim-publications.com /Meaning/Chesil.html.
[18] Tyson, *She Brought*, 223-4.

hallucinations on the night before the invasion of Cyrus. In this last example, I discuss the scene in Daniel 5 as being shadows flickering on the wall, caused by the lamp that is mentioned (i.e., as a blatant clue to the scene's interpretation, as otherwise, the lamp is inconsequential); Nabonidus sees these flickerings as divine writing but everyone else just sees shadows (Daniel exploits the king's state of mind to press home his own negative impression of the man).

If Nabonidus is identified as Orion, "the fool," then he must also be identifiable with Osiris, for the two legendary characters are virtually synonymous. In the exodus narratives we do indeed see Nabonidus taking on certain aspects of Osiris, both in Egypt and at Sinai, in the context of the rebirth of Re, the Egyptian solar deity. In fact, the overall representation of Moses "striking" multiple things (the Nile, the rock, etc.) with his wooden staff emulates the Egyptian rendering of Osiris the hunter, who would use a wooden stick to beat birds as they flew up from the marshes (represented by the Pleiades). This is how he was envisioned as a constellation:

> Osiris, on the day of caching birds with the throwing stick...raise thyself up...the sky weeps for thee; the earth trembles for thee...hands wave for thee, when thou ascendest to heaven as a star.
>
> Pyramid Texts, Utterance 553 §1362b

So, the "Ascent of Akrabbim," in both contexts seems to point to Nabonidus' Osirian/solar-based activity on the top of Mount Sinai, and the Jews' rejection thereof.

CALENDRICAL CLUES

The constellation Scorpius has its heliacal rising at the autumn equinox, on one of the last days of September, that is, in the month Tashritu, the month of "beginning."[19] This is the month of Moses and the Israelites' arrival at Sinai, according to my calculations.[20] Tashritu was also Nabonidus' favourite "auspicious" month, i.e., he chose this time to

---

[19] W. Muss-Arnolt, "The Names of the Assyro-Babylonian Months and Their Regents," *Journal of Biblical Literature* 11.2 (1892): 160-76, here 160.
[20] Tyson, *Arabian Sinai*, 115.

leave Tayma for Babylon in 543 BCE (Nabonidus 17, [i 1-11]; 47 [ii 3-11]), and the fall of Babylon itself occurred in this month (Nab Chr [iii 12-16].[21] I claim this was partly a deal made with Cyrus for a peaceful handover so Nabonidus could return to Tayma). The great Shamash (i.e., solar deity) temple at Ebbabar was begun in this month (Nab 28 [ii 60-5]).

Shamash, the Sun god, ruled the month of Tashritu, making it the perfect month for Nabonidus to begin his solar-based rituals at Sinai, but this also reiterates the solar allusions within the "Ascent of Akrabbim" and the symbolic mirroring of Sela. Whether chronologically precise or fabrication, this seems to suggest that the group arrived at Sinai in Tashritu (Sept/Oct), and that at the Sinai-twin Sela, the same auspicious timing is inferred. Where Sinai saw the *veneration* of the solar aspect of divinity, at Sela, with Nabonidus gone, we suddenly see the opposite, with a symbolic attack on the "Sun" (the deity) that Nabonidus had 'invented' and forced the Jews to worship (cf. Daniel 3).[22]

The allusion to the destruction of the solar aspect might, on the other hand, be intended by another familiar calendrical curiosity, i.e., the Babylonian "eighth month" (Oct/Nov) has as its symbol the scorpion. The zodiacal image represents the "sun-slaying darkness."[23]

As a calendrical clue, the rising of Scorpius (aka "the Ascent of Akrabbim") could suggest the crossing of the Jordan Valley did not take place in Nisan, as tradition holds.

In *Arabian Sinai* I assess the significance of retaining "Abib" in Exod 13:4, which the author chose to use, rather than simply saying "Nisan," which was the Babylonian/Jewish "first month." There, I argue that "Abib" is retained because it is the Arabic name for Ipip, the Egyptian month of June/July; this has significance both astronomically and in terms of the flooding of the Nile.[24] I also worked out that, at least potentially, Nabonidus and those he took with him to Egypt, spent ten

---

[21] Nabonidus inscriptions from Frauke Weiershäuser and J. Novotny. *The Royal Inscriptions of Amēl-Marduk (561-560 BC), Neriglissar (559-556 BC), and Nabonidus (555-539 BC), Kings of Babylon*, The Royal Inscriptions of the Neo-Babylonian Empire, Vol. 2 (University Park: Eisenbrauns, 2020).

[22] Tyson, *Arabian Sinai*, 345-8.

[23] Muss-Arnolt, 167.

[24] Tyson, *Arabian Sinai*, 110-16.

months there, as he searched for "Joseph's bones."[25]

If Joshua and his cohort make this symbolic transition to mirror the alleged emancipation from Egypt as depicted in Exodus (or rather, the authors depicted it as such), then a parallel calendar must be implied. The group (whether actually or symbolically) spend ten months at Sela before heading out for Jericho. That is, they arrive in September, marked by the heliacal rising of Scorpius, and they cross over in June/July (Abib) the following summer, i.e., the "time of harvest" mentioned in Josh 3:15.

Although barley was harvested around the time of Nisan, it does seem odd that this is not made clear, which might well have supported a Nisan reading of "first month." Instead, the "harvest" is purposefully oblique. In Num 13:17-24, however, when Moses sends the spies into Canaan, he tells them to bring back fruit, which is a much later harvest. In Canaan, the grapes, figs, and pomegranates that the spies bring back with them can only have been procured, *at the same time*, in the months of August and September.[26] This tallies with the arrival at Sela around this time, as gleaned from the rising of Scorpius.

I have argued that the calendrical clues in the exodus narratives have been purposefully obscured in order to suppress the Nabonidus/Arabia context and highlight the subsequent Jewish perspective. The integrity of the authors, however, in terms of them keeping true to the historical events, is to be lauded, for they must have deemed lying about what really happened, or purposefully omitting incriminating or uncomfortable material, a sin against God. They include, I think, everything they know about what happened, it's just that much is hidden, manipulated, and refashioned to suit the wholly Jewish narrative subsequent to Nabonidus' departure. Therefore, when the Jewish authors speak of the "harvest" at the time of the Jordan flooding, of course this *must* tally with the chosen Nisan dating of their *symbolic* crossing, i.e., this *would* be the barley harvest in March. Throughout the HB, at least in the exodus narratives, there are two tales being told; one is historical, one is theological/symbolic but they are inextricably linked via the authors' ingenious wordplay.

---

[25] Tyson, *Arabian Sinai*, 113-14.

[26] "The Grain and Fruit Harvest Times in Israel," §The Sowing and Harvesting Times in Israel, https://bible-menorah.jimdofree.com/english/calendar-and-feasts /barley-wheat-harvest-israel/. This article provides a good explanation for the verb *abib*, as used in Exod 9:31.

So, why the "tenth day"? This is clearly to link back to Exod 12:3, to reiterate the symbolic mirroring of the emancipation and the preparation for Passover, culminating on the evening of the fourteenth day. I have already discussed this timing in the Osirian context of "Abib" in Exodus:

> ... the phases of the waxing moon (Osiris) culminate on the fourteenth/fifteenth day, when Osiris officially "enters the moon" and shines as the bright full moon. This celestial opposition marks the starting point for Nabonidus' mission, which will ultimately end with a celestial conjunction, i.e., of Re and Osiris, at Sinai.[27]

Where the first deliverance of the Jews/"Israelites" was from bondage, as exiles in Babylonia (not Egypt), the second (the Jordan crossing) was from the tyranny of Nabonidus. Joshua's crossing of the Jordan on the tenth day allows for the Passover preparations but there is a lengthy description of circumcision before the Passover is again mentioned. This interjection represents *the passage of time* (this is another frequent scribal technique, as seen in the depiction of the plagues in Exodus[28]) i.e., the group arrives at Sela in September, marked by the Ascent of Akrabbim, they "cross over" ten months later, in June/July (Abib), and then they have their first Passover in Canaan the following Nisan (March/April).

This first Passover at Gilgal contains within it yet another assertion that this momentous event draws a line under the entire Arabian experience. Josh 5:10-12 states that once they had celebrated Passover, the manna the Jews ("Israelites") had eaten ended, i.e., the enforced obligations to their long-term Arabian hosts, via the Covenant of Salt, was officially negated. All ties to Tayma, etc., were now in the past.[29]

JERICHO AND MARDUK

Once Passover is 'dealt with', the attack on Jericho is discussed, and this is where the Osirian perception of the "full moon" comes into play:

---

[27] Tyson, *Arabian Sinai*, 111.
[28] Tyson, *Arabian Sinai*, 113-14.
[29] Tyson, *Arabian Sinai*, 146-54.

Joshua/Belshazzar is about to prove his loyalty to the Jews by denouncing his father's hold over them. The narrative's chronology gives the impression that the Passover and the attack on the "City of the Moon," Jericho, are to be linked, and that the assault began during the full-moon phase, thereby signifying the utter rejection of Nabonidus (who is represented by both the Moon and Osiris) and his most familiar and constant lunar deity, Sîn. In the narrative of Moses leaving Egypt (the second time, with the "Israelites"), we see a similar tactic of obscuring the true Nabonidus-based date in favour of emphasising a Jewish, symbolic one,[30] so there is continuity here (between father and son representations, i.e., Nabonidus/Moses and Belshazzar/ Joshua).

In *Arabian Sinai* I suggest that Joshua, Belshazzar's main (but not only) avatar in the HB, is an echo of Marduk, the warrior/saviour of Babylonian myth.[31] When you look at the constellations neighbouring Scorpius, you find the often forgotten Ophiuchus, the "Snake-bearer"; this constellation reaches its zenith in July, just as preparations for the "harvest" begin. It is also associated with Marduk, for the constellation is represented by a man seizing and/or tearing apart a large serpent, i.e., thought to be an allusion to Marduk slaying Tiamat.[32] If the context of the Jericho pericope *is* one of the testing of Belshazzar's allegiance to the Jews, the figure of the man destroying the snake, i.e., the latter being a prominent and underestimated symbol of Moses/Nabonidus,[33] the effect is one of reiterating that notion.

In the Neo-Babylonian *Great Star List*, the constellation Scorpius appears in connection with both Tiamat and the goddess Išhara, but note the "Sword of Heaven" attribute, i.e., Shamash himself is said to cut the mountain with a sword-like saw, and the word "scorpion" in Akkadian (*zuqaqipu*) is sometimes translated as "the cutter" (due to its claws):

---

[30] Tyson, *Arabian Sinai*, 110-14.

[31] Tyson, *Arabian Sinai*, 37-8; 388.

[32] Also, Marduk was traditionally associated with Jupiter; in this capacity he was sometimes given the name "Nebiru" which means "Crossing Point" (Francesca Rochberg, "Marduk in Heaven," *Wiener Zeitschrift Für Die Kunde Des Morgenlandes* 97 (2007): 433-42, here 435). What is happening at Sela? They are preparing to "cross over" under the leadership of Joshua (Belshazzar/Marduk).

[33] Tyson, *Arabian Sinai*, 275-85.

mul gir.tab	*dis-ha-ra*	The Scorpion	Ishara
mul gir.tab	*dmin ti-amat*	The Scorpion	ditto Tiamat
mul gir.an.na	*mul gir.tab*	The Sword of Heaven	The Scorpion[34]

Compare, then, the subtle symbolic imagery of Josh 5:13-15: Immediately prior to the description of the attack on Jericho, Joshua sees a "man standing before him with a drawn sword"; this man says he is the commander of God's army. The preparation for Joshua's destruction of Jericho begins with an order to remove his sandals, just as his father had been told, on Sinai, forcing the imposition of Nabonidus into this pericope on a subliminal level. We are expected to be able to make this connection. I think we are also expected (as a 6th Century BCE Jewish/Babylonian audience) to see the drawn sword of a heavenly being as an astrological sign. It is reiterating the hidden meaning of the "Ascent of Akrabbim" *and* the calendrical context.

Looking at this from the perspective of the exodus narratives and how I have interpreted them in *Arabian Sinai*, we see Joshua/ Belshazzar taking on the role of Ophiuchus, tearing asunder the serpent, i.e., Nabonidus, with his hands, while his foot stamps on the head of the scorpion.[35] Considering the Babylonian heritage of the Jews who leave and live with Nabonidus is vital here, too, for the arachnid scorpion was a strongly *feminine* symbol of reproduction, being associated with the goddess Ishara, the unwed, childless goddess of … marriage and procreation,[36] just like Ishtar, with whom she is often identified. Ishtar is one of the prime avatars of Nitocris, Nabonidus'

---

[34] Ulla Koch-Westenholz, *Mesopotamian Astrology* (Copenhagen: Museum Tusculanum Press, 1995), 189.

[35] Marduk/Joshua is figuratively stamping on the very creatures who protect and assist the Sun god, i.e., the scorpion-men who protect Shamash (and in the Babylonian myth, the scorpion-men, offspring of Tiamat, are indeed conquered by Marduk). This is merely an alternative interpretation; obviously the Jewish scribes might have had an utterly different understanding of the symbolism of the constellations, but I am merely attempting to reveal the richness and depth of astronomical allusions that can potentially provide new insight for exegetes. I rather liked the scorpion/Orion rendition, mentioned earlier, and this is the widely accepted interpretation, historically.

[36] For a discussion of the scorpion in this capacity see Gavin White, *Queen of the Night: The Role of the Stars in the Creation of the Child* (London: Solaria Publications, 2014), 73-8.

wife (i.e., in the Song of Solomon); Nabonidus' second-wife, Jehudijah, is depicted as a mother/midwife figure in the exodus narratives (*Arabian Sinai*). Both died prematurely but left an indelible memory on the Jewish psyche. Nabonidus and "his women" were a nightmare they wished to forget. The fear inspired by Scorpius mirrors the fear induced in the postexilic Jews concerning women; misogyny, an adverse reaction to the liberal, sexual 'deviances' of Babylon, was rampant in the Jewish generation that fled Babylonia, and it permeates the entire HB.

HIDDEN MEANINGS

Biblical authors used numbers in a similar way to words; they used wordplay and etymology for words, and gematria for numbers.[37] Gematria is the numerical value of a letter, word, or phrase, where each letter of the Hebrew alphabet has its own specific significance. Recalling the crossing of the Jordan river on the "tenth day" and the implied schism between an Arabian/Babylonian past and a 'Canaanite' future, the letter associated with "10" is the tenth in the Hebrew alphabet, i.e., *yod*. The meaning attached is simple and apropos: It means "Jew."

> The *yud* is also the first letter in the two names for a Jew. The first name is ישראל (*Yisrael*). Jews are called *b'nei Yisrael* – the children of Israel. … The second name for a Jew is *b'nei Yaakov* – the children of Jacob.[38]

Thus, the people who wrote both Exodus and Joshua (*at the very least*) were already identifying as "Jews" (not "Hebrews" or "Israelites"). This is their signature, if you like, just as the author of the Song of Solomon

---

[37] In my analysis of the Gospel of John, I argue that the gospel author created his own 'internal' calendar that fit the various episodes within the narrative. Hours were assigned to days, which spoke of particular festivals; most did not tally with the superficial/traditional understanding but fit the historical context of each scene they appeared in. It seems this scribal technique was handed down the generations (Janet Tyson, *The Testament of Lazarus: The Pre-Christian Gospel of John* [Norwich: Pirištu Books, 2023], 33-5).

[38] Rabbi Aaron L. Raskin, "Yod: The tenth letter of the Hebrew alphabet," https://www.chabad.org/library/article_cdo/aid/137082/jewish/Yod.

left *her* signature within the text of the Song.[39] They were postexilic scribes putting a Jewish slant on the history *they* were choosing to preserve, which had been, up to the point of the crossing of Jordan, entirely Babylonian/Arabian-influenced (at least for several generations).

It is probably not coincidental, therefore, that Josh 15:30 lists three names in sequence, buried deep within a long list (another regular tactic in the HB): 1) "Eltolad," which possibly means "the children of god" (*el*, "God," and *yalad*, "to bring forth/bear"; 2) "Chesil," as above, meaning "a fool"; and 3) "Hormah," from *haram*, i.e., "to dedicate for destruction/to exterminate." Take a step back and squint, and this *might* suggest: "The children of God put an end to the old fool," i.e., the Jews finally rid themselves of Nabonidus.

CONCLUSION

The "Ascent of Akrabbim" denotes both a geographical location, probably the rising banks of the wadi between the Dead Sea and Sela (and/or the ascent to the site of Sela itself, via staircases) *and* an astronomical reference to the heliacal rising of the constellation Scorpius in September. The literary allusion is to the ultimate segregation of the Jews from Nabonidus and his pro-solar interests, at Sela, and to the continued allegiance of Nabonidus' son, Belshazzar ("Joshua") to the Jewish invasion of Canaan.

BIBLIOGRAPHY

Abarim Publications. "Chesil." https://www.abarim-publications.com /Meaning /Chesil.html.

Allen, Richard Hinckley. *Star Names: Their Lore and Meaning.* New York: Dover Publications, 1963, 1899.

Baigent, Michael. *Astrology in Ancient Mesopotamia: The Science of Omens and the Knowledge of the Heavens.* Toronto: Bear and Co., 1994.

Crowell, Bradley L. "Nabonidus, as-Sila', and the Beginning of the End of Edom." *Bulletin of the American Society of Overseas Research*

---

[39] Tyson, *She Brought*, 216-17.

(*BASOR*) 348 (2007): 75-88.

Koch-Westenholz, Ulla. *Mesopotamian Astrology*. Copenhagen: Museum Tusculanum Press, 1995.

"The Grain and Fruit Harvest Times in Israel." §The Sowing and Harvesting Times in Israel. https://bible-menorah.jimdofree.com/english /calendar-and-feasts /barley-wheat-harvest-israel/.

Muss-Arnolt, W. "The Names of the Assyro-Babylonian Months and Their Regents." *Journal of Biblical Literature* 11.2 (1892): 160-76.

Nabataea.Net. "Sela." https://nabataea.net/explore/cities_and_sites/sela-1/.

Raskin, Rabbi Aaron L. "Yod: The tenth letter of the Hebrew alphabet." https://www.chabad.org/library/article_cdo/aid/137082/jewish/Yod.

Rochberg, Francesca. "Marduk in Heaven." *Wiener Zeitschrift Für Die Kunde Des Morgenlandes* 97 (2007): 433-42.

Tyson, Janet. *Arabian Sinai: Nabonidus and the Exodus*. Norwich: Pirištu Books, 2024.

_____. *She Brought the Art of Women: A Song of Solomon, Nabonidus, and the Goddess*. Norwich: Pirištu Books, 2023.

_____. *The Testament of Lazarus: The Pre-Christian Gospel of John*. Norwich: Pirištu Books, 2023.

Weiershäuser, Frauke and J. Novotny. *The Royal Inscriptions of Amēl-Marduk (561-560 BC), Neriglissar (559-556 BC), and Nabonidus (555-539 BC), Kings of Babylon*. The Royal Inscriptions of the Neo-Babylonian Empire, Vol. 2. University Park: Eisenbrauns, 2020.

White, Gavin. *Queen of the Night: The Role of the Stars in the Creation of the Child*. London: Solaria Publications, 2014.

Wright, Jacob L. *War, Memory, and National Identity in the Hebrew Bible*. Online Publication: Cambridge University Press, 2020.

8

TWO PROFOUND NUMERICAL CODES
IN THE HEBREW BIBLE

There are numerical codes within the texts of the Hebrew Bible; they are used to preserve 'secret' information. So far I have discovered two very significant examples, i.e., one in the Song of Solomon, the other in 1 Chronicles. Together, given the thesis of my continued investigations, they suggest Solomon and Moses are versions of the same historical person, i.e., Nabonidus, King of Babylon (556-539 BCE).

Song of Solomon
(This is an extract from *She Brought the Art of Women*, which available, Open Access, online; "Jehudijah" is Nabonidus' second-wife, i.e., the 'other woman' of the Song.)

Solomon's name is used seven times in the Song (i.e., 1:1, 5; 3:7, 9, 11; 8:11, 12); this follows the pattern of 2–3–2, in that his name appears twice close together at the beginning, then three times in the middle, then twice again at the end. This is a simple code. If we consider the numerical values of the second and third letters of the Hebrew alphabet, i.e., *bet* and *gimmel*, we find something rather fascinating. The letter *bet* (gematria of 2) means house, and this is alluded to twice; *gimmel* (gematria of 3) is used once, and its meaning is nourish (until ripe), wean. Recall the focus on the mandrakes' scent in Song 7:13, which occurs very briefly, when the "fruit" is "fully ripe."

The author, therefore, inserts into the narrative two references to a house, once at the beginning, and once at the end of the narrative. Who is it that nourishes and weans the "fruit"/child until Nitocris and Nabonidus take her (when she is "ripe")? The woman of the "nut orchard," the fertile "field," the "lily" down in the valley. The letter with a gematria of 7 (i.e., 2+3+2) is *zayin*, and this means a crown. Jehudijah is, I submit, claiming to be associated with the crown, King Nabonidus; *she* is the biological mother of Ennigaldi, and she lives (as nanny) first in one of the palaces (house) in Tayma, and then in Ur (house/temple)[1] with Nitocris and the girl.

1 Chr 3:20-3
(This is an extract from *Arabian Sinai*).[2]

Just as in the Song of Solomon, where Jehudijah leaves us her signature by hinting at her specific role in the royal court via the distribution of the name "Solomon,"[3] so here, in 1 Chronicles, we are provided a potential confirmation that "Solomon" is/was "Moses." In the genealogies of the "descendants of Solomon," we find a curious numbering: In 3:20 we have the number "five," in 3:22 is "six," in 3:23 is "three," and in 3:24 is "seven." This entire genealogical list is full of mystery, which I am still working on, but these numbers are unique in such a context. They total 21. In terms of gematria, this equates to the word *'ehyeh* (in *'ehyeh 'ăšer 'ehyeh*: "I am who I am"); it *equates* to "I AM." Thus the "descendants of Solomon" ultimately equate to those who experienced, or followed, "I AM," the deity of Sinai, of Moses/Nabonidus.

Some may suggest I am seeing what I want to see in these numbers. I can only respond by saying I don't have a good enough imagination to make such a clever puzzle 'fit' the text *and* the proposed history, let alone twice. Make of it what you will. There will be further examples, I am certain.

---

[1] Ziggurats were often called "House." Clinton Briar, "Sunshine and Shadowplay: An Archaeoastronomical Study of Dūr Kurigalzu" (2019): 10, https://www.academia.edu/45577518/.

[2] Janet Tyson, *Arabian Sinai: Nabonidus and the Exodus* (Norwich: Pirištu Books, 2024), 334.

[3] Janet Tyson, *She Brought the Art of Women: A Song of Solomon, Nabonidus, and the Goddess* (Norwich: Pirištu Books, 2023), 216-17.

9

NABONIDUS, ABRAHAM, AND THE BURAQ
A CASE OF MISTAKEN IDENTITY?

A stunning horse/rider petroglyph near Tayma is reputed to be of Nabonidus, King of Babylon (556-539 BCE) astride a stallion in full gallop (*Figure 1*), yet it is not mentioned in any of the academic monographs or articles I have come across which focus on the inscriptions surrounding Tayma (or the wider Hijaz region). Is this because these

Figure 1: Author's rendition of the Tayma glyph (after photo by Richard T. Bryant, Arabian Rock Art Heritage, https://saudi-archaeology.com/horses/nabo nidus-horseman-tayma/)

scholars believe it to be a fake? *My* first response to seeing it, over five years into my Nabonidus research, was just that, i.e., "it's a fake." Only a few websites, primarily composed by tourists to the area, present images of the glyph (which has, apparently, become one of the 'bestselling' logos on merchandise in the Tayma gift shop).[1] It seems *too* anatomically detailed to fit into the overall pattern of horse petroglyphs from the region (even from Nabonidus' day) which are, almost without exception, quite primitive, even abstract.[2]

---

[1] E.g., Sheila Russell Frgs, "On The Trail Of Nabonidus In Tayma," Living Museum (20 Apr 2023), https://www.livingmuseum.com/en/deepdive histories/nabonidus.

[2] For a one-stop comparison of horse glyphs near Tayma see Sandra L. Olsen, "Arabian Rock Art Heritage," 2014, https://saudi-archaeology.com/subjects /horses/. Interestingly, Olsen's paper, "Insight on the Ancient Arabian Horse from North Arabian Petroglyphs" (*Arabian Humanities* 8 [2017], https:// www.academia.edu/60149032), does not include the glyph of the "King of Babylon" on horseback.

The associated Thamudic writing mentions "Malik Babl," i.e., "King of Babylon" but this is not in keeping with Nabonidus' known reliefs/inscriptions produced during his reign, which all refer to him by name, as (at the very least) "Nabonidus, King of Babylon," even when a third party is referring to him (rather than in the first person, as in his royal inscriptions). For instance, an inscription found (1999) in an area south-west of Tayma called Ramm bears an inscription written by someone who arrived at Tayma with Nabonidus, and there the king is given this fuller, official name.[3]

The glyph is a strongly Assyrian image, reflecting both the positioning, tack, and other details found in the reliefs discovered in the palace of King Ashurbanipal (645-635 BCE) in Nineveh by Austen Layard in 1846-7 (*Figure 2*). Note the similar 'leaping' poses;[4] the

---

[3] Hani Hayajneh, "First Evidence of Nabonidus in the Ancient North Arabian Inscriptions from the Region of Taymā'," in *Proceedings of the Seminar for Arabian Studies, Vol. 31, Papers from the thirty-fourth meeting of the Seminar for Arabian Studies held in London, 20-22 July 2000* (Archaeopress, 2001), 81-95, here 82.

[4] Just as a point of interest, from a horseperson: Until the famous 1870s photographic collection called "Animals in Motion," by Eadweard Muybridge ("Flights Of Fancy," American Museum of Natural History, Horse Exhibition https://www.amnh.org/exhibitions/horse/how-we-shaped-horses-how-horses-shaped-us/trade-and-transportati on/gaits), the galloping gait of the horse was misunderstood. Moving at such speed it was difficult to tell, but the moment at which the horse fully leaves the ground is when the feet come close to one another, not when they are the farthest apart. This latter pose is how many civilizations represented the galloping animal (they seem to be flying). In the Tayma glyph and the Assyrian reliefs, however, the horses' hind legs are together *on the ground*, not flying out behind them; there is no way any horseman, or skilled artist, would see a horse as 'galloping' like a deer (springing from the hind legs). Initially, I wondered if it was possible that these royal hunting horses were trained in a fashion much like the Royal Lipizzaner horses of Vienna, Austria, i.e., they were taught specific movements for specific battle/hunting manoeuvres. This stag-like position might well have indicated the very moment before the kill, for instance, where the rider gains a height advantage over the prey/enemy by rearing up just enough, but not too much to de-seat the rider. There is an Assyrian relief showing just this sort of attack in the Assurbanipal reliefs (see *Figure 3*). In this example, the horse and rider attacking the lion is in the leaping pose, while the horse being attacked by the lion is in the "galloping" pose, with all four legs in the air. This certainly denotes a difference in the intended meaning behind the two depictions. The

tightly braided and/or tied tails; the extended legs of the riders, indicating bareback riding; the square blankets; and the bitted bridles.[5]

Figure 2: William Boutcher (19th C) illustrations from original discovery of Assyria (BM 2007,6024.457, https://www.british museum.org/collection/object/W_2007-6024-457)

Figure 3: Horse being pursued (galloping) and horse attacking (leaping), (BM 124876, https://www.britishmuseum.org/collection/object/W_1856-0909-48_6)

---

training of Lipizzaner horses uses innate abilities and natural defensive/offensive behaviours, but exaggerated, to create specific and controlled actions for the horse in the battlefield. The foal in *Figure 4* shows this 'leaping' ability is innate; the hunting/war horses perform it on command. In both Ashurbanipal's and Ashurnasirpal's reliefs (as in the source in Note 5), this 'leaping' pose is also used for chariot horses; in each case where it is depicted (that I can see), there is an 'enemy' right in front, or just knocked down, suggesting the horse itself might have been trained to lunge like this (which is actually quite a sophisticated training goal, as horses are averse to trampling people!).

[5] For a detailed analysis of horses in Assyrian reliefs, see Stephanie Baldwin, "Bit by Bit: An Iconographic Study of Horses in the Reliefs of the Assyrian King Ashurnasirpal II (883-859 BC)," MPhil Diss. University of Stellenbosch (2013), https://www.academia.edu/88430950.

Figure 4: Foal being chased by a hunting dog showing leaping pose, while mother trots (ibid)

The Tayma horse glyph was lovingly executed, the rider was not. In fact, when you look carefully, you can see that the horse was composed first and the rider added later, as if as an afterthought, for his body is not detailed and the horses' body is nowhere hidden from view by the human form, as it would be in reality. It's almost as if two very different artists (and motivations?) were at work, here.

Its Assyrian design is nothing like the Babylonian depictions of animals. Images of horses from Babylonian reliefs, etc., are extremely difficult to find (I have yet to see one); a search online reveals several undiscerning purveyors of images who claim there is a horse on the Ishtar Gate, but there isn't (there are only lions, bulls, and the 'dragon-like' creature, "Mushhushshu," the symbol of Marduk).[6] The Babylonian animals are mostly rigid, with all four legs on the ground, either standing or walking.

The rider's only identifying feature is the hair/headwear, which is clearly Mesopotamian in style but this alone does not make it undeniably an image of Nabonidus. The vague inscription (I have not been able to find a source that translates the entire text), "King of Babylon," leaves us guessing. I therefore present an alternative potential identification for this Babylonian king galloping through the desert: It is a representation of Nebuchadnezzar II, who was in the Hijaz and fighting the Qedarites at the Battle of Dhat Irq, in December 599 BCE.[7] He did not remain in the area for long, and his name would have been unpronounceable to the locals, probably.

---

[6] Joachim Marzahn, *The Ishtar Gate: The Processional Way/The New Year Festival of Babylon* (Berlin: Verlag Philipp Von Zabern, 1995), 22.

[7] "Nebuchadnezzar," Encyclopedia of the Bible, https://www.biblegateway.com/resources/encyclopedia-of-the-bible/Nebuchadnezzar.

If it was related to a royal campaign, why is the inscription in Thamudic and not cuneiform, and why the informality regarding his title? Why is the rider lacking any other identifying details; Assyrian reliefs are very meticulous and detailed.

Studies of the horse within the Arabian Peninsula suggest that the beast was first introduced sometime in the second half of the first millennium BCE, i.e., Nabonidus' era; many horse glyphs from Tayma to al-Ula are dated to this period.[8] Ezra mentions that the Jews leaving Babylon took horses with them (Ezra 6:22).[9] In other words, a horse would have been a rare sight at this time, so only someone already familiar with horses could execute such a detailed image as the one in *Figure 1*. Even if the Arabians owned horses, why would they choose to draw one in a strikingly Assyrian style?[10]

Could this be a fake, to draw attention to Tayma, Nabonidus … and the gift shop?

Shifting tack (unexpected pun!) for a moment, if I were to attempt to substantiate the claim that this glyph *is* of Nabonidus, I might offer the following evidence.

From the Neo-Assyrian period there is a cylinder seal depicting the Sun god Shamash as a winged human figure standing on a horse, between the usual symbols for Ishtar and Sîn.[11] Intriguingly, its wings are supported by two "bull-men," just as "Moses'" arms are held up by Aaron and Hur in Exod 17:12-13.

Moses, of course, is an avatar of Nabonidus, who was originally identified as a Moon-god worshipper but, with the events at Sinai (so I

---

[8] Jérémie Schiettecatte, Abbès Zouache, "The Horse in Arabia and the Arabian Horse: Origins, Myths and Realities," *Arabian Humanities* 8 (11/09/2017): 1-34, here, 10 (¶33), https://www.academia.edu/66492033.

[9] *Cambridge Bible for Schools and Colleges* states: "Before this time we do not find mention of the use of the horse among the Israelites for peaceful purposes. Hitherto the horse had been used for war and for pomp. The considerable number here mentioned is another proof of the presence of considerable wealth. The horse was the possession of the rich and well-armed" (https://biblehub.com/commentaries /ezra/2-66.htm).

[10] There are several arguments against the horse being in Arabia before the first millennium BCE. See Schiettecatte and Zouache, "Arguments a silentio," 7-8.

[11] Jeremy Black and Anthony Green, *Gods, Demons and Symbols of Ancient Mesopotamia: An Illustrated Dictionary* (London: British Museum Press, 1992), 103, *Figure 82*.

have claimed), becomes synonymous with solar worship. This was a case of his 'vision' being misconstrued at the time, and ever since. My previous books and papers reveal how this came about, i.e., why the solar aspect became such a 'big deal' to Nabonidus, and how he chose to depict this as part of his desire to come up with a universal deity that combined Sun, Moon, and Stars.

So, looking at the horse glyph near Tayma with this in mind, it is just *possible* that someone, i.e., from Babylonia, who had come to the region on the exodus with Nabonidus and who had witnessed similar images to Ashurbanipal's reliefs (perhaps an artist in training), chose to commemorate this new 'solar aspect' of Nabonidus as him riding on a horse. While I find this enticing, I think it's a case of wishful thinking, for it raises even more questions than it answers, e.g., as well as the issue with the language, the incomplete name, and the Assyrian style, we must ask how anyone other than those involved with the Sinai events would know of this very subtle allusion. Why is there no mention of the Sun anywhere? Or Shamash's icon, to serve as a clue?

As this is the only possible rationale for this being figure *being* Nabonidus that I can think of, I am compelled to suggest that the glyph in question is from the reign of Nebuchadnezzar II, perhaps drawn by soldiers on his campaign to mark their passing through the region on the way to Mecca and the confrontation at Dhat Irq. The unspecific Thamudic identification was possibly added later or written by a 'translator' who didn't know how to write the king's long name. The only other option, I feel, is to accept it as a convenient fake.

If we do accept the image to be of Nebuchadnezzar II, by whatever machinations of fate (concerning 'why' and 'how' the image came about), there is one significant connection to Islamic tradition that might just swing the pendulum back in Nabonidus' favour, for on his route through the Hijaz from Damascus, Nebuchadnezzar would probably have travelled right through the Tayma region, it being one of the most important oases.

The Islamic legends name a certain Adnan, who was the leader of the Hijaz tribes that united against Nebuchadnezzar; this Adnan supposedly sent his son (Ma'ad ibn Adnan) to Mecca for safety but when the Babylonian king conquered Mecca, "Jeremiah and Baruch" (of HB renown) apparently took the boy to Harran.[12]

The founding of Mecca, of course, is traditionally attributed to Abraham and Ishmael, though in the legend it is Hagar and Ishmael who first stumble across the site when they flee from Sarah's home.

In effect, the horse glyph near Tayma represents 'a Babylonian king riding a horse toward Mecca' (I would like to know if the glyph faces in that direction). This tallies with the Islamic tale of Abraham riding on a swift horse (Buraq) to visit Hagar and Ishmael in Mecca:

> Sometimes Abraham visited Hagar and Ishmael in Mecca. According to some sources, he made three visits to Mecca from Palestine. Upon Allah's command, he made his first visit with Buraq (horse), under the guidance of Archangel Gabriel.[13]

The Tayma horse glyph with a king of Babylon riding bareback through the sands of the Hijaz seems to have stumbled into the world of Nabonidus accidentally. It was a strange coincidence that Nebuchadnezzar had previously come to the region of Tayma, and that someone had marked his fleeting presence, but it is a known trait of humans to jump to conclusions that suit them. I would have been thrilled for this to be the man I have been studying but I concede to the evidence, potentially to the contrary. As it turns out, it still has significance in the history of Nabonidus through its possible adoption by the earliest of Muslims, who saw in this artistic depiction their heroic and once-Babylonian forefather, Abraham ... who turns out to *be* Nabonidus.

(When Nabonidus married Nitocris II, high-priestess daughter of Pharaoh Ahmose III, as part of the 549 BCE alliance against Cyrus [between Egypt, Babylon, Sparta, and Lydia)],[14] he gained access to the riches of Egypt. This inspired his insatiable "greed" that would be deemed one of the weaknesses that brought him low in the eyes of God

---

[12] William Muir, *The Life of Mahomet*, Vol. 1 (London: Smith, Elder, & Co., 1861), Chapter 3, §4, "Origin, and early History, of Mecca," https://www. answering-islam.org/Books/Muir/Life1/section4.htm.
[13] "Prophet Abraham," June 21, 2013, LastProphet.info, https://lastprophet. info/the-prophet-muhammad-saw/prophethood/18/prophet-abraham.
[14] Janet Tyson, *She Brought the Art of Women: A Song of Solomon, Nabonidus, and the Goddess* (Norwich: Pirištu Books, 2023), 7-10.

and the Jews; "Apart from having married a Gentile … the king transgressed two other biblical laws. He kept many horses, which a Jewish king ought not to do, and, what the law holds in equal abhorrence, he amassed much silver and gold."[15] Our Tayma glyph could easily be mistaken for a representation of the horse-mad "King Solomon.")

(As a corollary to this, please see my short Note, "The Kaaba and Moses' Black Box.")

BIBLIOGRAPHY

Baldwin, Stephanie. "Bit by Bit: An Iconographic study of horses in the reliefs of the Assyrian king Ashurnasirpal II (883-859 BC)." MPhil Diss. University of Stellenbosch, 2013. https://www.academia.edu /88430950.

Black, Jeremy and Anthony Green. *Gods, Demons and Symbols of Ancient Mesopotamia: An Illustrated Dictionary*. London: British Museum Press, 1992.

Cambridge Bible for Schools and Colleges. https://biblehub.com /commentaries/ezra/2-66.htm.

Encyclopedia of the Bible. "Nebuchadnezzar." https://www.biblegateway .com/resources/encyclopedia-of-the-bible/Nebuchadnezzar.

Frgs, Sheila Russell. "On The Trail Of Nabonidus In Tayma." Living Museum. 20 Apr 2023. https://www.livingmuseum.com/en/deep divehistories/nabonidus.

Ginzberg, Louis. "The Marriage of Solomon," *Legends of the Jews* (1909), 4.5, (22), https://www.sefaria.org/Legends_of_the_ Jews.4.5.

Hayajneh, Hani. "First Evidence of Nabonidus in the Ancient North Arabian Inscriptions from the Region of Taymā'." Pages 81-95 in *Proceedings of the Seminar for Arabian Studies, Vol. 31, Papers from the thirty-fourth meeting of the Seminar for Arabian Studies held in London, 20-22 July 2000*. Archaeopress, 2001.

LastProphet.info. "Prophet Abraham." June 21, 2013. https:// lastprophet.info /the-prophet-muhammad-saw/prophethood /18/prophet-abraham.

---

[15] Louis Ginzberg, "The Marriage of Solomon," *Legends of the Jews* (1909), 4.5 (22), https://www.sefaria.org /Legends_of_the_Jews.4.5. Cf. 1 Kgs 4:26; 10:26-9.

Marzahn, Joachim. *The Ishtar Gate: The Processional Way/The New Year Festival of Babylon*. Berlin: Verlag Philipp Von Zabern, 1995.

Muir, William. *The Life of Mahomet*, Vol. 1. London: Smith, Elder, & Co., 1861. https://www.answering-islam.org/Books/Muir/Life1/section 4.htm.

Muybridge, Eadweard. "Animals in Motion," American Museum of Natural History, Horse Exhibition https://www.amnh.org/exhibitions/horse /how-we-shaped-horses-how-horses-shaped-us/trade-and-transportation/gaits.

Olsen, Sandra L. "Arabian Rock Art Heritage," 2014, https://saudi-archaeology.com/subjects/horses/.

_____. "Insight on the Ancient Arabian Horse from North Arabian Petroglyphs." *Arabian Humanities* 8 (2017):1-41. https://www.academia.edu/60149032.

Schiettecatte, Jérémie and Abbès Zouache. "The Horse in Arabia and the Arabian Horse: Origins, Myths and Realities." *Arabian Humanities*, 8 (11/09/2017): 1-34. https://www.academia.edu/ 66492033.

Tyson, Janet. *She Brought the Art of Women: A Song of Solomon, Nabonidus, and the Goddess*. Norwich: Pirištu Books, 2023.

The wind of heaven is that which blows between a horse's ears
Arabian Proverb

10

THE KAABA AND MOSES' "BLACK BOX"
NABONIDUS' 'SOLAR' ARK AND TABERNACLE
AS KAABA INSPIRATION

This Note follows on from the paper, "Nabonidus, Abraham, and the Buraq: A Case of Mistaken Identity?" but more significantly, from the discussion in *Arabian Sinai* that describes how Moses (i.e., Nabonidus) recreates the perfect conditions for the Egyptian Sun god, Re by creating the ark and the tabernacle.[1]

In a nutshell, Nabonidus, as "Moses," is on a mission to create what he sees as the will of heaven, i.e., to devise a universal theory of divinity by hybridising the Sun, Moon, and Stars; this is "I AM" (not Yahweh). Each cosmological aspect is represented by a character: Moses is the Moon, Aaron the Sun, and Miriam the Stars. Due to Nabonidus' jealous nature, he and Aaron soon fall out and Nabonidus finds himself without a solar aspect for the ritualistic 'creation' of this new deity. This is where "Joseph's bones" come in, for they represent a significant historical figure very much a part of Nabonidus' life, and it is these bones that take Aaron's place, at Sinai.

Moses/Nabonidus attempts to recreate an ancient Egyptian rite that will (symbolically) bring the bones 'back to life', i.e., as a representation of the power of the Sun god, but this can only happen when the solar aspect is hidden in darkness. The process involves treating the bones as if they belonged to Re, and the rituals on Sinai pertain to the passage of this Sun god through the darkness of the night. Once reborn, the new "Sun" remains in the darkness, to be witnessed only by Nabonidus (Moses), Joshua (Belshazzar), and their chosen assistants.

The ark, I have claimed, can be likened to a portable "glory machine" in which the fire of the Sun (literally, a burning ember used to begin the ritual ignition of the Glory/Shekinah) is carried, in total darkness, from place to place (I also claim the ark is an olfactory

---

[1] Janet Tyson, *Arabian Sinai: Nabonidus and the Exodus* (Norwich: Pirištu Books, 2024), 225-66

mechanism for combining various elements, making a hallucinogenic vapour that Moses would then inhale from between the cherubim and thereby 'talk' with God). The solar aspect is the only tangible part of "I AM."

The tabernacle, by extension, becomes a residence for "I AM" while the group camps; the solar energy is kept smouldering within, hidden by the heavy, black curtains.

The Kaaba, the large black cube around which devout Muslims walk seven times as part of the Hajj, is said to have been constructed by Abraham and his son. "The interior contains nothing but the three pillars supporting the roof and a number of suspended silver and gold lamps";[2] might these pillars have once represented the Sun, Moon, and Stars, and the lamps, the light of the Sun? (Cf. Moses erecting pillars to emulate the twelve attendants of Re.[3]) Reza Assasi suggests, on the other hand, that the Kaaba was originally a solar-influenced structure with *no roof*, i.e., "the Kaaba is located right under the celestial seat of the Sun, where it reaches the zenith right in the middle of the longest day of the year."[4] Either way, the Kaaba's roots in the worship of the Sun needs far more attention.

With respect to my previous paper, "Nabonidus, Abraham, and the Buraq," I mentioned that the Mesopotamian Sun god, Shamash, is sometimes depicted as a humanoid (with wings), standing upon a horse; this is his means of traversing the sky. If the horse/rider petroglyph near Tayma is genuine, we can begin to see how such a myth about Abraham riding to Mecca on a swift horse might be derived. Those on the same route taken by Nebuchadnezzar II (whom I claim this glyph represents),

---

[2] Britannica, "Kaaba," https://www.britannica.com/topic/Kaaba-shrine-Mecca-Saudi-Arabia.

[3] Tyson, 258-9.

[4] Reza Assasi, "Kaaba: A House Built Under the Sun," 1-5, here 3, https://www.academia.edu/41324836. Assasi also mentions the Quran passages (Surah 6:74-80) that tell of Abraham challenging those who claim to know and worship the heavens. This sounds very much like Nabonidus, whose fascination with astrology, omens, etc., led him to challenge the interpretations of the greatest of the astrologers! The exodus narratives reveal a man who clearly had his own ideas about how the heavens worked and what sort of a deity might control them. See the Verse Account of Nabonidus 5.4-6, (Livius.org, https://www.livius.org/sources/content/anet/verse-account-of-nabonidus/VA).

perhaps Muslim pilgrims on their way to Mecca, witness the rock image of the Babylonian king galloping through the desert and hear stories of the man from Tayma who brought the Jews out of Babylon and worshipped the Sun in a "black box." That man is then identified as "Abraham" (rather than "Moses") and he is linked to the Kaaba via the original "black box" at Sinai. I think this suggests the earliest Muslims were already perceiving a potential link between Moses and Abraham, i.e., Nabonidus, the man from Tayma who became an honorary Arab.

BIBLIOGRAPHY

Assasi, Reza. "Kaaba: A House Built Under the Sun." https://www .academia.edu/41324836.

Britannica. "Kaaba." https://www.britannica.com/topic/Kaaba-shrine-Mecca-Saudi-Arabia.

Livius.org. "Verse Account of Nabonidus." https://www.livius.org/sources /content/anet/verse-account-of-nabonidus/VA.

Tyson, Janet. *Arabian Sinai: Nabonidus and the Exodus*. Norwich: Pirištu Books, 2024.

11

Nabataeans, Nabonidus, and the Tribe of Dan

Nabonidus, King of Babylon (556-539 BCE) is known primarily for his chronicled absences from duties in Babylon due to his preference for residing in Tayma, Arabia, and for his worship of the lunar deity, Sîn. There were only a couple of renowned scholars writing about him until relatively recently, i.e., Raymond P. Dougherty[1] and Paul-Alain Beaulieu.[2] Today, focus is less on understanding the man and more on preserving and fine-tuning the translations of the inscriptions left in his wake, from the famous Verse Account written by the Persians after the seizure of Babylon, which ridicules and castigates him, to the lofty billboard-sized inscription at Sela, presumed to be a declaration of his conquest over Edom.[3] Emphasis is now on linguistics, with the early, more romantic appreciation for the ancient figure and his exotic world seemingly deemed outmoded and subjective. I, however, approach the subject from both angles; I am fascinated by the character the Hebrew Bible (HB) preserves, in the context of elaborate narratives, but I also find the precise language used to convey a plethora of minute details remarkably riveting.

Having assessed the Song of Solomon as an account of Nabonidus' years in Tayma, and his toxic marriage to the Egyptian high-priestess, Nitocris II, I continued the investigation into the exodus

---

[1] Raymond P. Dougherty, *Nabonidus and Belshazzar: A Study of the Closing Events of the Neo-Babylonian Empire,* 1929 repr. (Eugene: Wipf & Stock, 2008); "Nabonidus in Arabia." *Journal of the American Oriental Society* 42 (1922): 305-16.

[2] Paul-Alain Beaulieu, *The Reign of Nabonidus King of Babylon 556-539 B.C.* (New Haven: Yale University Press, 1989); "Nabonidus the Mad King: A Reconsideration of His Stelas from Harran and Babylon," Pages 137-66 in *Representations of Political Power: Case Histories from Times of Change and Dissolving Order in the Ancient Near East,* M. Heinz and M. Feldman, eds. (Winona Lake: Eisenbrauns, 2007).

[3] Megan Sauter, "The Nabonidus Inscription at Sela: Investigating a Neo-Babylonian inscription in modern Jordan," Biblical Archaeological Society, https://www.biblicalarchaeology.org/daily/the-nabonidus-inscription-at-sela/.

narratives, for I had picked up on several allusions to Moses I couldn't otherwise explain. I was stunned by the degree of sophistication and the sheer quantity of new and substantiating evidence I could glean from texts *tradition* holds were written hundreds of years before Nabonidus was born! I discovered so much more about the man, which not only followed seamlessly from the depiction of him in the Song, but also tallied with historical references, that I have now written over a million words on the subject – and counting! I may have a good imagination but I couldn't make up the etymological connections, the wordplay, the allusions; the biblical scribes were *masters* of their craft and perhaps cannot be excelled.

With a strong, convoluted but consistent rendition of Nabonidus *after* the fall of Babylon now in a workable format, for others to challenge, cite, or utterly reject, I now make a bold declaration: The 4th Century BCE Nabataeans were the descendants of Nabonidus' most loyal and local followers. They named themselves after Nabonidus, they remained in the same general area, and they are accounted for in the HB as the tribe of Dan.[4]

This is not a history of the Nabataeans, but a speculative review of the key elements of what we know about them *as these reflect the Nabonidus I have been presenting* in my books and papers. I am sure someone could use this as a springboard for a lengthier treatise. I will assume you are familiar with the basic premise of my work, i.e., that Nabonidus is depicted in the HB under several pseudonyms including "Abraham," "Moses," "Samson," and "Solomon."

AT SELA IN THE 6TH CENTURY BCE?

There are several theories for the origin of the Nabataean people, including that they were Aramaic Babylonians;[5] they were a tribe of the Nabaiat-Nabaiati, who were mentioned in texts dating to the reign of the Assyrian King Ashurbanipal (668-627 BCE); or, they were the

---

[4] This is an argument for the *rise* of the Nabataean nation; their natural evolution goes beyond the scope of this paper.

[5] Robert Wenning, "The Nabataeans in History," in *Politis, Konstantinos D. (Hrsg.): The World of the Nabataeans*, Vol. 2 of the International Conference "The World of the Herods and the Nabataeans" held at the British Museum, 17-19 April 2001, Stuttgart 2007, S. 25-44, here, 26.

descendants of Nebaioth, the firstborn son of Ishmael, in Gen 25:13.[6]

The Nabataean people, Sánchez suggests, were "probably the result of a confederation of tribes that were united by a common interest."[7] I would concur with this, as I claim their "common interest" was Nabonidus.

One of the most interesting finds concerning this argument, for me, is a fascinating, lengthy work from a Muslim linguist who states:

> Shuaib (2014) stated that the inflectional terminations detected in "Assyrian texts (*a-ti*), Biblical texts *(-ôt)*, and Jebel Ghunaym texts (*-t*) seem … to indicate the root *nby* rather than either the root *nbṭ* or *nbt*" as indicated by Eph'al (1982). Furthermore, he referred to Winnett and Reed (1970) who suggested that 'Nabayāt', **which came into view in the sixth century BCE in northern Arabia**, might have originated from "the root *nby* rather than *nbt*". Accordingly, the name Nabataean is not to be equated with the Assyrian 'Na-ba-a-a-ti' and the Biblical 'Nebaioth'.
>
> **… such a spelling of *Nbyt* in the north Arabian inscriptions, dated to the 6th century BCE ….**[8]

This potentially corroborates my dating of the "exodus" of Moses (Nabonidus) and the original crossing of the Jordan Valley at Sela; as a consequence of these events, the Nabataeans, perhaps, arose first at Sela and its immediate environment, then migrated to Petra sometime in the 4th Century BCE; "Petra in 311 BCE was not, up till that point of time, the headquarters of the tribe and definitely not the religious epicenter of the Nabataeans."[9] *Sela was* (I argue). In fact, it has been made clear by Wenning that in the account of the Nabataeans provided by Diodorus Siculus (4th Century BCE), the distance between the Dead Sea and "Petra" has been misconstrued, i.e., the journey is correctly assigned a distance of …

---

[6] Francisco del Río Sánchez, *Nabatu the Nabataeans Through Their Inscriptions* (Barcelona: Universitat de Barcelona, 2015), 24-25.

[7] Sánchez, 20.

[8] Heba M. I. M. Enein, "Glimpses into the Archaeological History of Makkah," Vol. 1, 2 (2021), here Vol. 2, 341-2, https://www.academia.edu/49274496.

[9] Enein, 350.

> 300 stades ... that is about 34 miles. The distance from the famous Petra to the Dead Sea would be about 74 miles. The distance reported in Diodorus locates the site of Khirbet es-Sela. Therefore the 'Petra' of Hieronymus and Diodorus should be identified with Khirbet es-Sela. The site also fits the description in Diodorus as a natural refuge with an easibly (*sic*) defendable ascent.[10]

It should also be remembered that in my reassessment of Sela, in terms of Nabonidus and his departure from the Jewish contingent, Sela is to be identified with both "Nebo" *and* "Pisgah," i.e., the former relating to Nabonidus' large inscription on the walls of the wadi at Sela, the latter to the geology of the site, with its 'twin peaks' and its symbolic link to Sinai.[11] Thus, "Nabatu" becomes not just a play on "Nabû-na'id" (Nabonidus), as evidenced in the inscription,[12] but also on the physical attributes of Sela that make it the Jews' 'last stand' against Nabonidus and his solar-based vision/dream.[13]

Healey concludes that the Nabataeans "are probably not to be associated with the *Nebayot/na-ba-a-a-ti/nbyt* of biblical/ Mesopotamian/Taymanite sources," and states that both "the Nabataean inscriptions and later Greek sources associate them with another tribe, the *slmw/salamu* ...."[14] Recalling the Tayma Stone, and my interpretation of the inscription as it might pertain to Nabonidus as "Salm," this is surely worth further investigation.[15]

---

[10] Wenning, 28. See Diodorus 19.95.2 and 19.98.1 (*The Library of History of Diodorus Siculus,* Vol. 10 of the Loeb Classical Library edition, 1954; https://penelope.uchicago.edu/Thayer/E/Roman /Texts/Diodorus_Siculus/19E*.html#ref80).

[11] Janet Tyson, *Arabian Sinai: Nabonidus and the Exodus* (Norwich: Pirištu Books, 2024), 173.

[12] Bradley L. Crowell, "Nabonidus, as-Sila', and the Beginning of the End of Edom," *BASOR* 348 (2007): 75-88, here 88.

[13] For this discussion see my paper, "Scorpion Rising: Nabonidus and the Ascent of Akrabbim."

[14] John F. Healey, *The Religion of the Nabataeans: A Conspectus*, Religions in the Graeco-Roman World, R. Van Den Broek, H. J. W. Drijvers, H. S. Versnel, eds., Vol. 136 (Leiden: Brill, 2001), 25.

[15] Tyson, *Arabian Sinai,* 297-301.

SUN WORSHIPPERS

There is another way of interpreting "Nabatu," based on a breakdown into Nab + atu. The former part retains its identification with Nabonidus/Nebo but the –atu suffix proves to be wonderfully apropos! Atu is an alternative rendering of Utu, the Sumerian Sun god (whose sister Ayu, otherwise known as Inanna, is the lunar crescent).[16] If you have read *She Brought*, at the very least, you will see why this is so exciting; in *Arabian Sinai*, of course, the solar worship aspect is fundamental to everything Nabonidus does in the exodus narratives. In effect, "Nabatu" becomes *something* like: the people of "Nabonidus, the Sun (worshipper)"; the ex-king's reputation for being a lunar worshipper was outshone (pun intended) by the Sinai years and the emphasis on the Egyptian solar rituals. The Nabatu were known for being Sun worshippers; according to Strabo, "They worship the sun, building an altar on top of the house, and pouring libations on it daily and burning frankincense" (16.4.26).[17]

Intriguingly, Strabo continues (*ibid*) that "They eat their meals in companies consisting of thirteen persons"; might this have been to ritually emulate Nabonidus and his "twelve" solar-related pillars (as Moses in Exod 24:4[18]) or his twelve districts (as Solomon), with the "king" as number thirteen?

IMBIBERS OR NOT?

Intriguingly, the descriptions from the two main classical sources, i.e., Diodorus and Strabo, provide contrasting assessments of the Nabataeans' attitude toward alcohol. According to Diodorus, the Nabataeans did not drink wine; this could well be a backlash from Nabonidus' over-indulgence and the negative connotations of wine as "blood"; this was something everyone seemed to want no part in after

---

[16] David Olmsted, "Mediterranean and Alphabetic Akkadian Lexicon 2nd Edition - February 2021," 23, https://www.academia.edu/45091402.

[17] Strabo, *The Geography of Strabo* published in Vol. VII of the Loeb Classical Library edition, 1932; https://penelope.uchicago.edu/Thayer/E/Roman/Texts/Strabo/16D*.html.

[18] Tyson, *Arabian Sinai*, 258-9.

the exodus years.[19] Diodorus, also suggested that the Nabataeans refrained from growing grain and fruit, i.e., from which alcohol is produced: "They follow this custom because they believe that those who possess these things are, in order to retain the use of them, easily compelled by the powerful to do their bidding" (19.94.2-6). Once you know how Nabonidus behaves in the HB, and how the Jewish authors painted him as the drunken tyrant, etc., this makes complete sense.

Strabo, on the other hand, claims that the "king holds many drinking-bouts in magnificent style, but no one drinks more than eleven cupfuls, each time using a different golden cup" (16.4.26). Did Strabo receive a slightly different rendition of the mythology surrounding the Nabataeans? Was he more aware of the true nature of their founding father, Nabonidus, and extrapolated from this description? Note how similar it is to the pericope of Dan 5:23, where the partying king is blatantly drinking out of the gold and silver goblets/vessels that were allegedly destined to be returned to Jerusalem. The "golden cup" is a matter of discussion in the assessment of the Song of Solomon; it relates to the occult rite of imbibing the Elixir Rubeus.[20]

There was clearly a focus on the notion of imbibing but it is still without consensus; it was, I posit, either a reaction *against* Nabonidus' influence, or a practice inspired *by* it. Perhaps both situations existed but at different times, e.g., the first generations adhered to what they remembered of the man himself but subsequent generations, growing farther away from those memories, rebelled and became more austere and, maybe influenced by the Jews themselves, came to consider this aspect of Nabonidus' legacy reprehensible. Abstinence became the byword and one of the fundamental features of *their* 'new' religion.

(For a few thoughts on the notion of eleven vs. twelve tribes, please see the Postscript, below.)

---

[19] The chief deity of the later Nabataeans was Dhū Sharā, described as he " 'who drinks no wine, who builds no home,' the patron of the nomads" ("Pre-Islamic Deities," https://www .britannica.com/topic/Arabian-religion/Pre-Islamic-deities).

[20] Janet Tyson, *She Brought the Art of Women: A Song of Solomon, Nabonidus, and the Goddess* (Norwich: Pirištu Books, 2023), 30-4. It is the golden cup of "abominations" in Rev 17:3-5.

TRADERS/LANDOWNERS

As we saw in the analysis of "Moses," Nabonidus seems to return to Tayma with the sole agendum of building a lucrative trading empire, now that the local (Arabian) economy was shifting from its land-based trading routes to those on the Red Sea and Nile. Pharaoh Ahmose III, Nabonidus' father-in-law, had reinstated the ancient Punt expeditions and Nabonidus (with his friend Hiram III) was probably one of the first, along with his son Belshazzar, to make the most of this difficult but profitable market. As "Abraham," Nabonidus travelled through the Levant, a train of camels following him, all laden with "goods" destined not for a struggling Jerusalem, but for his own coffers back in the Hijaz. As "Solomon," he owned the fleet of ships at Ezion-geber, on the eastern shore of the Red Sea (i.e., at al-Wajh) that would take vast loads of luxurious items from Punt, on the coast of Nubia/Eritrea, up into the Nile Delta, to Naukratis, for export via Thonis-Heracleion.[21]

We learn that the Nabataeans were also strongly focussed on international trade; Diodorus wrote of the Nabataeans (or Nabataei) that they exploited the bitumen eruptions in the Dead Sea (when others had steered clear, due to its stench and detrimental effects on human health) and the unique, indigenous balsam, which they sold to apothecaries.[22] He also claimed they were "fond of accumulating property," and considered a lack of the drive to do so reprehensible.[23]

Nabataean territory was vast, like the Qedarites' before them, stretching from southern Syria right down to Tayma and the Red Sea.[24] This is, basically, the territory of "Solomon" (cf. 1 Kgs 4:21) and a great part of the Neo-Babylonian Empire. Abraham's formal land purchase (Genesis 23), in the context of a burial site for Sarah, demonstrates Nabonidus' desire to legitimize his *post-royal* presence in the region; the legal specifics of the account, though the arrangement was made between friends, shows us that this was a vital aspect of Nabonidus' Levantine and Arabian business interests.[25]

---

[21] See my paper "Nabonidus, Tarshish, and Ophir."

[22] George Livingston Robinson, *The Sarcophagus of an Ancient Civilization; Petra, Edom and the Edomites* (New York: Macmillan, 1930), 465.

[23] Robinson, 473.

[24] Sánchez, 20.

[25] Tyson, *Arabian Sinai*, 75-81.

WATER EXPERTS

The English word Nabataean comes from *Nabatu* – a term which frequently appears in the inscriptions and seems to be related to the concept of "irrigation, watering, channelling water."[26]

This is not an understanding that has any reliance on the etymology of "Nabatu" but from the inherited perception of the Nabataeans from ancient writers. For instance, Diodorus writes:

> … whenever a strong force of enemies comes near, they take refuge in the desert, using this as a fortress; for it lacks water and cannot be crossed by others, but to them alone, since they have prepared subterranean reservoirs lined with stucco, it furnishes safety. As the earth in some places is clayey and in others is of soft stone, they make great excavations in it, the mouths of which they make very small, but by constantly increasing the width as they dig deeper, they finally make them of such size that each side has a length of one plethrum. After filling these reservoirs with rain water, they close the openings, making them even with the rest of the ground, and they leave signs that are known to themselves but are unrecognizable by others (19.6-8).

While I clearly have an alternative understanding of the name "Nabatu," this perception of the Nabataeans does bring to mind the scenario in Herodotus of Cambyses having to ask for assistance from the "king of the Arabs" to get through the desert from Gaza to Egypt (*Hist.* 3.1.8-9). In *Arabian Sinai* I suggest that Nabonidus might well have been this particular "king of the Arabs" at that time,[27] i.e., the "Arabs" in question being his own (nomadic) supporters who then dominated the corridor territory between Edom and the Mediterranean. The Nabatu, I suggest, in their *earliest* phase, perhaps even before they identified themselves as such, might well have been these water-savvy Bedouin who guided Cambyses to the watering holes.

In *Arabian Sinai*, I discuss Doughty's 19th Century journey through this region, and how he witnessed for himself the secrecy

---

[26] Sánchez, 21.

[27] Tyson, *Arabian Sinai*, 96-7.

amongst the nomads not only concerning the location of water sources but also the landmarks (i.e., rocks) used to locate them.[28]

ROCK DWELLERS

> There is also in the land of the Nabataeans **a rock** (*petra*), which is exceedingly strong since it has but **one approach**, and using this **ascent** they mount it a few at a time and thus store their possessions in safety (Diodorus, 2.48.6).

> But when the time draws near for the national gathering at which those who dwell round about are accustomed to meet, some to sell goods and others to purchase things that are needful to them, they travel to this meeting, leaving on **a certain rock**their possessions and their old men, also their women and their children. This place is exceedingly strong but unwalled, and it is distant two days' journey from the settled country (Diodorus, 19.95.1-22).

The "rock" (i.e., *petra* in Greek, not emphatically the location we now call Petra) with one "approach," i.e., ascent, is most likely Sela.[29] Robinson quotes this passage from Diodorus but adds that the access point was "made by hand"[30]; this must allude to the stairs carved in the rock.

Obviously, Moses and "rocks" go together. There is the rock in the desert where he sits to watch Joshua and Amalek battle; the "split rock" near Tayma he names; the rock he strikes to procure its "water" ("Miriam's Well"); the "Way to Shur" is the "Way to the Rock"; Sinai is a "rock" (mesa); as is God himself (Deut 32:4 and many of the Psalms); and there are the toponyms "Sela" (Hebrew) and "Petra" (Greek), both translated as "Rock."

After the initial phase at Sela, perhaps after the first couple of generations, the population must have begun to outgrow the facilities there, and the group spread out into the surrounding territory, making their indelible mark on the other rocks, which became their legacy.

---

[28] Charles M. Doughty, *Travels in Arabia Deserta* (New York: Random House, 1921). Tyson, *Arabian Sinai*, 162.

[29] See my paper "Scorpion Rising: Nabonidus and the Ascent of Akrabbim."

[30] Robinson, 169.

Influenced by Hellenistic and Roman architecture, they created palatial tombs in the desert, a sign of their affluence and self-aggrandisement, something they would have learned from Nabonidus!

PIRATES/SEA MERCHANTS

The Nabataeans had an early reputation for piracy on the Red Sea, which might be attributable to the 'less than honourable' behaviour not only tolerated but positively encouraged by Nabonidus, e.g., as both "Abraham" *and* "Moses," Nabonidus presses his followers to steal silver and gold from first the Babylonians, and then the Egyptians. As their trading acumen and scope increased, however, the Nabataeans became legitimate merchants with two major ports on the Red Sea, i.e., one at the tip of the Gulf of Aqaba, at Aila, which is *conventionally* considered to be the location of Solomon's "Ezion-geber," and the other, more significant port, at Leuke Kome (White Village).[31] Leuke Kome is now called al-Wajh ("Laban" in Deut 1:1), and this is where I have claimed Ezion-geber *really* was.[32] Al-Wajh was Nabonidus' (Solomon's) port on the Red Sea; it was the site to which he and his contingent of followers headed for after escaping Egypt (with the bones of "Joseph"), having taken small boats from Aila, or another port in the vicinity.[33]

It seems a natural progression, from being (potentially) Nabonidus' supporters at Sela, to being, perhaps, sailors in his fleet of Tarshish boats; over the years their dominance in the region grew, until they took over Nabonidus' main trading hubs and routes. Diodorus suggests "the Nabataeans far surpass the others in wealth" (19.94.4); Nabonidus would have been proud!

AND THEN THERE WAS DAN …

The tribe of Dan is an anomaly.

✸ The account of Dan and its allotted lands in Josh 19:47 suggests that

---

[31] Zaraza Friedman, "Did Nabatean Seafaring Exist?" *Michmanim* 25 (2014): 23-30, here 26-7, https://www.academia.edu/10783439. Strabo, 16.4.23.

[32] Tyson, *Arabian Sinai*, 130-5.

[33] Tyson, *Arabian Sinai*, *Fig. 11*, 138.

they were provided territory close to the coast of the Mediterranean, i.e., "opposite Joppa"; Joppa was a port well-documented by the 15th Century BCE (Thutmose III is reported to have captured it, so it is one of the few *confirmed* locations of the Bible).[34] This, presumably, was due to their association with "boats," made so evident in Judg 5:17: "… and Dan, why did he abide with the ships?"[35]

This quotation was actually the first thing to catch my eye in this attempt to tally the Nabataeans with a group of people connected with Nabonidus. The Nabatu began as pirates, recall, then became seasoned merchants utilizing Nabonidus' old port and trade routes on the Red Sea. In *Arabian Sinai*, I posit the idea that Belshazzar, Nabonidus' son (who is depicted in part as "Joshua"), continued to assist the Jews in conquering lands in Canaan before heading back to reside at Tayma, with his father; the two built a lucrative trading business based at Eziongeber. It is plausible that he assigned this section of Canaan to "Dan" for the sole purpose of ensuring a capable (and loyal) faction might take control of Joppa, which could later serve as a key link in Nabonidus' trading empire (i.e., he was already partnering with Hiram III of Tyre, farther along the coastline, so this would seem the perfect halfway point).[36]

The story continues with Dan losing Joppa (to the Philistines) and subsequently conquering a place called "Laish"/"Leshem," which they renamed "Dan" after their (founding) father. "Laish" means "Lion," from the noun *layish*. "Dan" means "Judge" or "Governor," from the verb *din*, "to judge or govern." The tribe of Dan is heralded as a "lion's whelp" in Moses' blessings, according to Deut 33:22, even though Gen 49:9 declares *Judah* as such; recall that Genesis is a later document, pushing the new, elitist Judaite agendum. This is but one of many, many aspects assimilated from the Nabonidus/Belshazzar/ Arabian context of the exodus narratives into the early Jewish perspective.

---

[34] Petrie Flinders, ed., *Egyptian Tales Translated from the Papyri.* Second Series, 18th to 19th Dynasty (New York: Frederick A. Stokes, 1913, 1899), § "The Taking of Joppa," https://pages.ucsd.edu/~dkjordan/arch/egypt/Petrie /PetrieTale7.html#joppa.

[35] Cf. Ezek 27;19, which links Dan with Javan in the context of trade with Tyre by sea.

[36] For a brief reassessment of the tale of Solomon receiving cedar wood from the Lebanon via Joppa (2 Chr 2:16), see "Nabonidus, Tarshish, and Ophir," 43-5.

In this current context, this suggests that Laish is a commission name, i.e., an invented toponym that serves a purpose in the narrative (it may or may not have been a physical location); that purpose being to represent Nabonidus as a figurehead. I have claimed that the attack on Jericho was Joshua's ultimate test of loyalty to the Israelites; it was a symbolic conquest over his father's tyranny.[37] The razing of Laish is a similar situation; if Laish is the "lion," and Dan is the "lion's whelp," this corresponds to the former representing Nabonidus, and the latter his son, Belshazzar/Joshua. The tribe of Dan one might suggest therefore, is strongly associated with Nabonidus via his son.

✦ Joshua (Belshazzar) was allotted Timnath-serah, in Ephraim (Josh 19:50); this was a 'gift' from the Israelites as payment for services rendered. Thus, Belshazzar *also* owned land in the Levant, i.e., near Shechem, in Ephraimite territory; this is why he is said (retrospectively) to hail from the tribe of Ephraim, in Num 13:8. The name "Timnath-serah" means "extra portion," from *mana*, "to count or assign," and *serah*, "excess." That is, Joshua was *not* from one of the Israelite tribes, originally; his portion was "extra." This is probably the reason why Revelations 7 does not mention Dan.

This link to Timnath-serah has a deeper level of meaning, for according to Josh 24:30, it becomes Joshua's burial site. As I have argued before, the HB's treatment of the deaths (and ages) of the main characters, such as Moses, Aaron, Joshua, and even Miriam is one of manipulation and concealment by the authors. Certain information was considered to be on a 'need to know' basis and was therefore encoded into the etymology of names, and/or hidden in the gematria of words or phrases. This is a case in point, for "Timnath-serah" changes to "Timnath-heres" in Judg 2:9, and this name means "portion of the Sun"! (Note how "heres" is a virtual anagram of "serah.")

In the exodus narratives "Joseph's bones" are a tangible relic of Pharaoh Ahmose III, Nabonidus' father-in-law. He represents the solar aspect of "I AM."[38] Therefore, we have Belshazzar, son of Nabonidus, being "buried" (according to the HB authors, when historically, he

---

[37] Tyson, *Arabian Sinai*, 387-9.
[38] Tyson, *Arabian Sinai*, 228.

seems to have gone back to Tayma[39]) in the same region that "Joseph's bones" ("the Sun") were interred (Josh 24:32), i.e., in the place called "Portion of the Sun."

Shechem, recall, was the very first place Abraham (Nabonidus) set up an altar at the tree of Moreh (Gen 12:6-8); to the later Jewish mind, this was hostile territory, i.e., Samaria. The authors of Joshua thus reject "Joseph's bones" and *symbolically* send them to the heathen high places of the north, befitting their opinion of the much maligned Egyptian element in early Judaism. It would appear they do the same with the 'remains' of Joshua; I have also previously shown how the Jewish perception of Belshazzar shifted after his return to Tayma,[40] further substantiating this idea of an ultimate rejection of Nabonidus' son, despite what he did for them.

✡ Just as a point of interest, when Joshua made this announcement,

"Sun, stand still at Gibeon,
And Moon, in the valley of Aijalon."
And the Sun stood still, and the
Moon stopped,
Until the nation took vengeance on their enemies.
Josh 10:12-13

he did so (allegedly) on the day he conquered the Amorites, whose territory boundary sat at Sela (Judg 1:36); this is probably the launching site of the attack. The name "Gibeon" means "hill" (from the noun *gibeah*, "hill"); Sela is a hill but as the mirror of Sinai[41] it is also a solar site, so it is the Sun that is told to stop here. To me, this is a declaration that Nabonidus' solar religion is to stop from this point onward (and these are words written by the authors of Joshua, for impact, i.e., to serve as a statement from the Jews, placed on the lips of their once hero).

―――――――――――――――

[39] This is a topic I won't go into again here, as it permeates *Arabian Sinai*. Abraham's, Moses', and Aaron's deaths are also treated in this dual manner, with hidden allusions to what 'really happened' deep within the text. Miriam's death also has a highly symbolic element.

[40] Tyson, *Arabian Sinai*, 306-8; see also my paper "Shishak and Rehoboam in a Nabonidus-based Paradigm."

[41] Tyson, *Arabian Sinai*, 171-4.

On the other hand, the name "Aijalon" means "protrude" from the noun *ayil*. This term is strongly linked to "Elim" and "Eloth," via the same noun; Elim is Tayma, and Eloth is the point just below Ezion-geber (on the Red Sea).[42] Around Tayma is the Wilderness of Sîn, and the town becomes synonymous with Nabonidus' long-term dedication to the lunar deity, so it is apt that the Moon be ordered to stop there. The 'miracle' lasted as long as long as it took the Jews to defeat "their enemies," suggesting that Joshua (Belshazzar) seized control of his father's 'divinely inspired power' (over the heavens, i.e., another aspect of Nabonidus' personality that is demonstrated even before he left Babylon[43]), for as long as it took him to secure the Jews' new territory. (The phrasing of Josh 10:12-13 also hints at a future end to Belshazzar's dealings with the Jews, for once the land is conquered, he goes back to Tayma; there he returns to his own inherited ways and is no longer deemed such a role model in the Jewish collective mind.)

Combined, what we are seeing in this potent verse is a confirmation that everything Moses (Nabonidus) had done, i.e., imposing his own conflation of the Sun, Moon, and Stars on the Jews, was now deemed null and void … thwarted by the hand of his own son.[44] This, in turn, plays on the Nile scenes in Exodus 7, where Moses was basically being 'set up' by the scribes, to be his own foil in the narrative; the entire scenario of the "bloody water" is a fabricated 'in-joke', to suggest Moses' (Nabonidus') Egyptian-influenced aberrations will (i.e., as a 'prediction' in hindsight) be for nought.[45] At Sela, with Joshua's alleged announcement, Exodus 7 comes full circle.

★ It should come as no surprise that one of the avatars of Nabonidus in the HB is Samson, identified as a Danite in Judges 13.[46] "Samson" means "man of the Sun," from *shemesh*, "sun." Judg 13:25 reads: "The

---

[42] Tyson, *Arabian Sinai*, 136 (Eloth); 146-7 (Elim).

[43] Tyson, *She Brought*, 1-7, et al.

[44] This should be seen in light of Joshua's battle with Amalek (Exod 17:8:13), where he takes on the challenge of 'defeating'/nullifying Nabonidus' unsavoury past (see *Arabian Sinai*, 176-181), and his involvement in the "Eldad and Medad" incident (pp. 183-4). Each scenario is one of Belshazzar doing a bit of damage-limitation on behalf of his father.

[45] Tyson, *Arabian Sinai*, 120-2.

[46] Tyson, *She Brought*, 18-20.

spirit of the Lord began to stir him in Mahaneh-dan," and this is exciting because "Mahaneh" means "camp" (from *mahaneh*, "camp"); "Mahaneh-dan" therefore means "camp of the governor/judge." Now *mahaneh* is also used in the Song of Solomon (Song 6:13), where the Egyptian emissaries begin their taunting 'praise' of Nitocris (Nabonidus' Egyptian wife) and she questions their motives; she refers to the "dance before two armies (Mahanaim)" but this is actually a reference to Jacob's dichotomy in Genesis 32.[47] The point is that Judges is purposefully signalling that we need to remember this term in the Song; it means that "Mahaneh-dan" is being used as a commission name for Tayma, where the Song's narrative actually takes place. Tayma was, indeed, the 'camp of the governor', Nabonidus (and Belshazzar). This is where Nabonidus has his religious vision to create a hybrid deity.

Mahaneh-dan is situated, we are told, between two other locations, i.e., Zorah and Eshtaol (Judg 13:25). "Zorah" means "leprous," from *tsara*, "to become leprous." This pertains to the pericope of Miriam's punishment with "leprosy" in Hazeroth, a pseudonym for a region near Tayma,[48] in Num 12:10-15. "Eshtaol" means "to ask, enquire," from *shaal* ("to ask, enquire"). Although this verb is used several times in the exodus narratives, the most germane example I can find is in Exod 18:7, where Moses and Jethro meet in the wilderness surrounding Sinai (Paran); "each asked after the other's welfare." So this leaves us with Mahaneh-dan, i.e., Tayma, sitting between the place where Miriam was excluded from the camp, which I have claimed is *south* of Tayma, and the place where Moses meets Jethro, near Sinai, further *north*. The location for Tayma (as Mahaneh-dan) is vague but correct, i.e., sitting between the two other sites.

As a point of interest, the Brown-Driver-Briggs Hebrew and English Lexicon states: "… in form like the infinitive of the Arabic VIII. conjugation from שָׁאַל: so אֶשְׁתְּמֹעַ from שָׁמַע. Perhaps Arabic-speaking tribes may have settled in parts of south of Judah …."[49] It wasn't "Arabic speaking tribes" in Judah, but Hebrew-speaking tribes in Arabia!

---

[47] Tyson, *She Brought*, 164-5.

[48] Tyson, *Arabian Sinai*, 210-14.

[49] Brown-Driver-Briggs Hebrew and English Lexicon, "847. Eshta'ol," Unabridged, Electronic Database. 2006, https://biblehub.com/hebrew/847.htm.

So, when Gen 49:16 declares, "Dan shall judge his people, as one of the tribes of Israel," this is a statement that the tribe of Dan is given an honorary place amongst the tribes of Israel, just as Pharaoh Ahmose III was given an honorary place in the history of Judaism—because both served as agents of God in releasing the Jews from the bondage of Babylon and bringing them 'home'. Joshua, or rather Belshazzar, in the early days at least, was a hero but because of his rejection of this honour, and his insistence on returning to be with his reprobate father, they had to, in the end, ostracise him … along with the Sun of Nabonidus' creation.

✸ The Danites were always deemed a negative force, i.e., they were "idolaters." In Judges 18, after naming Laish "Dan," they erected their idols and who should become their priests? The descendants of Moses (i.e., Nabonidus, as opposed to Aaron, which, once you read *Arabian Sinai*, will seem so fitting)![50]

In the *Legends of the Jews*, we read:

> The tribe of Dan had already at the time of the exodus from Egypt been possessed of the sinful thought to fashion an idol. To counteract this "dark thought" Asher was made its comrade, from whose soil came "the oil for lighting"; and that Dan might participate in the blessing, Naphtali, "full with the blessing of

---

[50] I have reiterated often that I argue for a wholly exilic/postexilic HB, meaning that nothing was written before the Babylonian exile. References to anything previous is simply the embellishment of a vague oral history for a new narrative, or pure (but remarkably clever) invention. Names such as "Ishmaelites" and "Danites" become part of the narrative only with hindsight and changing perspectives. At the *time* of these recorded events, such names did not exist. Thus, to say that the priestly line of "Jonathan son of Gershom" served Dan "until the time the land went into captivity" is a manipulation of the 'truth' to suit a retrospective tale. In effect, it makes Dan wicked from the time 'before Jewish history'; they were a "mixed crowd" of unsavoury characters (as judged by the Jews) who supported and followed Nabonidus and Belshazzar, so they 'must' have been evil from distant days! The "house of God" was not at Shiloh until the ark went there; the ark was made at Sinai. Sinai *did not* predate the "captivity."

the Lord," became its second companion.[51]

In other words, Asher's role was to counter, or negate, the detrimental influence of Dan.

Ginzberg goes on to suggest that Dan held the position of the Northern standard bearer as an allusion to its "dark" and sinful ways. Recalling the concept of "North" in the exodus narratives, which was part of the analysis of Baal-zephon in *Arabian Sinai*,[52] the intimation may be that Dan is again associated with Nabonidus' escapades in the 'North', i.e., his dealings with Hiram, his associations with Pharaoh, etc.

Legends describes how the standards had above them certain letters from the names of Abraham, Isaac, and Jacob. In the case of the standard of Dan, the letters were: *mem* for Abraham, *kof* for Isaac, and *bet* for Jacob.[53] These are the *final* letters, just like Joshua's allotment was an "extra portion," a last thought, etc. In gematria terms, this proves interesting:[54] *Mem* stands for 40 and means "water" and/or "womb"; it denotes metamorphosis. One thinks of the forty years with Moses, the forty days and nights on Sinai, etc. *Kof* stands for 100 and means "monkey"; it is a significant letter/number in the ages provided in the HB, and is associated with the dealings of Solomon.[55] It suggests death, falsehood, and impurity. *Bet* is 2 and means "house/home"; this is one of the signature elements of Jehudijah in the Song of Solomon. It alludes either to the ex-king's home, i.e., Tayma, or to Nabonidus' second-wife and the mother of his children.

The sum of these letters is 142; in gematria this has two potential associations that suit our anti-Nabonidus-based interpretation of the HB.[56] One is the name "Balak," from *balaq,* "to lay waste, devastate" (Numbers 22-3. i.e., possibly a later insertion). There are reasons to delve deeper into this long and convoluted pericope with Balaam and Barak and the cursing of Israel, especially as there may be a link to Jehudijah (as "Zippor," i.e., one of her avatars, recall, is "Zipporah"),

---

[51] Louis Ginzberg, *The Legends of the Jews* (1909), 3.4.15, https://www. sefaria.org.

[52] Tyson, *Arabian Sinai*, 49-51.

[53] Ginzberg, 3.4.45.

[54] The letter meanings taken from Rabbi Aaron L. Raskin, Letters of Light: The Meaning of the Hebrew Alphabet, www.chabad.org.

[55] Tyson, *Arabian Sinai*, 76; 370.

[56] From Bill Heidrick, Hebrew Gematria, #142, www.billheidrick.com.

but this is not the place for that discussion. Just the insinuation of "waste/devastation" however, via 142, is enough to suspect this association is intended; Nabonidus, the forty years, the Sinai 'fiasco'— it was all waste and devastation for *many*.

The other is *beliyyaal*, meaning "worthlessness." In several etymological analyses this notion of "worthlessness" comes up, e.g., it is a factor in the understanding of the names "Elim" and "Eloth" (Tayma and the location of Ezion-geber[57]) and in the Song of Solomon's curse on Nabonidus' name (by Jehudijah[58]). It is a consistent (negative) identifier of Nabonidus in the HB narratives.

A third word with gematria of 142, though appearing only once in 2 Sam 23:25, is the name "Elika," meaning "God vomits out," or "God loathes," from *el*, God, and the noun *qe'*, "vomit."

One might suggest, therefore, that the number 142 in the HB is decidedly negative.

✦ A fascinating little comment from the *Legends* plays on the notion of inversion as a sign of evil, i.e., something I discuss in the analysis of Song 5:10-16[59]; anything reversed, upside down, etc., invokes a negative response and denotes chaos, witchcraft, doom, etc.

> Dan's stone was a species of topaz, in which was visible the inverted face of a man, for the Danites were sinful, turning good to evil, hence the inverted face in their stone.[60]

✦ Furthermore, the tribe of Dan had as its emblem a snake.[61] This could not be any more apropos, as I demonstrate in *Arabian Sinai*, the snake is perhaps the most significant symbol for Nabonidus' Sinai experience.[62] The snake is not merely to be understood in terms of the Nehushtan, the brazen serpent on a stick; it becomes the sole identifying symbol for "I AM" (Nabonidus' hybrid deity), and is etched

---

[57] Tyson, *Arabian Sinai*, 136; 146..
[58] Tyson, *She Brought*, 50.
[59] Tyson, *She Brought*, 143-4; 166 f.
[60] Ginzberg, 3.3.43.
[61] Ginzberg, 3.4.35
[62] See Tyson, *Arabian Sinai*, 275-85 and 302-6.

into the Nabonidus rock reliefs/inscriptions in the very area the Nabataeans dominated. I have argued that these serpents were added at a later date than the royal inscriptions, as they appear slightly off-kilter, as if someone deemed the emblems of the trinity of Sîn, Shamash, and Ishtar (the deities appearing on Nabonidus' inscriptions) no longer apt, or 'enough', as the Sinai years had changed everything. Is it possible that the Nabatu (aka "Dan"), i.e., the mysterious, reclusive, pro-Nabonidus clan that hid amongst the rocks of the desert were the ones responsible for etching the snake onto Nabonidus' old reliefs? It was *their* symbol; they laid claim to the heritage *and* the sites.

> *Dan shall be a snake by the roadside, a viper along the path,*
> *that bites the horse's heels so that its rider falls backward*
> Gen 49:16-17

✻ 1 Kgs 12:26-30 tells of the rivalry between Rehoboam and Jeroboam.[63] Rehoboam is Solomon's son; Solomon is Nabonidus, so Rehoboam is Belshazzar.[64] The name "Rehoboam" means something like "a widespread people"; it is derived from the verb *rahab*, "to be or become large or wide," and the noun *am*, "people." Dan was supposedly the second-largest group after Judah, and in Jewish lore they refused to fight with Judah when the ten northern tribes broke away, choosing instead to go into exile.[65] Strabo mentions several times that the Nabataeans were a peaceful people (e.g., 16.4.18, 21, 26), clearly choosing isolation in the desert, rather than living in populated areas, keeping a small standing army, basically for emergencies. Similarly, Diodorus says, "whenever a strong force of enemies comes near, they take refuge in the desert, using this as a fortress; for it lacks water and cannot be crossed by others, but to them alone …" (19.94.2; cf. 96.2 and 97.4).

So, I suggest that "Dan" slipped quietly into the crags and crevices of the same desert rocks we now consider Nabataean territory.

---

[63] Dan is singled out as the only tribe to accept the idols of Jeroboam (Ginzberg, 3.4.33).

[64] See my paper, "Shishak and Rehoboam in a Nabonidus-based Paradigm."

[65] "A Few Notes on Dan," Hebrew Nations, https://hebrewnations.com. According to this account, Dan ended up in Cilicia (southeast Turkey), Anatolia, Libya, Greece, Cyprus, Crete, Scandinavia, Britain, and Ireland.

Consisting primarily of those who originally supported Nabonidus and his son, who were commissioned with protecting the Levant's major port (albeit unsuccessfully) and thus access for the traded goods coming to and fro from Egypt and Tyre, these were the sea-faring proto-Nabatu. Others, naturally, had their own reasons to go farther afield and assimilate into other societies.

✦ Another quotation from Strabo, concerning the Nabataeans, caught my eye:

> One woman is also wife for all; and he who first enters the house before any other has intercourse with her, having first placed his staff before the door, for by custom each man must carry a staff; but she spends the night with the eldest. And therefore all children are brothers. They also have intercourse with their mothers; and the penalty for an adulterer is death; but only the person from another family is an adulterer (16.4.25).

Nabonidus and his staff, the most vivid aspect of Moses/Aaron iconography, seem to have left an impression on the Nabataeans; this is the way he is depicted in the numerous rock reliefs in the region; that every man carries one is an echo of Num 17:1-3, where the leaders of each tribe are to have an identifying staff.

The attitude toward women mirrors that of Nabonidus/Moses (and even Abraham), in that they are sexually subservient (nothing new there), but note that they also sleep with their mothers; is this a rumour arising from the Jewish Ashmedai myth and its attempted rationale for the alleged deviances of Solomon at court? In *She Brought*, I explain that this myth of the King of the Demons was devised to explain why Nabonidus (Solomon) behaved as he did whilst living at Tayma, i.e., while he was under the 'spell' of Nitocris and her Elixir Rubeus.[66] In this deranged state, it was said, the king demanded that menstruating women … and even his mother … were to be brought to him (for sex). The Nabatu would not be the only ones to base their practices (especially in terms of liturgy) on the lives of Nabonidus and Nitocris.[67]

---

[66] Tyson, *She Brought*, 28-9.
[67] Tyson, *She Brought*, 32.

✷ Alternative Danite emblems include the eagle, dragon, or griffin.[68] Nabonidus was renowned for creating huge guardian statues for his temples in Babylonia; following Esarhaddon's and Ashurbanipal's example, he "installed copper(-plated) statues of *mušḫuššu*-dragons as gateway guardians ...."[69] In the Persian Verse Account (i 6-7). Nabonidus is said to have erected statues of the Anzu bird, i.e., the "Storm Dragon," a hybrid, griffin-like creature. The eagle is potentially alluded to in "Baal-zephon" and Nabonidus' relationship with Hiram of Tyre.[70]

✷ In my paper on the "Ascent of Akrabbim" I posit that this toponym, identified with the approach to Sela, is largely astronomical, and that it pertains to the constellation Scorpius.[71] The chief star in Scorpius, i.e., Antares, which the Egyptians identified with Isis, became another symbol of the tribe of Dan. In astrological lore from Mesopotamia, Antares was known as "the Lusty King"[72]—perfectly fitting to allude to the Nabonidus the early Jews knew!

CONCLUDING COMMENTS

The Nabataeans derived from the earliest and closest followers of Nabonidus (as "Moses"). They were probably comprised of Arabian locals, the offspring of those who stayed with Nabonidus on the longer sojourn to Tayma and chose not to become part of the new Jewish society, and friends and family who joined him when he left Harran.[73]

---

[68] "A Few Notes on Dan," Hebrew Nations, https://hebrewnations.com.

[69] Frauke Weiershäuser and J. Novotny. *The Royal Inscriptions of Amēl-Marduk (561–560 BC), Neriglissar (559-556 BC), and Nabonidus (555–539 BC), Kings of Babylon,* The Royal Inscriptions of the Neo-Babylonian Empire, Vol. 2 (University Park: Eisenbrauns, 2020), 11, n. 88.

[70] Tyson, *Arabian Sinai,* 51-5; 59; 66.

[71] Janet Tyson, "Scorpion Rising: Nabonidus and the Ascent of Akrabbim."

[72] William Tyler Olcott, *Star Lore of All Ages: A Collection of Myths, Legends, and Facts Concerning the Constellations of the Northern Hemisphere* (New York: Putnam's/Knickerbocker Press, 1911), 329.

[73] Interestingly, there is a latter-day tribe in Arabia called "the Slayb," which became the focus of study of a certain 19th Century explorer residing in Arabia, Colonel Lewis Pelly; they claimed descent from the 'original Arabs'

(I have often wondered if the "Samaritans" derived from one of these pro-Nabonidus groups, rejected by the Jews who remained in Canaan, i.e., because they were not 'of the faith' and swore allegiance to "Moses" (Nabonidus) and "Joshua" (Belshazzar), who had strong connections with Shechem.)

As demonstrated, there are several levels of comparison between the Nabataeans and what has been discovered about Nabonidus and Belshazzar by reassessing the HB in terms of etymology, gematria, and symbolism. One or two potential allusions would pass as intriguing but would be dismissed as coincidence; here, we have seen eight distinct areas of potential connection, and eleven possible links just to the tribe of Dan.

Without the context of Nabonidus and the Babylonian exile, without the location of Arabia, the patterns within the etymology and gematria no longer make sense. It's like trying to discern meaning using an Ottendorf cypher, without having the correct book in your hand! Once the 'mad' Babylonian ex-king is given permission to reveal himself once more, having been banished to the shadows of the HB for two and a half thousand years by the early Jews who abhorred his ways and deemed his name anathema, the cypher works and the messages are not only clear but consistent and profoundly enlightening.

POSTSCRIPT

Why would Strabo mention the Nabataeans' "eleven" golden cups? Might this pertain in some way to the number of Jewish tribes?

It has been my constant attestation that we have been erroneous in our dating of much of the HB; in my humble opinion, not one book of the Hebrew Bible predates the exile. Genesis, considered the beginning of the Hebrew story, is actually a much later addition, serving as a sort 'legend' (as in the corner of a map), to guide us to the overriding structure of early Judaism. It provides information on context and relationships that *anticipate* the exodus narratives in certain

---

(i.e., those whom Nabonidus would have known) and had as their place of pilgrimage, Harran, Nabonidus' home city. "Who are the Nabataeans Today?" § The Slayb, Nabataea.net, https://nabataea.net/explore/history/who-are-the-nabataeans-today/.

detail; there is no way it could have been written *before* Exodus, Numbers, Deuteronomy, etc.[74]

With this in mind, we are forced to re-evaluate the long-held convention of there being *twelve* tribes, for it soon becomes evident that various HB authors had other ideas. In fact, "scholars are now beginning to recognize that most twelve-tribe lists are in fact late, Judahite lists, and that the twelve-tribe concept is a late, Judahite idea."[75] Tobolowsky, for instance, suggests that the original version of the blessings in Deuteronomy 33 "covered only eight tribes: Benjamin, Joseph, Zebulun, Issachar, Gad, Dan, Naphtali, and Asher"; the tribes Reuben, Levi, and Judah, he argues, "were added later, and Simeon was not added at all."[76]

The explanation for this omission of Simeon is a little confusing but in *Arabian Sinai* I argue that Zimri, the man killed along with the woman Cozbi, by Phinehas (Num 25:6-15), was none other than Aaron.[77] Aaron was a Qenite, Nabonidus' (Moses') son-in-law, and Jethro's sacerdotal 'assistant'/"brother." As "Zimri" he is said to hail from the tribe of Simeon. I didn't deal with this in the book, as it wasn't relevant to the immediate discussion; "Simeon," however, comes from a very similar etymology to "Ishmael," i.e., both stem from the verb *shama*, "to hear." Those who were deemed "Ishmaelites" and those who were symbolically referred to as "Keturah's children" dwelt/remained on Arabian soil, i.e., the new Jewish society rejected them, considered them inferior, dangerous even.

Aaron, though a Qenite, lived farther afield, away from Sinai, away from Jethro; he is given this tribal name, perhaps, to signify that although he was an Ishmaelite (an Arabian), he was a singular example. Aaron, rather than Moses was posthumously adopted by the early Jews, who made him their priestly figurehead[78] (i.e., Aaron was considered a

---

[74] See my paper, "Nabonidus and the Arabian Genealogies (Genesis 10 and 11); also, Janet Tyson, *Nabonidus and the Queen of Sheba: Roots of a Legend* (Norwich, Pirištu Books, 2024), 119 (Appendix).

[75] Andrew Tobolowsky, "Did Israel Always Have Twelve Tribes?," §Introduction, TheTorah.com, https://www.thetorah.com/article/did-israel-always-have-twelve-tribes.

[76] Tobolowsky, §2.

[77] Tyson, *Arabian Sinai*, 361.

[78] Tyson, *Arabian Sinai*, 283-4. Aaron as a "Levite" is a much later and convoluted phenomenon but I offer an alternative understanding of the original levites in the context of the Sinai experience in the Hijaz.

priestly character, originally, due to his sacerdotal role within a highly ritualised form of metallurgy/smithing; he knew spells and rites, could write, inscribe stone, etc. As his popularity with the people increased, Moses/Nabonidus became peeved and began to demote Aaron, until eventually, he got rid of him altogether[79]).

It is in Deuteronomy, a predominantly pro-Moses text, that we find a negative perspective of Aaron; it is quite subjective, I feel, and included in a very subtle way, but it would seem at least one of the authors of Deuteronomy had a problem with Aaron:

> The traditional "Mount Hor" location for Aaron's death is preserved in both Numbers and Deuteronomy; the latter calls the place both "Hor" (Deut 32:50) *and* "Moserah" (10:6), which proves enlightening.
>
> "Moserah" is a virtual anagram of "Ramose/Rameses," ("Son of the Sun"), i.e., Moserah is "Ramoseh." Something that is reversed in the HB often signifies a negative intention, such as dark spells, evil intentions, etc. (by introducing chaos into order, on a symbolic level, e.g., the procedure for making the magical poppet in the Song of Solomon, for instance).[80] It may be that Moses sees Aaron as a pretender to the sacerdotal "throne"; by reversing the highly symbolic name "Rameses" the pro-Moses Deuteronomy author admonishes Aaron and marks him for eternity as a dissident who got what he deserved.[81]

It is no wonder, then, that the Deuteronomy tribal list would omit Aaron, i.e., "Zimri from Simeon"; it is a snub. Just as with the twelve disciples of Jesus, which become eleven with the death of Judas, so the Jewish tribes reduce to eleven after the death of Aaron (and with "Joseph" having unwanted connotations, too, it was inevitable that this name would also be struck from the list and replaced with two others, Ephraim and Manasseh, making the list 'twelve' again).

According to Exod 26:7, the tabernacle was to be made with *eleven* curtains, presumably one representing each tribe but in Exod 24:4 Moses sets up *twelve* pillars, it is said, *suspiciously obviously, to represent "the twelve tribes"*; I see this a later addition to the text, to

---

[79] This is a sweeping statement but is substantiated throughout *Arabian Sinai*.

[80] Tyson, *She Brought*, 135-42.

[81] Tyson, *Arabian Sinai*, 361. The reference to "Rameses" here must be understood in context.

explain the pillars, which had quite another association. I have interpreted these as a physical acknowledgement of the solar aspect of Nabonidus' mission at Sinai, i.e., the twelve pillars represented the twelve attendants of the Sun god Re as he passed through the night, something that is fully explained in *Arabian Sinai*.[82] Even Solomon's (Nabonidus') "twelve districts" (1 Kgs 4:7) was a *non-tribal* delineation based on imposed service to the Babylonian king.[83]

I think, therefore, the influence of Moses' apparent (but misconstrued) interest in "twelve" may prove to be the inspiration for the "twelve tribes" tradition. It is possible that by the time of Strabo's account of the Nabataeans, Deuteronomy's biased, anti-Simeon tribal list, that also pushes the agenda of the three tribes denoting the new Jewish nation, had yet to be imposed upon the simpler, original list of eight.[84]

In Gen 37:9, Joseph says: "I have had another dream: the sun and the moon and the <u>eleven</u> stars were bowing down to me. In the context of the narrative, Joseph has a dream of his eleven brothers' subservience, but note the sun/moon/stars context, anticipating precisely what happens at Sinai with "Joseph's Bones." This is another example of Genesis authors' precognition of the events detailed in books that *supposedly* come later, chronologically. It also highlights "eleven," where Joseph is external to this group.[85]

BIBLIOGRAPHY

"A Few Notes on Dan," Hebrew Nations, https://hebrewnations.com /articles/tribes/dan/a-few-notes-on-dan.html

Beaulieu, Paul-Alain. "Nabonidus the Mad King: A Reconsideration of His

---

[82] Tyson, *Arabian Sinai*, 257-9; and the whole of Chapter 13, "Joseph's Bones."

[83] Tyson, *Arabian Sinai*, 258.

[84] In both Hebrew and Christian ideas of symbolic numbers, eight represents resurrection, new beginnings, etc. In the context of the final days at Sela, when the Jews are ready to begin their new life in Canaan, this seems apt.

[85] I think the Genesis tale of Joseph is worthy of its own forensic analysis, in light of everything discovered thus far about Nabonidus' relationship with the early Jews and the *truly* Egyptian identity of "Joseph."

Stelas from Harran and Babylon." Pages 137-66 in *Representations of Political Power: Case Histories from Times of Change and Dissolving Order in the Ancient Near East*. Edited by M. Heinz and M. Feldman. Winona Lake: Eisenbrauns, 2007.

______. *The Reign of Nabonidus King of Babylon* 556-539 B.C. New Haven: Yale University Press, 1989.

Britannica.com. "Pre-Islamic Deities." https://www.britannica.com/topic /Arabian-religion/Pre-Islamic-deities.

Brown-Driver-Briggs Hebrew and English Lexicon. Unabridged, Electronic Database. 2006.

Crowell, Bradley L. "Nabonidus, as-Silaʿ, and the Beginning of the End of Edom." Bulletin of the American Society of Overseas Research (BASOR) 348 (2007): 75-88.

Diodorus. *The Library of History of Diodorus Siculus*. Loeb Classical Library, Vol. 10. 1954. https://penelope.uchicago.edu/Thayer/E/Roman/Texts /Diodorus_Siculus/19E*.html#ref80).

Dougherty, Raymond P. *Nabonidus and Belshazzar: A Study of the Closing Events of the Neo-Babylonian Empire*. 1929 repr. Eugene: Wipf & Stock, 2008.

______. "Nabonidus in Arabia." JAOS 42 (1922): 305-16.

Doughty, Charles M. *Travels in Arabia Deserta*. New York: Random House, 1921.

Enein, Heba M. I. M. "Glimpses into the Archaeological History of Makkah." Vol. 1,2. 2021. here https://www.academia.edu/49274496.

Flinders, Petrie, Editor. *Egyptian Tales Translated from the Papyri*. Second Series, 18th to 19th Dynasty (New York: Frederick A. Stokes, 1913, 1899). § "The Taking of Joppa." https://pages.ucsd.edu/~dkjordan/arch /egypt/Petrie/PetrieTale7.html#joppa.

Friedman, Zaraza. "Did Nabatean Seafaring Exist?" *Michmanim* 25 (2014): 23-30. https://www .academia.edu/10783439.

Ginzberg, Louis. *The Legends of the Jews* (1909). https://www.sefaria.org /Legends_of_the_Jews.3.3.43?lang=bi&with= all&lang2=en.

Healey, John F. *The Religion of the Nabataeans: A Conspectus, Religions in the Graeco-Roman World*. Edited by R. Van Den Broek, H. J. W. Drijvers, H. S. Versnel. Vol. 136. Leiden: Brill, 2001.

Heidrick, Bill. Hebrew Gematria. ww.billheidrick.com.

Olmsted, David. "Mediterranean and Alphabetic Akkadian Lexicon 2nd Edition - February 2021." https://www.academia.edu/45091402.

Olcott, William Tyler. *Star Lore of All Ages: A Collection of Myths, Legends, and Facts Concerning the Constellations of the Northern Hemisphere*. New York: Putnam's/Knickerbocker Press, 1911.

Raskin, Rabbi Aaron L. Letters of Light: The Meaning of the Hebrew Alphabet. www.chabad.org.

Robinson, George Livingston. *The Sarcophagus of an Ancient Civilization; Petra, Edom and the Edomites.* New York: Macmillan, 1930.

Sánchez, Francisco del Río. *Nabatu the Nabataeans Through Their Inscriptions.* Barcelona: Universitat de Barcelona, 2015.

Sauter, Megan. "The Nabonidus Inscription at Sela: Investigating a Neo-Babylonian inscription in modern Jordan." Biblical Archaeological Society, https://www.biblicalarchaeology.org /daily/the-nabonidus-inscription-at-sela/.

Strabo, *The Geography of Strabo.* Loeb Classical Library, 1932. https://penelope.uchicago.edu/Thayer/E/Roman/Texts/Strabo/16D*.html.

Tobolowsky, Andrew. "Did Israel Always Have Twelve Tribes?," §Introduction. TheTorah.com. https://www.thetorah.com/article/did-israel-always-have-twelve-tribes.

Tyson, Janet. *Arabian Sinai: Nabonidus and the Exodus.* Norwich: Pirištu Books, 2024.

____. *Nabonidus and the Queen of Sheba: Roots of a Legend.* Norwich, Pirištu Books, 2024.

____. *She Brought the Art of Women: A Song of Solomon, Nabonidus, and the Goddess.* Norwich: Pirištu Books, 2023.

Wenning, Robert. "The Nabataeans in History." Pages 25-44 in *The World of the Nabataeans.* Vol. 2 of the International Conference "The World of the Herods and the Nabataeans" held at the British Museum, 17-19 April 2001, Stuttgart. 2007.

Weiershäuser, Frauke and J. Novotny. *The Royal Inscriptions of Amēl-Marduk (561–560 BC), Neriglissar (559–556 BC), and Nabonidus (555–539 BC), Kings of Babylon.* The Royal Inscriptions of the Neo-Babylonian Empire, Vol. 2. University Park: Eisenbrauns, 2020.

"Who are the Nabataeans Today?" § The Slayb. Nabataea.net.https://nabataea.net/explore/history/who-are-the-nabataeans-today/.

INDEX

PIRIŠTU BOOKS

JANET TYSON

The Testament of Lazarus
The Pre-Christian Gospel of John
(2023)

She Brought the Art of Women
A Son of Solomon, Nabonidus, and the Goddess
(2023)

Arabian Sinai
Nabonidus and the Exodus
(2024)

Nabonidus and the Queen of Sheba
Roots of a Legend
(2024)

www.ingramcontent.com/pod-product-compliance
Lightning Source LLC
Chambersburg PA
CBHW052356030726
47599CB00014B/1095